Proper Brummie:

A Dictionary of Birmingham Words And Phrases

Compiled by Carl Chinn and Steve Thorne

**BREWIN
BOOKS**

First published by
Brewin Books Ltd, Studley, Warwickshire
in November 2001
Reprinted January 2002
www.brewinbooks.com

ISBN 1 85858 207 5

British Library Cataloguing in Publication

A catalogue record for this book is available
from the British Library

Typeset in Times Roman and
made and printed in Great Britain by
Supaprint (Redditch) Ltd
Redditch, Worcestershire.
Website: www.supaprint.com
E-mail: admin@supaprint.com

Contents

Acknowledgements

Books of this kind are necessarily dependent on the work of others, and the many publications and unpublished manuscripts which provided us with vital raw material are all listed at the back of the dictionary.

It would not have been possible to authenticate any of the entries in *Proper Brummie* without the corroborative material we received by letter, e-mail, phone call and word-of-mouth from Brummies, honorary Brummies and expats alike. In this regard we would thank particularly Betty Adams; David and Gill Adams; J. R. Acland; John and Dorothy Adkins; F. E. Allison; E. Aplin; Susan Ashley; Barbara Aston; Betty Atkins; J. Austin; Nancy Bainbridge; Gwen Baker; Dennis Barker; J. Barklam; B. M. Barnard; S. H. Bate; Marge Baylis; G. F. Beasley; F. C. Bedford; Richard Best; Rod Birch; Elsie Birks; Rob Blaxland; Mary Bodfish; Eric Bosworth; F. Brittain; Janet Broome; O. Brown; V. Brown; Geoff Bryant; Graham Buckley; J. Burgess; Roger Butt; John Carr; Ken Carruthers; A. J. Cattell; Jo and Pete Chance; Pat Chapman; Albert Charles; Margaret Clarke; S. Cleverley; Frank Collins; Gloria Cornish; W. E. Cossons; Mike Cotton; Robert Couling; Joan Davis; Kath Davis; Steve Deane; O. Deeley; D. Dodd; Bill Drew; June Eastlake; Pauline Edwards; Janet Emery; John Essex; Dot Evans; K. M. Felton; Eric Foakes; Colin Forknall; Fred Gill; Larry Gombley; Christine Goodall; David Grainger; C. C. Green; Albert Grice; Mary Grosvenor; Richard Haddock; Therese Hadley; Eileen Hands; E. Hawker; Ray Holmes; Bob Houghton; J. E. Houldey; C. W. Hughes; Ann James; K. G. Jenks; Sue Kelly; Christine Kendell; Linda Key; B. King; T. L. King; Trevor Knibbs; Johnny Landon; D. W. Lee; Robert Lowe; Gill Manning; Jason Mansell; V. P. Mattiello; Geoff Moore; Dick Morris; P. M. Nardell; Marie Oakes; B. Osborn; L. E. Page; Usha Parmar; Nigel Penn; Christine Penton; Jennifer Percival; Margaret Perry; Melanie Pettit; M. Potter; Margaret Puffett; Robert Randle; M. Ravenhill; S. Rees; Mabel Revell; Joe and Laura Reynolds; E. Richardson; Yvonne Rideout; Jean Rider; Madge Rider; O. Roberts; Norma Rogers; Leslie Rowe; Maureen Rudge; Antony Sealey; John Shaw; Beat Sherlock; G. F. Sly; Jean Smith; Brian Stevenson; Dorian Stevenson; Patricia Stevenson; Win Tainty; Andy Tann; Margaret Taylor; O. D. Taylor; Olive Taylor; L. F. Thomas; Doreen and Ray Thorne; Betty Tidmarsh; Stuart Tomley; Albert Trapp; Philippa Travis; Ian Trow; Derek Vickers; E. Wakeling; Hilda Walker; Paul Walker; Ted Walker; Ken and Nellie Weekes; John Wellings; Amy Westwood; Fred Whitehouse; D. Whyle; Steve Wilcox; Dorothy Williams; Paul Williams; Dolly Wolstenhome; Stan Wood; E. Woodward Jephcott; Ernie Wooldridge; F. M. A. Wright; L. G. Yates; Ernie Yorke, and Graham Young.

We also wish to thank Jim Hunt at the *Virtual-Brum* website, as well as the following for their contributions to the BBC Birmingham Online website *Voices and sayings*: John Alldritt; Tony Beetlestone; Amy Blackwell; Yvonne Brissett; Colin Butters; Stephanie Chapman; Jamie Holt; Dave Jones; Tony Jones; Margaret Joy; Sophie Kay; Roger Phipps; Richard Powderhill; Betty Prettyman; Lee Purvin; Robert Reay; Samantha Robinson; Hilary Taylor; Sid Thomas, and Jeff Woodward.

This dictionary would not have been published without the unflagging encouragement offered by Gertrude, Dulcie, and Carrie Weekes. Nor would it have appeared without the technical support of Jeremy Paige, or the invaluable assistance we received from the staff at community centres, youth groups, clubs and associations all over Birmingham. We are also grateful for the patience and understanding shown by everybody in the Archives and Local History sections of Birmingham Library Services.

Last, but by no means least, a special debt of gratitude is also owed to the venerable Mr William Shakespeare for doing so much to keep the language of the English Midlands alive.

Foreword

When me and our kid, Darryl, were youngsters all of the family used to gather at our mom's on a Sunday afternoon. We listened raptly as the chat turned to the goings on down 'the old end'. Lively characters of the past were mulled over, noteworthy events of days gone by were knocked about and a forceful way of life was shaken into view. And as we took in the bustling histories of our families, their neighbourhoods and their city, without knowing it we also drew in the way in which these tales were told. For they were recounted in the vigorous speech of working-class Brum, a speech which pulled us unconsciously into the origins of the English language in the West Midlands.

In my mind's eye, those many Sunday afternoons are now one and as that day sped on, our granddad Perry would urge us not to forget that we were related to the Tipton Slasher, he would go 'Well, blige me' when something happened that he wasn't too keen on or which impressed him, and towards the end of the afternoon he would look at our mom and beckon her over. Sadly, our granddad had multiple sclerosis and couldn't walk so he'd gain our mom's attention by saying, 'Come ere ma wench.' 'What's that, our dad?', our mom would reply. 'Gie us a piece, wench, I'm clammed.' And off our mom would go to cut our granddad a piece of bread and so stop him feeling hungry.

Our granddad come out of Hick Street, Highgate and his broad Brummie sounds were shared by our nan and her sister, our Winnie, who come out of Whitehouse Street, Aston. Like so many Brummies, our nan's mom and dad originated elsewhere, but their kids grew up in back-to-back Brummagem and as with all those whose address was 'back of' their Brummie speech was inextricably bound to who they were and where they came from. Our nan would begenst and snever, teach us how to play glarnies and jackstones, warn us 'to mind the 'orse road', mek us doorstep sarnies and matter-of-factly point out that her leg was a-wailing her and playing her up. All the while, our Winnie would let us know how her'd traipsed all over the town and that her'd had a good mooch down The Cov, the Coventry Road, with her ta-ta bag, the big shopping bag her took with her everywhere. Then she and our nan would bring to mind their mom, great granny Wood. She was a hard collaring woman who had to mek do and mend every day of her life and could put together a filling meal with a few bacon bones and pot vegetables. Nobody give her nothing and day after day, she would be in the brewus maiding and dollying, blueing and rinsing and meking sure that her own kids wore clothes that were as spotless as were those she cleaned for the better off.

With sayings and words bouncing hither and thither, our mom would tell us to have no cotter with someone who was upsetting us and to tek no notice if we were teased by a cousin; she'd let us know how someone had come a right purler and scraged their legs; and she'd admonish us not to let anyone see us blartin if we'd had a bit of a dust up over the rec. Often our nan's brothers, our uncle George and our uncle Bill would pop in and put in their twopennyworth. Our Georgie was nicknamed the fat 'un and he'd bring to the fore how our great granddad Wood, the old mon, would tek no nonsense

8

from no-one and would have a set to with anyone, no matter how hard they were. Our uncle Bill was the big 'un, the oldest lad, and once when he saw someone he dain't like he asked the person whether or not they'd got their rings on their fingers from down the suff, 'where yo' come from yerself'.

Our dad worn't left out. He comes out of Studley Street, Sparkbrook and would fetch us over to 'Go and put that rubbish in the miskins' and when it was bedtime he'd alert us to the fact that it was time to get up the dancers. On other occasions, he'd evoke a lost world of illegal betting. It was a world peopled with tekers and runners, the folk who took cash bets for illegal bookies, coppers whom you bunged to let you know when they were going to nick you, cute punters who were clever with their betting, and old dears who had a flutter for a bit of fun and who boasted colourful monikers.

The old mon's accent was slightly softer than the flatter tones of our mom's Aston family and he shared this characteristic with his uncles. Great uncle Bill was born in 1893 in that part of Sparkbrook that had been in Balsall Heath, Worcestershire until two years previously. Both his mom and dad had been brought up locally, in what had been an agricultural outpost on the edge of Brum. They recalled the Spark when still it flowed down what is now the Stoney Lane and mentioned the hedgerows that had run along The Lane, the Ladypool Road. Growing up hard on the borders of Worcestershire with Warwickshire, their speech emphasised the melding of the tones of the rural West Midlands with the urban talk of Brum. Neither uncle Bill nor his younger brother, uncle Wal, said floor or door - always they pronounced such words as floer and doer - whilst cloth became clorth. To go shopping along the Ladypool Road was always a trip down The Lane, the town was the fanny brown, to have something on credit was to have it on the mace, and somebody who was seen as a bad 'un was a mongrel.

Although the sound of the voices of my Sparkbrook uncles differed slightly from that of my Aston relatives, the words they used and the way they put those words together in a sentence were all but the same. They spoke the same dialect and were proud to be 'proper Brummies'. Their mom, great granny Chinn, was a wardrobe dealer - a posh way of saying someone who flogged second-hand clothes - and a couple of times a wick she would tek her clobber up the old Rag Alley, lay it out on the floor and pull the buyers in with her banter. Uncle Wal mimed for me how she would lift up a pair of the old-fashioned ladies' bloomers - the type which had no covering at the front and were just two holes for the legs and were tied together by string. Our great gran would lift up the underclothes and bawl out to a woman, 'Ee are ma wench. Look a' these! Ow about these! Come on now, if yo fancy a pair of freetraders these'll do y'. Come on now!'

In those days of the 1960s you didn't hear anyone talking like my family on the wireless or on the television - except for those who mocked or denigrated our accent. Anyone who was well educated and in positions of authority spoke 'posh', and it is not surprising, then, that many working-class parents wanted their children to converse in standard English. It was felt, probably rightly, that this speech would allow youngsters to get on better in life. Our mom and dad were no different. They tried to get me and our

Darryl to speak properly, as they thought. I can understand why they and so many other moms and dads did so. It is not their fault that society was so prejudiced against dialect speakers and that those with strong accents were so often discriminated against. And I blame no mother or father who seeks to impress upon their youngsters the need to speak standard English. Indeed it is essential that everyone has a sound command of this dialect. However, it must be borne in mind that standard English is a dialect and as well as acknowledging its importance we ought also to assert the significance of local dialects.

From an early age I rebelled against speaking differently from my family and against the belief that their way of talking was wrong. In my youthful eyes, they were the ones who spoke properly. I was too young to rationalise my actions or to justify what I was doing, all I knew was that I didn't want to be different, that I wanted to speak like our nan and granddad, our Winnie and our Georgie, my uncle Bill and my uncle Wal. They are all dead now, but I know that they were proud not only that one of them got on, but also that I continued to be one of them and did not forsake their tongue. And I know that our mom and our dad feel the same as well.

Now that I am older, I can express my feelings about my language. I have benefited from a good education, an education that was denied to all the members of my family until I came along. I have had a choice, a gift that was withheld from all my forebears until my time. I can be who I want to be and speak as I wish to. And still I wish to speak like them. For they made me what I am. They scratted and saved, toiled and moiled so that someone in the future had a future, had opportunities, had possibilities. I owe it to them to grasp hold of the chances they laboured for but I also owe a duty to them not to turn my back on their lives. I shall never forget that debt nor that responsibility and so never will I seek to pretend that I do not come from them. I will speak as they did for if I forswear their dialect I will have cast aside my heritage and disowned my family.

God knows that our folk had nothing to give us in terms of money and property. They had no gold nor silver, nor houses or lands, nor jewellery or finery. Yet, they passed on to us precious things. They gave us their examples of hard work. They showed us how to make strong neighbourhoods in the midst of a dark and hostile environment. And they handed us their words. Even if they are no longer used commonly, we have a responsibility to give our words to our children and to their children. For these words call us to the beginnings of our city and to those who made us first. If we abandon our words as worthless we give up our past as meaningless. And if we do that we throw out something vital of ourselves, for a people who lose their language are a people who lose their soul.

These are things I feel deep in my heart and my being. They are made all the more powerful by the years I have spent researching the lives of tens of thousands of other working-class Brummies who lived not only in Aston, Sparkbrook and Highgate but also in all those other working-class heartlands of the city from Winson Green in the west to Saltley in the east, from Summer Lane in the north to Small Heath in the south. And when many of those folk were moved on during the post-war redevelopment of Brum, they took their language with them to areas like Pype Hayes, Quinton, Weoley Castle, Yardley

Wood, Sheldon, Lea Hall, Chelmsley Wood, Shard End, and Castle Vale. Here the accent and dialect of the old end has been carried amidst the new surroundings and housing. In other places, such as Acocks Green, Cotteridge and Ward End, the Brummie town speech has been tinged by the rural-tinged tones of those who lived in what were villages in Worcestershire and Warwickshire.

A more remarkable development has occurred in the redeveloped central areas such as Lea Bank and Hockley and also in Handsworth. Here the Brummie language has been influenced deeply by the inward movement of people speaking the patois of Jamaica and other Caribbean islands. In such localities, the accent that is now common amongst young people owes almost as much to the West Indies as it does to Brum. At the same time, certain African Caribbean words have made their presence felt. Similarly, in Kings Heath, Erdington and Sparkhill there is an Irish Brummie accent noticeable amongst the sons and daughters and even grandchildren of those Irish men and women who have come to live and work here since the 1930s. And increasingly, it is easy to pick out amongst the teenagers of Alum Rock, Bordesley Green, Lozells and other neighbourhoods a South Asian Brummie accent - itself owing much to the speech of Black Brummies.

It is likely that in forthcoming generations a newer Brummie twang will appear that will look for its roots not only to the English of Warwickshire, Worcestershire and Staffordshire but also to the West Indies, Ireland and South Asia. This shift in the accent will be accompanied by the emergence of a modern Brummie dialect which will be influenced both by local and external forces. These outside effects are evident already, for example, in the spread of the glottal stop of Estuary English. This speech form is now common amongst young people. Often they drop the 't' in words such as bitter leading to the pronunciation of bi'er. As the newer form of Brummie strengthens, probably, it will spread outside the city's boundaries along with big city accents and dialects elsewhere in the country. As a result, the traditional Brummie dialect will gradually decline - although some of its words and grammatical forms will live on in the new speech.

That is as it should be. The people of Birmingham are changing and their dialect must reflect this transformation. Language is a vital thing. It cannot and should not be put in a jar and sealed. We are on the cusp of a major linguistic shift and those of us from older generations have an important role to play in that process of alteration. We can hark back to the older words and phrases, we can listen to and take note of the shifting of sounds and words in our city, and we can try and make sense of the speech that will emerge. No matter how hard we may wish that we could, we cannot force words which are dear to us on to younger people. But what we can do is to seek to explain the history of the traditional Brummie dialect, we can stress the importance to our present of those who spoke the words of the past, and we can try and help maintain a bond between the Brum which has gone and the Brum which is to be. In that way, our forebears will live on and will not be strangers to their descendants.

Carl Chinn

Preface

> There was only one more thing which had to be done, a last message to leave behind on the last day of all: and so he gathered up his strength in the midst of a long stretch of silence and framed his lips to say to me quite clearly the one word *Dictionary* (Wright, 1932).

Proper Brummie represents the first attempt ever to comprehensively document the Birmingham dialect. I'm sure it will come as a great surprise to many, as indeed it did to me, that there has never been anything like it before. When I first started researching this dictionary I was astounded by the lack of information on the language of England's 'second city'. Apart from the odd humorous take on Brumspeak, like Ray Tennant's *Book of Brum* booklets, one of the only published works I could find which takes a serious look at the Brummie tongue was one which proposes to do away with it – Frank Jones' (1918) *Brummagem English: being an account of the peculiarities of pronunciation commonly heard in Birmingham and District together with a course of phonetic exercises to correct them*. The other, Hans Oskar Wilde's (1938) *Der Industrie-Dialekt von Birmingham*, is written entirely in an almost impenetrable form of academic German. For those who want to find out about the dialects of other parts of England, on the other hand, there is an abundance of published material available in any public library; from books on how to *Larn Yersel Geordie* (Dobson, 1969) to a glut of Scouse, Cockney, Glaswegian and even Black Country dialect dictionaries. Anybody hoping to familiarise themselves with the Birmingham dialect, however, might well end up believing that such a thing does not exist.

I've heard it said that Brummie, unlike other British English dialects, does not have a large collection of specifically local words or phrases, but this is patently untrue – as, I hope, the amount of entries in this dictionary will prove. Birmingham has its own instantly recognisable dialect, which us Brummies – contrary to popular opinion – are fiercely proud of, and yet it has been ignored by linguists and lexicographers. Brummie, furthermore, is an historic tongue. Along with dialects spoken in surrounding areas of the English Midlands, it is probably the closest you're ever going to get to the way Shakespeare spoke. Shakespeare's plays are peppered with dialect words and phrases which many Brummies still use today, but popular attitudes towards the Shakespearean and Birmingham dialects couldn't be any more different; Shakespeare's language is celebrated all over the world, whereas a Brummie still can't open his or her mouth without making some other English person cringe.

The aim of this dictionary, therefore, is not just to provide the definitive guide to the Birmingham dialect, but also to shatter a few of the myths, common misconceptions, and prejudices surrounding the language of this city and its people. It seems perverse that at a time when discrimination on the basis of sex, race, age, gender, religion, disability or sexual orientation is generally condemned, prejudice against people who speak certain dialects should be allowed to continue unabated. I am not, of course, under the illusion that prejudice against those who do not 'speak proper' will vanish overnight, but, with any luck, this dictionary may help a little in turning the tide. Since, as the poet Tony Harrison (1992, p.121) warns us, "the dumb go down in history and disappear," it appears to be of the utmost importance that our language and the language of our ancestors is recorded before it's too late. There is nothing wrong with the way we speak. Our language is as good as any other, and we should celebrate its distinctiveness and vitality. Brummies have, up until now, been denied a voice; silenced; written out of history, and I think it's about time we stood up and made ourselves heard.

Steve Thorne

Historical introduction

The history of the West Midlands stretches back long before Germanic invaders arrived from the later fifth century to wrest control of the region from the British - those people whom now we would call the Cymry, the Welsh, and the Cornish. There have been finds of Old Stone Age tools, left behind by hunters passing through the region; there is evidence from the Sandwell Valley to indicate the presence of hunter-gatherers from the Middle Stone Age; whilst the burial mound at Kingstanding may have been made at the end of the New Stone Age or at the beginning of the Bronze Age - the era from which date the Burnt Mounds that have been found in places such as Moseley Bog.

In the ensuing Iron Age, it would seem that settlement in the West Midlands was marginal and that the region fell across the borders of two Celtic tribes: the Cornovii to the north west and the Corieltauvi to the north east. These peoples were overcome by the Romans in the first century AD, and once they had been pacified each boasted a capital - Wroxeter and Leicester respectively. There is no evidence of anything so substantial in the Birmingham area, although the Romans did establish a fort at Metchley in the modern Edgbaston. This was occupied for over a century and became the focus of a number of roads, but no noteworthy civilian settlement grew up alongside it.

But if human activity, no matter how little or how great, can be traced back tens of thousands of years, then it was the Germanic invaders of the West Midlands who have left their mark most firmly upon our area in its place names and language. Arriving from the mid-400s from northern Germany close to the border with modern Denmark, large numbers of Angles, Saxons, Jutes and Frisians settled heavily in East Anglia (the land of the East Angles), Kent, Sussex (South Saxons), Essex (East Saxons), southern Hampshire, Lindsey in Lincolnshire, the east riding of Yorkshire and the upper Thames valley. All bar the last of these were coastal areas. Inland, the British were still in control, although by the early 500s there is evidence indicating the presence of small numbers of Saxons in the Avon Valley.

Overall, not much is known about the emergence of the Anglo-Saxons in the English Midlands but it does seem that the region was settled by Angles who arrived from the mid-500s at the latest. These pioneers did not take over from the Welsh in a sudden conquest. Instead they came as groups of men and women under the command of a leader seeking land to till. Consequently, the Welsh were neither exterminated nor beaten out. Instead it is likely that both peoples co-existed and inter-married with each other. One of the main bands of Anglians were the Mierce, the boundary people, whose heartland was around Lichfield and Tamworth in Staffordshire. It has been argued that the boundary in their name referred to the Welsh from whom these Angles took control, but against this point of view it has been suggested strongly that these folk co-existed with the greater numbers of Welsh amongst whom they lived. In the opinion of such experts, the name boundary people related to the borders with the greater population of Angles in the East Midlands.

Amongst the Angles who came to make their home in the West Midlands was a leader called Beorma whose people (ingas) joined him in setting up a landed estate or homestead (ham) which became known as Birmingham. It may well be that Beorma and his clan took control of an area larger than that of the old manor of Birmingham. Whatever the case, Beorma's folk would have arrived by the late 500s, at a time when there was no great kingdom in the region and when the political situation in the region was in a state of flux. Within half a century, this state of affairs had changed dramatically. Under a ruler of the Mierce called Penda, who was in power from the early 600s to 655, other groups of Anglians - perhaps such as the Beormingas - were brought together to forge a powerful kingdom called Mercia. Its heartland was the middle Trent Valley - embracing what are today Staffordshire, Leicestershire, Nottinghamshire, southern Derbyshire and north Warwickshire. The whole of old Birmingham, Aston, Erdington, Saltley and Ward End - all in Warwickshire - and Handsworth and Harborne in Staffordshire would have been part of Mercia.

To the south in Worcestershire and south-western Warwickshire, arose another Anglo-Saxon entity known as the kingdom of the Hwicce. This was a place where Angles coming from the north east and Saxons arriving from the south had merged with each other and intermingled with the local Welsh. Those parts of Birmingham which once were in Worcestershire would have belonged to this kingdom. They included Norton (Kings Norton), Northfield, Weoley, Selly (Selly Oak) and Yardley. From the time of Penda, the Hwicce were under Mercian domination and by the end of the 700s they had lost their kings and had become a province of their greater northern neighbour.

Under first King Aethelbald (716-57) and then King Offa (757-96), Mercia became the most powerful kingdom in Anglo-Saxon England. By this time, the descendants of the original Welsh inhabitants of Mercia were increasingly mixed with the Anglo-Saxons - so much so that there was little difference between the two peoples away from border areas in Herefordshire and Shropshire - and by the later 800s, the speaking of Welsh had disappeared from most of the West Midlands. This was the case especially in north Warwickshire, Staffordshire and north-east Worcestershire. The dominance of the Old English language in this district is reflected in the rarity of Welsh place names. Indeed in Birmingham and the Black Country only the rivers Cole and Tame and the hills Barr and Penn are ancient Celtic; whilst Walsall alone refers to British people, probably meaning as it does the nook or cranny of land of a Welshman.

Following the death of Offa, Mercia continued to impose itself as a major force, but by the 820s Wessex - the kingdom of the West Saxons - had taken over as the most important Anglo-Saxon kingdom. Within a generation, however, all of Anglo-Saxon England was assailed by raiders from Scandinavia, and from the 850s, Danish forces began to stay throughout the year and not return home in the winter. Then in 873 the Danes gained control of north-eastern Mercia and drove the king into exile. Four years later, they partitioned the kingdom, taking the eastern half for themselves and placing the western portion under an Anglo-Saxon nobleman called Ceolwulf. He ruled until 879 but had no successor and within four years the English part of Mercia had been placed by King Alfred of Wessex under the control of Earldorman Aethelred. He later married Alfred's sister, Lady Aethelflaed. Known as the Lady of the Mercians, she ruled the western part of Mercia after her husband's death in 911 and was responsible for establishing a number of boroughs, fortresses, to defend her lands from the Danes. Amongst these were Tamworth and Stafford in 913 and Warwick in 914. After Aethelflaed's death in 918, her brother Edward the Elder annexed western Mercia to Wessex and conquered the Danish Midlands and East Anglia.

Edward's son, Athelstan, was the greatest ruler in Britain since the Romans. Although of the royal house of Wessex, he was brought up in western Mercia where he was fostered by his aunt Aethelflaed and uncle Aethelred. King Alfred had been keen to ensure that the west Mercians were not treated as a subject people and it was his decision that Athelstan should be raised in Mercia. It is also believed that Alfred's mother was a Mercian as was his mother-in-law. With a Mercian upbringing and education, Athelstan was proclaimed king by his Mercian friends in 924, following the death of his father and the sudden death of his brother who was the heir to the throne. It was a momentous decision, for within three years Athelstan went on to lead the English in defeating the Vikings of York and bringing Northumbria into the Kingdom of England. Athelstan was later acknowledged by the kings of the Welsh and the Scots as their overlord.

In the years following the forming of the kingdom of England, there were more invasions by the Danes but linguistically Old English triumphed. That is not to say that Norse did not have an impact. It did and many modern English words are from the Norse - such as fellow, score and beck. These and other words came to be part of the Old English language, and it is evident that in the formerly Danish-controlled parts of England that Norse had an even more pervasive influence on the local dialect. However, in west Mercia the linguistic effect of the Danes would have been restricted to those words that entered general usage. Similarly, Norse place names are largely absent west of the Watling Street, the dividing line between English and Danish Mercia. In west Mercia the overwhelming majority of the place names are Old English: ham for homestead or estate; leah (ley) meaning woodland clearing or glade; worth, signifying an enclosure or enclosed settlement; halh (hall), referring to a nook or corner of land; burh, relating to a fortified place; grene, indicating a grassy location or village green; and greot (greet), telling of a gravelly place.

How then did the Anglo-Saxons of west Mercia speak? Like all their folk from Northumbria in the north to Sussex in the south and from Essex in the east to Wessex in the west, their language was Old English. This was a Germanic speech which emerged amongst the Angles, Saxons, Jutes, Frisians and other groups from northern Germany and Denmark who arrived in the former Roman province of Britannia. Apart from a few inscriptions written in the runic alphabet, little written material survives from the fifth and sixth centuries and thus most of the evidence for the Old English language dates from the time of King Alfred (849-99).

By this period, Old English had emerged as a distinct form of speech with various dialects. Because of the success of its kings like Alfred and their role in the making of the kingdom of England, the particular form of Old English belonging to Wessex became the dominant form of writing in most Old English texts. This dialect was spoken south of the Thames, except in Kent. It is relevant to point out, however, that many later West Saxon texts do indicate a Mercian influence. This was because Mercian scholars were brought in by Alfred to help the literary rebirth which he energised.

Elsewhere in England, Northumbrian held sway above the line made by the Mersey and Humber Rivers, thus embracing most of northern England and the eastern lowlands of Scotland. Finally, Mercian was the dialect of the folk of the Midlands, East Anglia and also the London district - for this had belonged to Mercia. Like Northumbria, Mercia was a great area and it is not known if before the Danish conquests there were distinctions in the speech between its eastern and southern localities, or indeed between its northern and southern district. Unfortunately, there survive very few texts written in the Mercian dialect. However, those that do remain indicate that the Mercians turned an 'a' into an 'o' before a nasal consonant such as 'n', 'm' and 'ng'. Thus Mercians would have said mon for man, hond for hand and lond for land. It is remarkable that this feature survived strongly into the twentieth century in Birmingham and the Black Country.

Despite the emergence of England, Danish invasions continued - so successfully at some stages that Danish kings were imposed. Indeed, it was the Danish king Cnut (1016-1035) who made Mercia an earldom and placed over it Leofywyne, whose son was the Leofric who married Lady Godgifu (Godiva). The earldom of Mercia only survived by a few years the Norman Conquest of 1066, whereby all the English became a subject people. Old English now was the speech of the conquered and the dispossessed for French was the language of government, administration, literature and the Church - although Latin was used also in religious and administrative affairs. But the English tongue was not overwhelmed as had been the speech of the Celts when the Angles and Saxons had taken over what became England. Spoken by the great majority of the population, Old English proved itself to be hardy and adaptable and by the later twelfth century it had evolved into Middle English - a form which is more recognisable to speakers of Modern English.

Flourishing among the common people, and now the first language of the nobility, Middle English burst fully upon the national scene in the fourteenth century with a wonderful array of literature. Crucially, each work was put down in the dialect of the speaker, for there was no such thing as standard English. By this time, scholars have identified a number of major dialects: Northern, which covered the same area as the Old English kingdom of Northumbria; Southern, equating to the former kingdom of Wessex; Kentish in Kent; East Midland, holding sway over East Anglia and the eastern midlands; and West Midland or West Central, which was dominant in south Lancashire, Cheshire, Shropshire, Herefordshire, Warwickshire, Worcestershire and Staffordshire - equating to that part of Mercia which had not been conquered by the Danes.

Some dialect experts further sub-divide this area. In the case of Peter Trudgill, he identifies a Staffordshire dialect which embraces Staffordshire itself, most of Cheshire, northern Shropshire, parts of southern Derbyshire, north-western

Warwickshire and north-eastern Worcestershire. Whatever the fine distinctions, it must be borne in mind that dialects cannot be demarcated easily. They merge one into the other and the borders of a certain feature of speech may not fall on the line drawn by referring to another peculiarity. Still, it is obvious that what is now Birmingham and the Black Country fell clearly within the bounds of the West Midlands dialect, a distinct form of Middle English which had emerged from Old English and was less affected by Norse influences.

William Chaucer, the famed writer of The Canterbury Tales, recognised the varieties of English when he bemoaned the 'gret diversité / In Englissh and in wrytyng of oure tonge' (Troilus, 5. 1793-4). Compared to the Old English period, when most texts were written in the dialect of Wessex, and the Modern English period when a standard English form of writing emerged, there is no recognised speech for the writing of Middle English. Instead, as Chaucer indicated, poets and others all wrote in their regional tongue. Several major Middle English texts have been brought to us by people who lived in the West Midlands. Amongst them were Layamon's *Brut*, written about 1200. This poem tells the history of Britain and was written by a man who was the parish priest of Areley Kings in Worcestershire. Another important poem is *Sir Gawain* and the *Green Knight*, written in the dialect of the north-west Midlands by someone who may have come from the borders of Cheshire and Staffordshire. Thus the author would have fallen within the general area of the west Mercian variation of Middle English. He was also responsible for the poems *Pearl, Cleanness* (*or Purity*) and *Patience* - all dating from the later 1300s.

There are a number of texts from our dialect region such as *Ancrene Wise, St Erkenwald* and *The Vision of Piers Plowman*. The latter was written in the later 1300s by William Langland, a man who was probably brought up either in the Malvern Hills in Worcestershire or in the Clee Hills in Shropshire. In *The Vision* he makes three references to the Malvern Hills and the language of the poem does belong to this part of Worcestershire. Langland's work is noted as the most widely read of the Middle English alliterative poems - a form popular in the Midlands and the North. It was not the style used by his contemporary. Geoffrey Chaucer, the man who is praised as the first great poet of the English nation and who is regarded as gaining prestige for the written language of the London dialect. Neither Chaucer's work nor its profound effect on the development of the English language should be lessened, but neither should we neglect the importance of literature from the West Midlands dialect region.

By the later 1400s, Middle English itself had developed into Early Modern English. Great changes continued to occur in the language before Modern English fully emerged in the 1700s. And changes are taking place still. However, despite the development of a standard English in both the spoken and written word, the basic dialect map of England remained mostly the same as it had been in the Middle English period and so did the key differences between the dialects. Birmingham was clearly within the West Midlands dialect area. Beginning as a place of some importance from 1166 when it first had a market, it was a town that was clearly embedded within its rural hinterland.

For centuries it drew most of its people from the surrounding villages, and although we have little information on the Middle Ages a list does exist that gives the origins of almost 700 people who arrived in Birmingham to live between 1686 and 1726. Over 90% of them came from within twenty miles of Birmingham. Of these, more than 200 had migrated from within Warwickshire; a similar number had arrived from Staffordshire; almost 100 were Worcestershire people; and forty-odd belonged to Shropshire. Of the remainder, about 60 were drawn from Leicestershire, Cheshire, Derbyshire, Lancashire and Middlesex, and another 50 were from other parts of Britain.

The incomers did not leave their accents and dialects at the town's limits. They brought their speech with them and given the preponderance of incomers from the immediate locality, it is not surprising that the Brummie speech evolved from the dialect of north Warwickshire, south Staffordshire and north-east Worcestershire - the dialect which owed so much to the Middle English West Mercian tongue. In the nineteenth century, Birmingham became the magnet for people from further afield - in particular, from Cornwall, Wales, Scotland, Ireland, Italy and the Jewish pale of settlement in the Russian Empire. But local migrants continued to form the great majority of newcomers, and as late as 1951, 71% of Birmingham's citizens had been born in Warwickshire. Of course, the Brummie accent of the later nineteenth and twentieth centuries has developed into a distinctive urban accent but its roots lie within the wider West Midlands as do the words and grammatical formations of its dialect. The roots of that dialect pull us back to the misty origins of the English in this region.

Carl Chinn

Linguistic introduction

It is important to make a clear distinction from the start between accent and dialect, as many so-called dialect dictionaries frequently appear to confuse the two. Accents differ from one another in terms of pronunciation only, whereas dialects differ in terms of pronunciation, vocabulary and grammar. The words 'ackchullay' (actually), 'orsepickle' (hospital), and 'sirstificate' (certificate), for example, are not dialect words. Although each of these words have appeared in various dialect glossaries over the years, they are merely humorous attempts to represent words which normally appear in the standard English dialect but are sometimes pronounced differently in Brummie. Since an exhaustive account of how the Birmingham accent differs from other British English accents would almost certainly require a book of its own, this dictionary is concerned primarily with dialect differences[1]. If we are to fully understand the Birmingham dialect, however, a brief discussion of the main characteristics of the accent is essential.

Perhaps the most distinctive feature of the Brummie accent is the way in which the 'i' sound is formed in words such as 'lip', 'symbol', 'women', 'ladies', lettuce, and 'private'. In Birmingham speech the 'i' is very close, which means that the back of the tongue is tautened and pushed up as far as it will go against the roof of the mouth. No other dialect has a sound quite like this, and it can even occur in words such as 'bracelet' (*bracelit*), 'chocolate' (*chocklit*), 'necklace' (*neckliss*), and 'harness' (*harniss*). It must also be noted that the noun 'week' and the past participles 'seen' and 'been' are usually pronounced *wick*, *sin* and *bin* in Brummie EG "I 'en't sin 'er since last wick. She said she'd bin tryin' to find a job."

Bearing in mind that Birmingham is situated in the English heartlands, it comes as no surprise to learn that the accent associated with the area has both northern and southern characteristics. Brummie can be considered northern, for example, in that the 'a' sound occurring in words such as 'cat' and 'plait' is more open than in many southern dialects – a quality often described by people from southern dialect areas as 'flat'. Likewise, the Birmingham accent differs from most southern British English accents in that the 'a' sound also occurs in words such as 'fast', 'mask', 'grass', 'bath', 'daft', 'after', 'chance', and 'command', whereas in accents such as Cockney and Received Pronunciation there is a lengthened 'ar' vowel sound: *farst, marsk, grarse, barth, darft, arfter, charnce, commarnd*. This appears to be a more recent development, however, since older Brummie speakers often produce a lengthened 'ar' sound similar to that in Cockney EG "I throwed all me old clobber out larst wick."

There are also a few exceptions to this 'rule'. The words 'half', 'aunt', 'laugh', and 'laughter', unlike the way in which they are pronounced in many northern dialect areas such as Tyneside (*haff, ant, laff, laffter*), are generally realised in Brummie speech as *harf, arnt, larff*, and *larfta*, i.e. with an 'ar' sound. Notice, furthermore, the 'a' sound at the end of the Brummie pronunciation of 'laughter'. This is because '-er' (mother, computer, water, Christopher), '-re' (mitre), '-or' (doctor, razor), '-ar' (sugar, pillar), '-ure' (picture, mixture), '-ur' (sulphur), '-our' (colour), '-eur' (amateur), as well as '-a'

(China, dogma) word terminations invariably have a far less neutralised lip position in Birmingham speech, being realised as 'a' in most instances EG "The docta told us me motha weren't too well." To this extent, the Birmingham accent appears to share something in common with Cockney, along with many northern accents.

The vowel sound occurring in words such as 'need', 'these', 'disease', 'piece', 'receive', 'key', 'quay', 'people', and 'machine' is also much longer in Birmingham speech than it is in the majority of other British English accents. Whereas RP and some southern accents have a lengthened 'i' sound, Brummie articulation of this vowel is closer to an 'ay' sound EG "I lost me kays and couldn't get in the 'ouse." This also occurs where words end with '-y' or '-ey', as in 'pretty' (*prettay*), 'family' (*famlay*), 'money' (*monay*), and 'gulley' (*gullay*). The vowel sound in words such as 'do', 'mood', 'rude', 'group', 'flew', 'shoe', 'juice', and 'blue', moreover, is also very long in Brummie – sounding something similar to 'ow' EG "There 'en't arf a big growp o' people outside."

In RP and many southern British English accents the words 'took' and 'tuck' are pronounced differently. The vowel sound in 'took' is usually 'u', whereas in 'tuck' the vowel has more of an 'uh' sound to it. In Birmingham, as in the north of England, there is no such distinction, and minimal pairs such as 'took' and 'tuck', 'put' and 'putt', 'could' and 'cud', and 'stood' and 'stud' sound exactly the same:

RP / southern	RP / southern	Birmingham / northern
took = *tuk*	tuck = *tuhk*	tuck & took = *tuk*
put = *put*	putt = *puht*	putt & put = *put*
could = *cud*	cud = *cuhd*	cud & could = *kud*
stood = *stud*	stud = *stuhd*	stud & stood = *stud*

Brummie can also be considered southern to some extent, however, in that the vowel sound produced by Birmingham speakers in the words 'break', 'wake', 'way', 'waist', and 'weight' is very open, similar to that produced by Cockney speakers, and not at all like, for example, the kind of elongated 'air' sound produced by a Geordie in these words (*brairk*, *wairk*, *wair*, etc.). Note that, although Birmingham articulation of the vowel sound in the word 'says' is similar to RP in that speakers of both accents tend to produce an 'e' sound (*sez*), this tendency is also quite commonly extended in Brummie to other verb forms, such as 'make' (*mek*), 'made' (*med*), and 'take' (*tek*) EG "'Ow lung did it tek 'er to mek the cake?" "'Er sez she med it in about an hour."

Birmingham pronunciation of the vowel sound in the word 'one', as Hughes and Trudgill (1979) point out, is 'o', but in 'won' it is 'u'. The significance of this appears to be that the Birmingham accent (in this respect, at least) shares an affinity with neither southern or northern British English variants. In RP speech 'one' and 'won' sound the same: both being realised as *wuhn*, whereas in most northern varieties both words – although also pronounced identically – are realized as *wun*. But a tendency in Birmingham speech to produce 'u' in words where 'o' is normally present in RP English suggests that the 'one' / 'won' contrast is not as illustrative as it at first seems. The vowel sound in the word 'was', for example, has variants in the Birmingham dialect area ranging from 'o' through to 'u', and – for working-class and older Birmingham speakers in particular[2] – 'g**u**n' and 'g**o**ne', 'l**u**ng' and 'l**o**ng', and 's**u**ng' and 's**o**ng' quite often form homophonous pairs; the vowel sound in each word being realized as 'u'. Although the speech of younger Brummies appears to have succumbed to the influence of the prestige RP and Estuary variants, varying degrees of 'o' – 'u' substitution still detectable in the speech of others (and still largely retained in the speech of Black Country folk) suggests that such differences between Birmingham and northern accents did not always exist. It seems that the Birmingham accent once had much more in common with northern British English speech, but has gradually been pulled in the direction of the prestige southern variants.

The most widespread pronunciation of the vowel sound in words such as 'c**ure**', 'end**ure**', 'l**ure**', 'mat**ure**', 'p**oor**', 'p**ure**', 's**ure**', and 't**our**' is something similar to an 'or' sound throughout Britain. In Birmingham English, however, a sound similar to 'ooa' is pronounced EG "Our old mon never 'ad no money, and we was allus dead pooa." For speakers with the strongest Brummie accents, there is also virtually no audible difference between the vowel sound occurring in words such as 'f**i**ve' and 'n**oi**se'. Whereas the RP vowel in 'f**i**ve' approximates 'ai', and in 'n**oi**se' it is similar to 'oi', minimal pairs such as 'l**i**ne' and 'l**oi**n', 'f**i**le' and 'f**oi**l', 't**ie**' and 't**oy**' sound identical in Brummie speech:

RP	RP	Birmingham
line = *lain*	loin = *loin*	line & loin = *loin*
file = *fail*	foil = *foil*	file & foil = *foil*
tie = *tai*	toy = *toi*	tie & toy = *toi*
high = *hai*	hoy = *hoi*	high & hoy = *hoi*
heist = *haist*	hoist = *hoist*	heist & hoist = *hoist*
pint = *paint*	point = *point*	pint & point = *point*
kind = *kaind*	coined = *coined*	kind & coined = *coined*
buy = *bai*	boy = *boi*	buy & boy = *boi*
lighter = *laiter*	loiter = *loiter*	lighter & loiter = *loiter*

As well as vowel sounds, the Birmingham accent differs from other accents in the way that consonant sounds are either pronounced or, indeed, omitted. For example, the 'h' sound – whether occurring at the beginning of a word ('**h**appy', 'horse', 'hill') or in the middle ('per**h**aps', 'be**h**ind', 'man**h**ood'), is normally absent in working-class Birmingham speech EG "'Er's be'ind with the rent again, and 'er landlord 'en't 'appy." As is the case in many other urban working-class accents in Britain, no distinction is normally made in Brummie between words such as 'hill' and 'ill', 'high' and 'eye', or 'hair' and 'air'. Generally considered to be indicative of 'uneducated' speech, 'h-dropping' is perhaps most noticeable in Birmingham articulation of the words 'he', 'him', 'his', 'her', 'hers', 'have', 'has', and 'had' EG "'E sez 'e's 'ad enough of 'er blartin'."

The way in which younger Brummies articulate the 'g' sound in '-ing' word terminations is yet another prominent feature of the Birmingham accent. Whereas

22

speakers of accents such as Cockney, Geordie, Scouse, Glaswegian, and even RP regularly drop the 'g' ending in words such as 'hunting' (*huntin'*), 'singing' (*singin'*), and 'fishing' (*fishin'*), the 'g' sound is usually pronounced quite clearly in the speech of younger Brummies – whether it occurs at the end of a word (*sing*), in the middle (*singer*), or in both positions (*singing*). Again, this seems to be a recent development since it is not altogether true of the speech patterns of older Brummies, who quite often do drop the 'g' sound. There are, furthermore, relatively few glottal stops in Birmingham speech. For example, the 't' sound in the words 'daugh**t**er', 'cu**t**lery', and 'bu**tt**er' (articulated thus in Cockney: *daugh'er, cu'lery, bu'er*) is seldom dropped by Birmingham speakers. The same also appears to apply when the 't' sound occurs at the end of a word, as in 'fee**t**' (*feet*), and 'tha**t**' (*that*).

Brummies often produce what is referred to by linguists as a 'tap' when they speak. Gimson and Cruttenden (1994) describe a 'tap'[3] as "a sound made by a flexible organ on a firmer surface," and in the Brummagem accent it generally tends to be produced by a single voiced tap struck firmly (yet with less force than in Spanish, French, or some Scottish accents such as Glaswegian) by the tip of the tongue against the roof of the mouth near the teeth, so that it resembles a soft 'd'. 'Taps' are produced most noticeably by Brummie speakers in disyllabic words such as 'ma**rr**y', 've**r**y', 'so**rr**y', 'wo**rr**y', 'pe**r**haps', and 'al**r**ight', but they can also occur in monosyllabic words such as 'b**r**ight', 'g**r**eat', and 'c**r**eam'. Note that the 'l' sound in 'alright' – a popular form of greeting in Birmingham when used with questioning intonation, is normally silent EG "Orroight?" "Ar, orroight mate. 'Ow's it gooin'?" It must also be noted that the production of taps amongst Brummie speakers, as is the case with most of the phonological features discussed here, is by no means uniform and can vary considerably from speaker to speaker – even amongst those of the same age, gender, social class and/or ethnicity, and can sometimes even be adopted and dropped within the space of a single utterance. What has been formulated here is a generalised account of the Birmingham accent which should in no way be construed as typical of all Brummie speakers. However, if we add to this account certain lexical and grammatical features – many of which are discussed at length in the dictionary, we now have a fairly good idea of how the average working-class Brummie sounds when she or he speaks.

All of the words and phrases included in *Proper Brummie* are Brummagemisms of one kind or another, and each has been verified as such; either through cross-referencing with dialect surveys, academic studies, existing glossaries, or confirmation received from those who actually speak the Brummagem dialect themselves or have heard it spoken by others. Many words and phrases are purely local, whereas some are more than likely to be heard in the dialects of surrounding areas of England. Since it would not have been possible to trace each and every word or phrase back to its moment and place of origin, some of the words and phrases recorded in this dictionary, although proven to have been used by Birmingham people at some point or other, may have originated elsewhere. Everything has been done to ensure that the majority of entries are proper Brummie, and the remainder – if also common in other dialects – have all been acknowledged as such. "Dictionaries," as Samuel Johnson once wrote, "are like watches . . . the best cannot be expected to go quite true."[4] I hope therefore that any errors or omissions which may have escaped our scrutiny will be overlooked on the grounds that this dictionary is the first of its kind.

The sheer range, diversity and expressiveness of words and phrases included in *Proper Brummie* – from street cant, everyday idioms, betting jargon, euphemisms, Brummagem rhyming-slang, and the lingo of market traders, to pithy proverbs, old agricultural provincialisms, Shakespearean terminology, and the parlance of household appraisers – is sure to shock even those who consider themselves to be dyed-in-the-wool Brummies. Some words and phrases are no longer in general use, and may not be familiar to the majority of Brummie speakers. Others, however, will be instantly recognisable, and many are now commonly used all around the UK.

We hope you enjoy *Proper Brummie* as much as we have enjoyed compiling it – whether you plan to read it from cover to cover, or simply use it as a reference book. Future revised editions are planned, and we would be interested to hear from anybody who knows of Brummie words or phrases not included in this edition, or would like to query any that are.

Steve Thorne

Terms used in the dictionary

Anglo-Saxon: relating to the Germanic tribes of Angles, Saxons and Jutes who invaded Britain in the fifth century A.D., and whose language formed the basis for modern day English; see also *Old English.*

back-slang: slang used by Birmingham market-traders in which words are pronounced as if spelt backwards.

Black Country: a working-class dialect spoken in the South Staffordshire area of the English Midlands.[5]

Brummie: working-class Birmingham English.

Celtic: relating to a branch of the Indo-European languages including Breton, Cornish, Gaelic, Irish, Manx and Welsh, as well as the people who existed in Britain before the Roman invasion in the first century B.C.

Cockney: working-class London English.

Estuary: a form of English with an accent that identifies it as originating from London and the south-east of England (along the Thames and its estuary), but differing from Cockney in that the majority of its grammatical features conform to the standard.

Geordie: working-class Tyneside English.

Latin: relating to the language that the ancient Romans used to speak, and which was first introduced to Britain after the Roman invasion of the British Isles in the first century B.C.

Middle English: (ME) the second historical period of the English language, dating approximately from 1100 to 1500 A.D.

Norman: pertaining to the Norman-French dialect spoken by the Scandinavian people who founded the Duchy of Normandy in northern France at the beginning of the tenth century and invaded England in 1066.

Old English: (OE) the first historical period of the English language, dating approximately from 450 to 1100 A.D.

Received Pronunciation: (RP) a standardised form of pronunciation which is widely construed as the most 'correct' and used as a model for the teaching of English; can be subdivided into *marked, refined* or *upper-class* (U-RP),[6] and *unmarked* or *general* variants.

Scouse: working-class Liverpool English.

standard English: language scholars long ago denied that such a thing existed, and the concept (or 'myth', as many have labelled it) of a 'standard' continues to be a highly problematic one; generally accepted, however, as a dialect of English which is comparatively free from the more localised differences in accent, grammar and vocabulary which typify urban working-class dialects such as those listed above.

Key to abbreviations used in the dictionary

adj.   adjective; a word that describes or gives more information about a noun or pronoun EG "It's a busy street," "He's stupid"

adv.   adverb; a word that describes or adds information about a verb, adjective, preposition or other adverb EG "He fought bravely, but was defeated in the fifth round," "He got it completely wrong," "She jumped straight into the swimming pool," "Time passed very quickly"

au v.   auxiliary verb; the name given to the verbs 'be', 'have' and 'do' when they are used to help other verbs EG "I am going home," "The game had finished by 5 o'clock," "Do you understand?"

bsl.   back-slang

c.   circa; used before a year to show that it is the approximate date when something occurred

conj.   conjunction; a word that joins sentences or other words together EG "Your mom said that you were out," "I'm going down the pub after I've watched the match," "The dogs are scared of thunder and lightning."

dem.   demonstrative; a word that points out things or people and draws our attention to them EG "Those shoes are nice," "Look at that!"

esp.   especially

infin.   infinitive; the base form of a verb which does not have inflections EG "You must tell me everything," "Let me go!"

interj.   interjection; a word or phrase used to express a strong feeling EG "My God!," "Oh no!," "Wow!"

n.   noun; the name of a person or thing EG "I bought a new car last week," "His name is John," "You could see the anxiety in his face"

nom.   nominative; the noun or pronoun which is the subject of a sentence is said to be in the nominative case EG "She fell over and broke her arm"

npl.   plural noun; a noun when it refers to two or more people or things EG "I bought a jacket and three shirts"

pa p.   past participle; the form of a verb used in compound tenses, such as the present perfect: "He's already done it," and the past perfect: "It had started to rain when we left the house," as well as in passive constructions: "This poem was written over four hundred years ago"

pa t.   past tense; the form of a verb used to describe past events EG "We spent about £100 on groceries yesterday"

ph v.   phrasal verb; these consist of either a verb + adverb ("She walked out"), a verb + preposition ("We couldn't get on the bus"), or a verb + adverb + preposition ("He's trying to cut down on smoking")

pr p.   present participle; the form of a verb used to describe something that is happening at or around the time of speaking EG "I'm learning to speak German"

prep.   preposition; a word that can describe either where or when something is EG

"You left your keys <u>on</u> the table," "I'll see you <u>in</u> two weeks"

pron. pronoun; a word used in place of a noun EG "<u>He</u> flew to Beijing last week," "<u>We</u> haven't seen either of <u>them</u> since last Sunday"

vi. intransitive verb; a verb that can be used without a direct object EG "He <u>disappeared</u>"

vt. transitive verb; a verb that takes a direct object EG "They <u>love</u> ice cream"

vulg. vulgar(ly); a slang or taboo term

Using the dictionary

Main entry words

All of the main entries in the dictionary are shown in bold type:

podge

Main entries, including hyphenated words and two-word compounds, appear in strict alphabetical order:

poke
poothery
pop
poppy-show
posher
pot alley

Part of speech labels

Parts of speech are shown in abbreviated form in italics:

pot-ball *n.*
pothery *adj.*

A second part of speech label may also follow the first definition if a main entry word can be used in more than one way:

arter *prep.* after; following, also *n.* afternoon.

Meanings

Definitions of each word appear immediately after the part of speech label:

powk *n.* a stye; an inflamed swelling on the eyelid.

Cross-references

Cross-references are also shown in bold type:

cat's eye *n.* a medium-sized marble; see also **alley**, **alley taw**, **blood alley**, **dogger**, **dummox**, **French alley**, **glarny**, **glass alley**, **gobbie**, **marley**, **pot alley** and **steelie**.

Variant spellings

All spelling variants are treated as separate entries:

huggermaugh *n.* see **huggermaw**.
huggermaw *n.* a type of hay knife; tool used to produce an 'Eton crop' on hay ricks.

29

Sources   Sources for each entry are shown in brackets:
                                proud-tailor *n.* the goldfinch (Timmins,
                                1889).

Examples   Examples, showing typical contexts of use and
                                grammatical structures, are given in speech marks:
                                trussen *vt.* to place trust in; to have
                                supreme confidence in something or
                                someone EG "I wun't trussen him far as I
                                could chock 'im."

Etymology   Word origins, if known, are also shown towards the
                                end of each entry:
                                abear *vt.* to like or endure EG "I can't abear
                                the sight of 'im" (Rhodes, 1950); from the
                                Anglo-Saxon 'aboeran'.

---

[1] For an in-depth account of how the Birmingham accent differs from other British English accents, as well as a discussion of associated linguistic, psychological and socio-cultural issues see Thorne (1999 and 2001).

[2] Note also that substitution of 'o' for 'u', although more widespread in the Black Country area, now appears to be confined mostly to the westerly parts of Birmingham.

[3] The International Phonetic Alphabet (revised to 1993, corrected 1996) makes reference to this sound as a 'flap'.

[4] From a letter to Francesco Sastres dated 24 August 1784.

[5] Like Brummie, Cockney, Geordie and Scouse, Black Country speech has also retained many of its distinctive lexico-grammatical features.

[6] Wells (1982), for example, uses this definition, whereas Gimson and Cruttenden (1994) favour the *refined/general* method of differentiation. This variant is also popularly known as *upper-crust* or *the Queen's English*, whereas other forms of RP are commonly referred to as *BBC* or *university-educated* English.

A

a *vt.* commonly used as a contracted form of the verb 'have' in continuous speech EG "Who'd a thought it?," "You shouldn't a done it" (Rhodes, 1950), also "as a prefix to the participle" (Skeat, 1876) EG "We're a-comin' directly," "As I was a-walking to Birmingham fair, I saw pretty Nancy a-combing her hair" (*A New Song Called Young Ramble-away*, 1845-1861). In *The Vision of Piers Plowman* by William Langland, written in the West Mercian dialect in the late 1300s, there is the line "Tho was Peres proude and pott hem alle a-werk." The addition of 'a' before some verbs is still common and older Brummies would say they are going 'a-work'. 'A' is also used for 'of', as in "What kind a thing is that?"

abear *vt.* to like or endure (Skeat, 1876); to withstand; to bear; normally used in the negative form "I can't abear the sight of 'im" (Rhodes, 1950); Spenser uses 'abear' in this sense in his poem *The Faerie Queene*: "So did the faerie Knight himselfe abeare, And stouped oft his head from shame to shield" (Book V, Cant. XII, 19); from the Anglo-Saxon 'aboeran'.

abed *adv.* or *adj.* in bed; asleep (Skeat, 1876) EG "You have not been abed, then?" (Shakespeare, *Othello*, Act III, Sc. I).

abide *vt.* see **abear** (Skeat, 1876); 'abide' has the same meaning as 'abear' and is derived from the Middle English 'abyde', meaning 'to endure' EG "I carn abide that kind a thing."

ablish *adj.* competent; qualified EG "'E's an ablish sort."

abost *vt.* to assault EG "A Bretone, a braggere, A-bosted Piers als" (from *The Vision of Piers Plowman*); see also **bost**.

abrook *vt.* to endure with patience; to tolerate (Alexander, 1951) EG "Sweet Nell, ill can thy noble mind abrook" (Shakespeare, *Henry VI (Part 2)*, Act II, Sc. IV).

Absey-book *n.* an ABC book; "a catechism, hornbook or primer used for teaching children the rudiments of reading" (Halliwell, 1855); "a book used to teach the alphabet" (Alexander, 1951) EG "And then comes answer like an Absey book" (Shakespeare, *King John*, Act I, Sc. I).

ackern *n.* pronunciation variant of 'acorn', also *vi.* to gather acorns EG "I'm a-gooin' ackernin' tomorra" (Rhodes, 1950); in other dialects it is 'aitchorning' (Halliwell, 1855).

ackidock *n.* pronunciation variant of aqueduct (Rhodes, 1950); in the twentieth century the normal pronounciation is 'ackerdocks', hence the Ackers, an activities site on part of the grounds of the old BSA factory in Greet.

acky *n.* see **acky vortis** (Rhodes, 1950).

acky-one-two-three *n.* see **I-acky**.

acky vortis *n.* a crude form of nitric acid used by jewellers and brass founders (Rhodes, 1950).

a-corning *n.* see **a-Thomasing**.

Adam's ale *n.* cold water EG "To slake his thirst he took a drink of Adam's ale from river's brink" (Jeffrey, 1868); 'Adam's wine' is the variant heard in some Scottish dialects.

adlan *n.* "part of a field left, for convenience of working, unploughed till the very end" (Alexander, 1951); "those butts in a ploughed field which lie at right angles to the general direction of the others" (Halliwell, 1855).

adone *vt.* and *vi.* contracted form of 'have done' EG "Adone, will yer?," "Why can't you adone shoutin' when I tell yer?" (Northall, 1896).

Aerly Baerd *n.* a racing paper in which tips appeared; borrowed, perhaps, from Cockney rhyming slang (Rhodes, 1950), also used in the expression "Afore I could say Aerly Baerd" (Squiers, 1916, p.3), which appears to be similar in sentiment to today's "Before I could say Jack Robinson."

Aerbut and Gaertie *n.* characters in a series of Birmingham dialect monologues penned by Graham Squiers (1916-31) entitled *Aerbut Paerks of Baernegum*, *Aerbut and Gaertie in War-Time*, *More about the Paerkses*, *The Rotary Bawl*, *Aerbut and Gaertie get Raphaelitis* and *The Aerbut and Gaertie Sketches*; according to Ainsworth (1989), Squiers also recorded his monologues for the Columbia Gramophone Company: "The resultant shellac discs – 78 rpm, of course – were very popular locally in the twenties and early thirties."

afeard *adj.* see **afeared**.

afeared *adj.* afraid; frightened; scared EG "Our nipper's afeared of the dark," "No more, I pray thee; I am half afeard" (Shakespeare, *The Merchant of Venice*, Act II, Sc. IX).

afterclap *n.* a sudden or unexpected subsequent event, consequence, or result; usually of an unpleasant kind EG "For he [the devil] can give us an afterclap when we least weene" (Latimer, 2000).

ag *vi.* to pester or nag EG "Stop yer aggin' 'n' gerron with it" (Rhodes, 1950).

aggy-face *n.* a term used for someone who is either in a bad mood, miserable or sulking.

agin *prep.* near; close by; near at hand EG "'Er as lives close agin us is in the old pickle" (Skeat, 1876).

agnail *n.* "a hang-nail, either on the finger or toe" (Halliwell, 1855).

a-gooding *n.* see **a-Thomasing**.

ah *adv.* see **ar** (Rhodes, 1950).

aigle *n.* an icicle (Marshall, 1796).

aince-awhile *adv.* now and then; once in a while; at intervals (Skeat, 1876).

airy *adj.* lightly clad, hatless and coatless.

aisins *npl.* see **easings**.

aitchbone *n.* butcher's joint, or – more precisely, "the edge-bone" (Halliwell, 1855).

aive *vi.* to lift; pronunciation variant of 'heave'; "in some parts of the Midlands, Easter Monday used to be celebrated as 'Aivin' Day' when men had the privilege of lifting women, perhaps as a crude reminder of the Resurrection" (Northall, 1896); see also **heaving day**.

alder-liefest *adj.* beloved; "dearest of all" (Alexander, 1951) EG "With you, mine alder-liefest sovereign" (Shakespeare, *Henry VI (Part 2)*, Act I, Sc. I).

alley *n.* a marble; a small hard ball used in children's games; "a choice taw, made of alabaster, is so called by boys" (Halliwell, 1855); probably an abbreviation of alabaster, and – since Dickens uses this word in *The Pickwick Papers*, its use was more than likely not restricted to the Birmingham dialect area alone; see also **alley taw**, **blood alley**, **cat's eye**, **dogger**, **dummox**, **French alley**, **glarny**, **glass alley**, **gobbie**, **marley**, **pot alley** and **steelie**.

alley taw *n.* see **alley**; "a taw was the 'business' marley" (Rhodes, 1950).

allus *adv.* every time; continually; pronunciation variant of always, as used in the nineteenth century Brummagem street ballad *Poverty Knock*:

> Lizzie is so easy led.
> Ah thinks that 'e teks her to bed.
> She allus was skinny, now look at her pinny.
> It's just about time they was wed.

along of *prep.* on account of EG "It was all along of that Bill Hancox' fancies, that the master kep' me in school" (Skeat, 1876).

alright *interj.* hello; pronounced as 'oroyt', this is the usual form of greeting in Birmingham. The response is not to launch into a litany of your woes but to state, "Not bad. You alright?" This reply usually elicits an "Ar, alright" from the first person.

Alum Rock *n.* area of Birmingham incorporating that part of Saltley east of Bowyer Road and Highfield Road, and that part of Little Bromwich between the Aston and Stechford and the Rugby to Birmingham railway lines. Both localities came into Birmingham in 1891, at which date Alum Rock remained a largely agricultural district. Its name is rumoured to have been derived from the discovery of alum in the area when Southall's set up a manufactory on the Alum Rock Road, although a map dated 1759 shows an Allum Rock Estate already in existence, and a document dated 1718 also mentions an Alom Rock.

alum rocks *npl.* Brummagem rhyming slang for socks (K. Carruthers).

an *interj.* an expression used by waggoners to make the horses move towards the left (Palmer, 1976) see also **eet**, **comming-gen**, **gee-gen** and **gee-whoop**.

an'all *adv.* see **annawl**.

ancere *interj.* encore (Rhodes, 1950).

anenst *prep.* see **anunst**.

anent *prep.* see **anunst**.

an-hond *adj.* in hand; "i.e. in his power" (Halliwell, 1855) EG "Me to wreken ye schul go / Of a treytour that is mi fo, / That is y-come up mi lond, / Wer he thenketh to bring me an-hond" (from *The Famous History of Guy, Earle of Warwicke*, 1620, p.43).

anigh *prep.* near; close to EG "'E en't bin anigh the place," and "Don't go anigh 'im" (Skeat, 1876).

annawl *adv.* too; also; as well; in addition EG "'E 'as annawl," "Ain't there a fleekin' crowd an'orl" (Squiers, 1916, p.16); a contraction of 'and all'.

33

an'orl *adv.* see **annawl**.

anty-tump *n.* an anthill.

anunst *prep.* against; in contact with; in opposition to EG "It's the 'ouse anunst hisn" (Raven, 1978).

any road *adv.* see **any road up**.

any road up *adv.* anyway; anyhow; at any rate; in any case EG "We would listen, but wouldn't murmur, trying to get the gist of their conversation, but we never did, because we were too young to understand, but we would listen any road up, for it brought a certain comfort and security just knowing our Dad wus at 'um" (Smith, undated); still in common use.

appund *n.* see **aprond**.

aprond *n.* apron; adding a 'd' to the end of nouns appears to have been common practice for Birmingham and Black Country speakers alike; see, for example, **gownd**, **lawnd**, **riband** and **saucepand** EG "Ah, it's a haprond, yo gotter tie it on yer like that cove theer" (Squiers, 1916, p.2).

aqua fortis *n.* see **acky vortis** (Rhodes, 1950).

ar *adv.* yes; okay; affirmative (Skeat, 1876); used to express approval, acceptance or compliance; also common throughout surrounding counties, though its future use in the West Midlands seems threatened by the continuing spread of the standardized form, 'yes' (see Upton, Sanderson and Widdowson, 1987, p.216); Ainsworth (1989) also states that "if intoned in a questioning manner, this response can imply a high degree of disbelief, rather than agreement," so that when one person says something that does not induce confidence, the listener may respond, "Oh ar." The phrase can also be used when defying somebody EG "You'd better watch it or I'll clock you one!" "Oh ar, you and whose army?"

Ardintone *n.* see **Erdington**.

Aristotle *n.* Brummagem rhyming slang for 'bottle'.

arley-barley *interj.* see **barlay**.

armhole *n.* armpit; also used as an exclamation when something goes wrong EG "Oh, armhole!" When someone raises their arm and rubs one hand under their armhole then that signifies distaste for something.

aroint *interj.* go away; be off (Alexander, 1951) EG "Aroint thee, witch!" (Shakespeare, *Macbeth*, Act I, Sc. III). It occurs three times in Shakespeare's works in this sense, and is applied in each instance to witches; probably of Anglo-Saxon origin, but Halliwell (1855) suggests that it may be derived from the Latin 'averrunco', "the participle of which may have been formed into 'aroint'."

arse-uppards *adv.* literally 'arse-upwards'; see also **arsy-versy**.

arsy-versy *adv.* topsy-turvy; Northall (1896) points out that Ben Jonson uses this term, probably obtained during one of his visits to Warwickshire, "but this is stretching a point; the word is, and has been common enough in the midlands."

arter *prep.* after; following (Skeat, 1876) EG "At Michaelmas and a little before, away goes the apple along with the core; at Christmas and a little bit arter, a crab in the hedge is worth looking arter" (Palmer, 1976), "Looking back I can see me queuing for the Tupp'nny crush on a Sat'day arternoon arter a look at ole mon Blackwell's, an' scroungin' some specks (fruit turning bad) ta stuff while we wus watchin' Buck Jones, Johnnie Mack Brown, or the Whisperin' Shadder" (Smith, undated), also *n.* afternoon EG "Gooin' to the match this arter?" Many older working-class Brummies use both the short and long vowel sound for 'a' so that 'after' can be pronounced as either 'arfter' or 'after'. 'Arter' is derived from the former sound. The long vowel is often used to stress something so that 'barstud' is even more a term of opprobrium than 'bastard'.

article *n.* Northall (1896) states that this word is commonly used as "an expression of contempt for man, beast or thing" EG "Yer daft article!" In the twentieth century, the word 'article' is regularly used when referring to a woman who was not regarded as clean, as in "'Er's a dirty article, 'er is."

arrand *n.* errand EG "Item given to a man to goe to Witton of an arrand" (Aston Parish Register, 1664).

as *conj.* commonly used in place of that EG "It worn't us as did it."

asiden *adj.* crooked; bent; bowed; possibly used to show disapproval (i.e., dishonest; corrupt); no longer in widespread use; see also **siden**.

ask *vt.* to publish the banns of marriage; see also **askings**.

asker *n.* a water-newt.

askings *n.* the publication of the banns of marriage (Northall, 1896).

assud-backud *adj.* back-to-front; literally 'arseward-backward' EG "That's an assud-backud way o' diggin' taters" (Northall, 1896); see also **arse-uppards** and **arsy-versy**.

Aston *n.* area of Birmingham. In the Domesday Book of 1086 it was recorded as **Estone**, meaning the east farmstead, manor or estate, though it was debatable as to which main settlement in particular it was to the east of.

atcha *interj.* greeting; hallo.

a-Thomasing *n.* on St Thomas's Day (21st December) the poor throughout Warwickshire went from door to door "collecting any sort of provisions against the coming winter, and Christmas . . . in some districts people specifically asked for corn (hence 'a-corning')," but the meaning of the variant 'a-gooding' is unknown (Palmer, 1976). A rhyme that poor people chanted as they went a-Thomasing ran thus:

> Little Cock Robin sat on a wall,
> We wish a merry Christmas,
> And a great snow fall;
> Apples to eat
> And nuts to crack
> We wish you a merry Christmas
> With a rap, tap, tap.

atredanz *npl.* see **hatredans**.

atte *prep.* at EG "And thanne seten somme / And songen atte nale" (from *The Vision of Piers Plowman*); see also **Rea**.

attwood *n.* an idiot or fool (Northall, 1894 & 1896); particularly common in those parts of Birmingham which were once in Warwickshire.

a-wail *vt.* to hurt; to cause pain to; to play up EG "'Er leg's a-wailin' 'er again."

awhile *adv.* shortly; soon; in good time EG "I'll do it when I can awhile" (Skeat, 1876).

ax *vt.* to ask, inquire or request EG "For my werke, nothing will I axe" (Chaucer, *The Canterbury Tales*), "Well then axe the mon into the parlour" (from the Brummagem street ballad *Christening the Wench Ben*, published anonymously in the 1870s); derived from the Anglo-Saxon 'axian' (to ask) and much older than the present standardized form; still in common use, though often looked upon as 'sub-standard' or 'vulgar'.

axe *vt.* see **ax**.

axings *n.* see **askings**.

axins *n.* see **askings**.

aysam-jaysam *adj.* equitable; fair and square; honest (Northall, 1894), also *adv.* EG "'E beat 'im aysam-jaysam." (Rhodes, 1950), and *n.* common sense EG "Use a bit of ayzum-jayzum" (Mary Bodfish); see also the phrase **upright and down straight**.

ayzam-jayzam *adj.* see **aysam-jaysam**.

ayzum-jayzum *adj.* see **aysam-jaysam**.

B

bab *n.* see **babby**.

babber *n.* betting terminology for the controller of a tossing ring.**babby** *n.* baby; child; the youngest in a family EG "Poor babby cried . . . till we got to Brummagem for the night" (Gaskell, 1882), "Our wenches, the young un's that is, Audrey, Dorothy, an' the Babby, our Bet" (Smith, undated); derived from the Anglo-Saxon 'babban'. The word is commonly shortened to 'bab' and is used as such not only towards children as in "Eeyar bab," but also towards younger women, "Thanks bab," and sometimes towards older women and men by their own age group, as in "Alright bab."

backarapper *n.* a cracker with several folds giving a rapid succession of explosions (Rhodes, 1950).

back'ards *adv.* pronunciation variant of 'backwards'; towards the back, as in the phrase "'Er 'en't back'ards in comin' forward," and the old Handsworth village crow-scaring rhyme from the early 1800s:

> Cooo-oo!
> I've got a pair of clappers,
> And I'll knock 'e down back'ards;
> I've got a great stone,
> And I'll break your backbone.

backarraper *n.* see **backarapper**.

backen *vt.* to keep back; to hinder, delay or retard EG "Them illnesses of 'isn backened 'im at 'is schoolin'" (Rhodes, 1950), "This frost'll backen the spring" (Northall, 1896).

backerapper *n.* see **backarapper**.

backfriend *n.* a piece of loose, irritating skin at the base of the fingernail (Northall, 1894 & 1896); Halliwell (1855), however, suggests that 'back-friend' was a word used in the old Warwickshire dialect for "a secret enemy" EG "A fiend, a fairy, pitiless and rough; / A wolf, nay, worse, a fellow all in buff; / A back-friend, a shoulder-clapper, one that countermands / The passages of alleys, creeks and narrow lands," (Shakespeare, *The Comedy of Errors*, Act IV, Sc. II), and Alexander's (1951) definition certainly seems to support this: "The officer who arrests you from behind."

backing *n.* slack for fires, "placed at the back of the coal" (Rhodes, 1950).

back of *prep.* behind; at the far side of; according to Tennant (1983), this was also "a reference to garret and backroom workers, who rented a single room, or even a hearth in someone else's house, to carry on their trade. The expression 'back of' someone's house was once quite frequent. The existence of one name per house would merely indicate the presence of the owner, chief tenant or rate-payer, or the man who opened the door to the publisher's canvasser. The little men would take no special steps to make their presence known for their reputation was with their neighbours and friends. They were typical Birmingham men and few of them had premises which could be shown to elegant visitors." 'Back of' was also the address of those tens of thousands of Brummies who lived in back-to-back houses that did not front on to the street. These were the great majority of such houses and were either directly backing on to front houses or down an entry and up a yard. Thus, when someone talks of 'all those whose address was back of', he or she is referring to the working-class Brummies of back-to-back Brummagem.

backrackets *n.* see **backarapper**.

backsetter *n.* "a stick or piece of wood placed outside the back of a slaughtered animal; each end of the stick being inserted into a slit, for the purpose of keeping the body open and extended" (Northall, 1896).

back-shift *n.* the late afternoon shift in a factory, mine, or mill (Raven, 1978); see also dead-man's shift.

backstone *n.* an iron for baking cakes, generally hung over an open fire; Northall (1896) states that "a stone was formerly used for the purpose, though the practice has given way to the more convenient material, iron." According to Halliwell (1855), the larger, "or double ones as they are called are about 28 to 30 inches by 16 to 20, and the smaller ones vary in size, 16 or 18 inches square"; see also the phrase **like a cat on a hot bake-stone**.

bad *adj.* late; behindhand, esp. when in arrears EG "I'm a quarter bad in me rent" (Northall, 1896).

bagsy *interj.* term used by youngsters laying claim to something, as in "Bagsy I goo first!"

baigle *n.* a corruption of 'beagle'; Northall (1896) claims that baigle was commonly used as "an opprobrious epithet" for "a depraved woman" EG "She's a beagle, true-bred, and one that adores me" (Shakespeare, *Twelfth Night*, Act II, Sc. III).

bain't *vi.* am not; negated form of the first person singular of the verb 'to be' EG "I bain't a-gooin' to work nex'wick" (Northall, 1896); now largely confined to the Black Country dialect, though still in use among older generations of Birmingham speakers.

bait *n.* a working lunch EG "I'm tekkin' me dad 'is bait," and "Ain't it time we 'ad us our bit o' bait" (Northall, 1896).

baiting-the-bear *n.* a children's game based on the cruel sport which was popular in Birmingham and surrounding areas up until the late nineteenth century. According to Palmer (1976), children who played this game would chant: "Here lies John Bull: if you don't hit him hard, I ull [will]," then take it in turns "to hit another, who crouched down and used his jacket for protection. The 'bear' had to try and identify one of his assailants, who then took his place."

bake-stone *n.* see **backstone**.

Balaam *n.* slang term for a horse (Jeffrey, 1868).

balched *n.* a nestling bird without feathers.

balks *npl.* the grass strips of ridges dividing ploughed lands in open common fields; a ridge of land left unploughed between the furrows; Northall (1896) suggests that in some areas of the Midlands the word 'balks' had much more of a negative connotation, meaning bad ploughing or generally uneven ground EG "Many bywalks, many balks: many balks, much stumbling" (old Midlands proverb).

ball and chalk *n.* Brummagem rhyming-slang for 'a walk' EG "I'm gooin' out fer a ball and chalk" (K. Carruthers).

balmpot *n.* see **barmpot**.

Balsall Heath *n.* area of Birmingham south of the city centre. The first mention of Balsall Heath is in a document from 1541 which describes the place as Bordishalle Hethe. W. B. Bickley was an expert on this part of Birmingham and he felt that Bordishalle was derived from Bordesley, which adjoined Balsall Heath. Thus, Bordesley was the clearing owned by a man called Bord, whilst Bordishalle was the place in a hollow owned by Bord. Bickley went on to explain that locally the name Bordesley was pronounced without the 'd', becoming Bor'sley. He deduced that this word was attached to 'heath' and thus led to Borsley Heath and then Borsall Heath. Certainly the will of Richard Grevis in 1600 mentions Borseley, which adds weight to Bickley's belief. Balsall Heath has been spelt in a variety of ways. In the Bordesley Tax Roll of 1552 a Bawsall Heath is recorded, and in July 1610, Joseph Rotton of Baulsole Heath was baptised at King's Norton Parish Church. By 1753 some people were spelling the name as Balsall Heath, as was shown by an advertisement in *Aris's Birmingham Gazette*. Still, fourteen years later the act which turnpiked the road to Alcester noted Ball's Hall Heath, whilst Boswell Heath was written down in 1795. Bickley's derivation certainly seems more likely than an attempt to relate Balsall Heath to Balsall Common. Those holding this view presume that someone from the Warwickshire village brought the name to what became the Birmingham suburb. In their opinion, Balsall is made up of the Old English words 'Baell' and 'hale', meaning Bael's place in the hollow.

balter *vi.* to gather, collect, accumulate or congeal; Northall (1896) writes that "when new-fallen snow collects on a horse's hoofs, so as to render it difficult for him to proceed safely, it is said to balter. In like manner, if, in mixing flour with milk or other liquids, it forms into lumps, the same expression is used."

balti *n.* from the Hindi for 'bucket'; a name first coined by the Kashmiri/Pakistani community of Birmingham for a style of spicy meat or vegetable curry cooked quickly over a high flame; also applied to the half-hemispherical steel or cast-iron pots with handles which balti dishes are typically cooked and served in. On *the Birmingham Balti Experience* website it is suggested that "to a certain degree, the utensil determines the cooking style, as a corollary of the 'form follows function' rule." Balti dishes are usually seasoned with spices such as cardamom, cloves, coriander, cumin and ginger, and served with a naan (a piece of thin leavened bread), which is broken into pieces and used as an eating implement. Contrary to popular opinion, Birmingham – known widely as the balti capital – is where the word was first used in this sense, and 'karai' (sometimes pronounced 'karahi' or 'karhai') is the equivalent term used in Kashmir and Pakistan for the same type of dish and cooking utensil.

balti belt *n.* the Sparkhill, Sparkbrook, Balsall Heath and Moseley areas of south Birmingham, so-called because of the high concentration of balti restaurants in the locality; home to the oldest and best balti restaurants in Britain.

bancel *vt.* see **bansel**.

bandogs *npl.* mastiffs used in bear-baiting; the entertainments laid on for Queen Elizabeth during her visit to Kenilworth Castle in 1575 included plays, ballad singing, hunting and bear-baiting: "The bandogs were tied up in the outer court, and 'thyrteen bears' were chained to posts in the inner court. Then the dogs were released and there was a fierce battle. These blood-thirsty sports were popular in Elizabethan times, and for several centuries after" (Palmer, 1976).

bandy *vt.* and *n.* Shakespeare uses bandy as a verb in *King Lear* (Act I, Sc. IV): "Do you bandy looks with me, you rascal!," and Alexander (1951) gives its meaning as "to exchange blows or words or looks (as strokes in a rally at tennis)." It seems much more likely, however, that Shakespeare was referring to hockey, since, as Northall (1896) points out, this was an early Warwickshire dialect word for the game; also *n.* the curved stick used in the game of hockey (Northall, 1894); see also **nun**.

bandy-legged *adj.* said of a person with an irregular gait or who seems unsteady on their feet; see also **bandylegs**.

bandylegs *n.* a person with shaky legs; someone who seems unsteady on their feet; a name often applied to people from Walsall, as in the old Warwickshire folk-rhyme:

Sutton for mutton, and Tamworth for beeves;
Walsall for bandylegs, Brummagem for thieves.

See also **knock-knees, hoppety-kick** and the phrase **Walsall whoffler**.

bangles *npl.* the larger pieces of wood in faggots (Skeat, 1876).

bang on *ph v.* exactly; precisely EG "Turn her out bang on four fifty or you'll let the housewife down" (from Ian Campbell's *The Apprentice's Song*; a ballad made up of recorded interviews with men from Saltley Gasworks). Today 'bang on' is commonly used when someone wishes to stress that everthing is fine, as in "What kind a do was it?" "Oh, bang on'; or, "Was everythink oroyt?" "Ar, bang on."

banksmen *npl.* see **bonksmen**.

bansel *vt.* to beat or drive EG "Bansel the dogs out" (Northall, 1896).

bap *n.* the softer type of small round loaf.

bar *prep.* except for; apart from; not including; a common term in horse racing, it is also used widely in Brum in expressions like "We all wen' out, all bar Our Kid."

bargain *n.* a baby EG "I see yer got yer bargain, Liz".

barge *n.* a strap which passes from the fore-wale of a horse's collar, in use c.1615 (Hoddinott and Nikitas); mentioned in a Solihull household inventory three hundred years before its first recorded use in the Oxford English Dictionary.

bark *n.* someone who is unsavoury, unliked and does nasty things EG "'E's a right bark 'e is, the way 'e guz on."

barkemill *n.* a mill in which bark is ground for tanning, in use c.1615 (Hoddinott and Nikitas), the date of the first recorded use of this word in a similar sense is given in the Oxford English Dictionary as 1824.

barlay *adj.* and *interj.* free; unhindered; without encumbrance; unrestrained. The same word appears in *Sir Gawain and the Green Knight*, the epic Arthurian poem written during the fourteenth century. Although the work is anonymous, the author's use of language marks them out as someone from the old region of West Mercia – south Lancashire, Cheshire, Shropshire, Staffordshire, Warwickshire and Worcestershire. At the beginning of the poem the gigantic green stranger at King Arthur's court challenges any man to strike him with his axe "so long as I shall have leave to launch a return blow Barlay." Here the word 'Barlay' means free or unchecked, and it's not hard to see how it came to be used by West Midlands kids in their play when wanting a break. Children still shout out 'barley!' or 'arley-barley!' when playing tig.

barley *adj.* see **barlay**.

barm *n.* yeast EG "And sometime make the drink to bear no barm" (Shakespeare, *A Midsummer Night's Dream*, Act II, Sc. I); from the Anglo-Saxon 'beorm'.

Barmegam *n.* variant of Birmingham listed in Langford (1868).

barmpot *n.* a silly or stupid person (K. Jenks) EG "'Ush, yer barmpot, it's in ther saervice" (Squiers, 1916, p.9).

barmy *adj.* dim-witted; stupid, also mad; insane; still in common use.

barnacles *npl.* spectacles; eyeglasses; Baker (1854) suggests that this was "a metaphorical application of the instrument applied by farriers to the nose of a restive horse whilst being shod," whereas Jackson (1879) describes an instrument, "like the figure of 8 in form, which is applied to the nose of a savage bull to subdue its violence."

barney *n.* a fight; a row or argument; still in common use.

barny *n.* see **barney**.

Barre *n.* see **Great Barr**.

barring-out *n.* a custom observed by Birmingham schoolchildren which involved arriving at school before the teachers on a traditional day and shutting them out in order to be given a day's holiday. Parson Thomas Hall, Curate of King's Norton and schoolmaster at the local grammar school where barring-out was practiced, was vehemently opposed to such goings-on: he "abhorred that lewd Custom of Schollers shutting their Masters out of doores & having broke in upon his boys severall yeares & drove them forth, at last (being too venturous & building too much upon former success) He had one tooth struck out, & two crazed; but since the breaking of his teeth broke the neck of Vile custom, it pleased him well" According to Palmer (1976), a barring-out used to take place at King Edward's School in Birmingham on 26ᵗʰ November, and there was also another famous barring-out at Nuneaton Grammar School. "According to Dr Johnson, Addison, in 1683, was the ringleader in an affair of this kind at Lichfield."

barrow *n.* pronounced as 'barrer', and used sarcastically - usually when somebody has done something unpraiseworthy - to imply that it is not out of character EG "That's just about his barrer" (i.e.: all he's good for).

Bartley Green *n.* area of Birmingham; noted in the Domesday Book of 1086 as Berchelai; from the Old English 'beorc leah', this means either 'the birch tree wood' or 'the clearing in the birch trees'.

basing *n.* rind, usually of cheese (Northall, 1896, and Rhodes, 1950).

bass *n.* "a hassock for kneeling on, covered with woollen yarn" (Northall, 1896).

bat *n.* a lump of unburnable coal; a slaty deposit found amongst coal EG "I found a lump o' bat in the scuttle" (R. Couling).

bat and wicket *n.* Brummie rhyming slang for 'ticket'. According to K. Carruthers, this term is often used when referring to someone who has been barred from a pub, "'E's 'ad 'is bat 'n' wicket."

batch-cake *n.* "a small cake made of the surplus dough after the batch of bread is moulded" (Skeat, 1876, and Northall, 1896); "a small 'oven-bottom' loaf made for immediate use" (Jackson, 1879).

batching *n.* "an unfledged bird" (Northall, 1896, and Skeat, 1876).

batch-loaf *n.* see **batch-cake**.

bat-fowl *vi.* "to catch birds at night by dazzling them with a light" (Alexander, 1951) EG "We would so, and then go a-bat-fowling" (Shakespeare, *The Tempest*, Act II, Sc. I).

bather *vt.* to buffet with the wings, as a foul EG "That new 'en don't 'arf bather the pullets" (Northall, 1896), also *vi.* to flap wildly; to flutter in the dust, whilst pruning the feathers, as birds do.

batler *n.* a wooden instrument used to beat clothes as they are being washed (Wise,

1861, and Alexander, 1951) EG "I remember the kissing of her batler" (Shakespeare, *As You Like It*, Act II, Sc. IV); see also **dolly** and **maid**.

batlet *n.* see **batler**.

batters *npl.* railway or canal embankments, esp. common in the Tamworth and Minworth areas of the Midlands (Northall, 1894 & 1896).

battin *n.* a truss of straw (Marshall, 1796).

battle-twig *n.* an earwig.

baulch *adv.* to fall 'baulch' is to fall flat on your face; to fall suddenly or heavily and in an undignified manner EG "The pony shied, an' I come down baulch on me back" (Northall, 1896).

baum *vt.* see **bawm**.

bauson *n.* a corpulent or obese person (Northall, 1896); no longer in common use.

bavin *npl.* easily-kindled brushwood (Alexander, 1951); "the scraps and scrapings of the faggot, in distinction to the faggot itself, and which so easily kindle" (Wise, 1861) EG "With shallow jesters and rash bavin wits, soon kindled and soon burnt" (Shakespeare, *Henry IV (Part 1)*, Act III, Sc. II).

bawcock *n.* an obese person; a "stout fellow" (Alexander, 1951); from the French 'beau' and 'coq' EG "Good bawcock, bate thy rage" (Shakespeare, *Henry V*, Act III, Sc. II).

bawk *vt.* to hinder, baffle or confuse; also common in the Black Country dialect.

bawm *vt.* to smear or daub; "to load a loose substance on thickly" (Mary Bodfish) EG "He's baumed his hands wi' cart grease" (Rhodes, 1950).

bawsen *n.* see **bauson**.

bazing *n.* see **basing**.

beano *n.* a party or celebration EG "We'm agooin' to 'ave a beano on this 'arf quid" (Squiers, 1916, p.24).

bear-herd *n.* see **bearward**.

Bearre *n.* see **Great Barr**.

bearward *n.* a person who keeps bulls for baiting (Northall, 1894); "one who keeps a bear for exhibition" (Alexander, 1951) EG "I will even take sixpence in earnest of the berrord, and lead his apes into hell" (Shakespeare, *Much Ado About Nothing*, Act II, Sc. I). At the last Birmingham bull-baiting in Handsworth, near Soho Pool in 1825, "the constables managed to secure two of the principals or berrods, as well as the bull itself" (Edwards, 1879). According to Rhodes (1950), "the word is a legacy of Elizabethan times, when bear-baiting was the chief sport of the bear-pits, and bull-baiting merely a minor variation." 'Bear-herd' appears to be an attempt to rationalize the spelling by false analogy with 'shepherd' and 'goatherd'.

beastings *n.* see **boistings**.

becall *vt.* to abuse, insult or condemn verbally EG "'Er becalled us all she could as lay 'er tongue to" (Northall, 1896); "to speak against a person" (Skeat, 1876).

bedlam *n.* "a game in which imprisoned players may be released by a visit from an uncaptured mate" (Rhodes, 1950); Northall (1896) describes the rules of the game as follows: "One party have a start, and, when the leader cries 'Bedlam,' the other party follow, and attempt to take prisoners. Any prisoner is conducted to a 'den,' on the outer line of which his captor must stand. Should one of the captive's friends dash through the den unchecked, crying, 'Release Bedlam,' the captive may make off again. Should the would-be releaser be caught in the attempt, he and his comrade must remain in the den. The game goes on until all are caught, and then the other party take their 'outing.' One player may guard any number of captives."

bed o' beef *n.* the flank of an animal, esp. its carcass; "in the living animal the intestines lie on it as on a bed - hence its name" (Northall, 1896).

bedwind *n.* small bindweed (Northall, 1896).

bee-skep *n.* a beehive (Skeat, 1876).

beetle *n.* latterly applied to any tool used for crushing or pounding, from a pestle in a chemist's mortar to a large wooden mallet, although Northall (1896) states that it was specifically applied, in the 1800s and much earlier, to a "heavy, iron-bound mallet, used for driving iron wedges into wood for the purpose of splitting it" EG "If I do, fillip me with a three-man beetle" (Shakespeare, *Henry IV (Part 2)*, Act I, Sc. II); from the Anglo-Saxon 'bytl' (a mallet); the Worcestershire dialect variant, 'clat-beetle', was a tool used specifically for breaking up hard clods of earth.

beetle-headed *adj.* stupid; wooden-headed (Northall, 1896).

beeza *n.* nickname for a motorbike made at the Small Heath factory of the British Small Arms (B. S. A.) Company Limited (Tennant, 1983).

beezum *n.* see **besom**.

begenst *conj.* when; at which time; by the time EG "Begenst we mek it to town, we'll 'ave us some dinner."

bellock *vi.* to bellow, roar or shout out loud (Rhodes, 1950); "used commonly of children crying" (Shaw, 1930).

belluck *vt.* see **bellock**.

bellus *n.* variant of 'bellows'.

belly-band *n.* see **belly-bun**.

belly-boster *n.* "a bad dive into water, falling flat on the stomach" (Rhodes, 1950).

belly-bun *n.* "a baby's binder" (Rhodes, 1950), also *n.* "the long loop on a kite face to which the flying string is attached" (Northall, 1896), and *n.* a cart-saddle girth (Marshall, 1796).

bellys *n.* see **bellus**.

bellytimber *n.* food; victuals (Northall, 1896).

bellyvengeance *n.* stale or weak beer (Northall, 1896); Halliwell (1855), however, gives "small beer."

belt *vt.* to hit or strike, "the belt being, metaphorically at least, the instrument of punishment" (Evans, 1881) EG "'E gi' 'im a right beltin'." Marshall (1796) also states that this is an old agricultural provincialism, meaning "to shear the buttocks and tails of sheep."

bennet *n.* "the peewit, or bastard plover" (Northall, 1896); mainly used in the Sutton Coldfield area of Birmingham.

Beringham *n.* variant of Birmingham listed in Langford (1868).

Berinyngham *n.* variant of Birmingham listed in Langford (1868).

Berkmyngham *n.* variant of Birmingham listed in Langford (1868).

Bermechagm *n.* variant of Birmingham listed in Langford (1868).

Bermengeham *n.* variant of Birmingham listed in Langford (1868).

Bermengham *n.* variant of Birmingham listed in Langford (1868).

Bermgham *n.* variant of Birmingham listed in Langford (1868).

Bermicham *n.* variant of Birmingham listed in Langford (1868).

Bermicheham *n.* variant of Birmingham listed in Langford (1868).

Bermigham *n.* variant of Birmingham listed in Langford (1868).

Bermimgaham *n.* variant of Birmingham listed in Langford (1868).

Bermincham *n.* variant of Birmingham; the surname 'de Bermincham' appears in a Patent Roll dated 1245 (Gelling, 1991).

Bermingeham *n.* variant of Birmingham given in the Domesday Book of 1086.

Bermingham *n.* variant of Birmingham listed in Langford (1868).

Bermyncham *n.* variant of Birmingham listed in Langford (1868).

Bermynehelham *n.* variant of Birmingham listed in Langford (1868).

Bermyngam *n.* variant of Birmingham listed in Langford (1868).

Bermyngeham *n.* variant of Birmingham listed in Langford (1868).

Bermyngham *n.* variant of Birmingham listed in Langford (1868).

Berningham *n.* variant of Birmingham listed in Langford (1868).

Bernynghem *n.* variant of Birmingham listed in Langford (1868).

berrard *n.* see **bearward**.

berrin *n.* literally 'burying'; a funeral or burial EG "A berrin, a berrin, A good fat herrin" (Children's game-rhyme at a mock-funeral, Warwickshire, mid-to-late 1800s).

Berringham *n.* variant of Birmingham listed in Langford (1868).

berrod *n.* see **bearward**.

berrord *n.* see **bearward**.

besom *n.* a birch broom (Rhodes, 1950), also *n.* "an opprobrious epithet applied to a female" (Northall, 1896); used in the children's game *Please old woman, will you come out?*:

> Please, old woman, will you come out,
> And help us out with our dancing?
> *(She remains silent, or says 'No')*
> If you won't come out, you shan't come out,
> You nasty, dirty besom, etc.

Fairly common in the Worcestershire and Black Country dialects, though no longer in use in Birmingham except among older generations of Brummie speakers.

best *n.* an acknowledgement of defeat or surrender; a token of submission EG "I med 'im gi' me best or I'd a tanked 'im one."

bettermost *adj.* superior; greater; preferred (Skeat, 1876).

bewist *interj.* keep quiet; shut up; in use c.1800 (Geoff Moore).

bezzle *vi.* to drink a copious amount, esp. of alcohol; also common in the Worcestershire dialect.

bibble *n.* pebble; grit (Rhodes, 1950).

bibble-babble *n.* "inconsistent chatter or nonsense" (Halliwell, 1855).

bibleback *n.* a person with broad, rounded shoulders; according to Northall (1896), "The metaphor is from the appearance of the ponderous family Bible."

bide *vi.* to stay; to remain, continue to be EG "Bide where you be a bit" (Northall, 1896, and Skeat, 1876); from the Anglo-Saxon 'bidan' (to dwell).

biggen *n.* a child's cap (Wise, 1861); a nightcap (Alexander, 1951) EG "As he whose brow with homely biggen bound" (Shakespeare, *Henry IV (Part 2)*, Act IV, Sc. V).

big'un *n.* an older brother or sister EG "That en't my shirt, it's the big'un's"; see also **little'un** and **babby**.

bilk *vt.* to cheat; to swindle, hoodwink or defraud EG "'Er bilked 'im of 'is pay." Now common in standard English.

billery-duck *n.* a period of sickness; a bilious or melancholic attack; a corruption, according to Northall (1896), of 'biliary duct'.

Billesley *n.* area of Birmingham lying north of the Chinn Brook and west of the River Cole. Meaning 'Bill's clearing in the wood', it is likely that the name Billesley emerged before the Norman Conquest of 1066.

Billy Button *n.* Ragged Robin (*Lychnis flos-cuculi*); sometimes called the 'cuckoo-flower'. According to Northall (1896), the white variety of this flower was called 'cheese-cup' in the Erdington area of Birmingham c.1890, whereas in nearby villages the red variety was known as 'red riding-hood' and the white 'white riding-hood', though the common term for the majority of Birmingham folk was 'Billy Button'.

billy-cock *n.* a hard gentleman's hat (K. Jenks) EG "If I close my eyes I can see him wearing his dark blue suit, white shirt with a stiff starched collar, a tie, always neatly in place, polished boots, waistcoat, with his silver watch and chain strung neatly across the front, and last, but not least, his billy cock (bowler hat) placed firmly and straight on his head" (Smith, undated). In the nineteenth century this was the headgear of the working class and in the twentieth century it tended to be worn by foremen, bookies and others amongst the working class who either were well off or who had high status.

bin *vi.* are; the plural and the second person (singular and plural) of the present tense of the verb 'to be', as in this inscription found on a brass at Hampton-in-Arden (reproduced in Palmer, 1976):

> Man, it behoves thee oft to have in minde
> That thou dealest with the hand that shalt thou find:
> Children bin sloathful, and wives bin unkind,
> Executors bin covetous and keep all they find.

bint *n.* a derogatory term for a woman (Jim Hunt).

bird *n.* a girl. Young lads would often be asked by older relatives, "'Ave yer gorra bird?" The Middle English poem *Patience* was written in the last quarter of the fourteenth century in the dialect of the North West Midlands, probably by someone who came from the borders of Cheshire and Shropshire. This locality had been part of the Kingdom of Mercia and was included in the area of the West

Mercian dialect. In it the poet mentions "burnes and beast, burdz and childer." In this sense 'burdz' means women and is derived from the Old English word 'byrde' which became the Middle English 'burde' signifying a maiden, lady or woman see also the phrase **to go birding**.

birds-in-the-bush *n.* a game of marbles, in which, according to Northall (1896), "one player holds any number of marbles in his clasped hands, saying, 'Birds in the bush, how many?' The other player guesses and wins the lot if he guesses correctly. If not, he must pay the number of marbles he is out in the reckoning. The guesser then becomes crier."

Birmincham *n.* variant of Birmingham c.1330 (Gelling, 1991).

Birmingcham *n.* variant of Birmingham listed in Langford (1868).

Birmingecham *n.* variant of Birmingham listed in Langford (1868).

Birmingeham *n.* variant of Birmingham listed in Langford (1868).

Birmingham *n.* according to Langford (1868) there have been over one hundred and forty different ways of spelling (and pronouncing) Birmingham, yet this is the variant that appears to have triumphed over all. In the city and in the West Midlands in general the word is pronounced with a strong 'g', as in Birmigum so that the 'n' is virtually silent. The retention of the pronunciation of the 'g' in the name of the city and in words such as 'long' and 'hang' is shared with dialect speakers in Central Lancashire, Merseyside and the West Midlands. Elsewhere in England, the 'g' is dropped so that Birmigum becomes Birminham. Birmingham folk, however, are not known as 'Birmies' after Birmingham, rather we are called 'Brummies' after Brummagem. This is the name used by working-class people both in Birmingham and the Black Country. Gelling (1991) explains that historical developments in the spelling and pronunciation of Birmingham "have left us with a 'correct' form: Birmingham, and a 'vulgar' form: Brummagem." This dichotomy arose because of a number of factors. First of all the 'r' and 'i' in 'Bir' were reversed. This occurred often; for example, the word bird was 'brid' in Old English. Thus in 1189 a document spells the surname de Brummingeham and in 1200 a property transaction notes Birmingham. This was a common spelling by the early fifteenth century and Morden's *Map of Warwickshire* in 1695 states Brimingham alias Birmingham. Secondly, early spellings of Birmingham vary between 'Bir', 'Ber' and 'Bur'. Finally, there is the addition of 'agem' for 'ingham'. The 'dg' substitution for 'ng' is not unique to the case of Birmingham and indeed is frequent in names where 'ing' is followed by a final syllable beginning with 'h' or 'w'. Sometimes 'ch' took the place of 'ng', as in 1245 when de Bermincham appears in a patent roll. When this variant was shortened by dropping the 'n' then Burmicham became apparent in 1317. With the reversal of the 'r' and the 'u' this shortened form became Brymecham in 1402. From this developed Brummagem and by 1643 this pronunciation had become accepted widely, as made plain in a pamphlet published during the Civil War which describes 'Brumegem'. As Gelling (1991) stresses, in Middle English many place names had two or more forms as the concept of a single correct name is peculiar to modern literate societies; see also **Brummagem**.

Birminghame *n.* variant of Birmingham listed in Langford (1868).

Birmygham *n.* variant of Birmingham listed in Langford (1868).

Birmyncham *n.* variant of Birmingham listed in Langford (1868).

Birmyngeham *n.* variant of Birmingham listed in Langford (1868).

Birmyngehame *n.* variant of Birmingham listed in Langford (1868).

Birymincham *n.* variant of Birmingham listed in Langford (1868).

bisnings *n.* see **boistings**.

bisson *adj.* blind; blinding (Alexander, 1951) EG "With bisson rheum; a clout upon that head" (Shakespeare, *Hamlet*, Act II, Sc. II).

bisus *adj.* turbulent; boisterous; rough EG "It's kickin' up a bisus wind" (Northall, 1896).

bittock *n.* a small part; a portion; a piece (Skeat, 1876).

bizzom *n.* see **besom**.

blaat *vi.* see **blart**.

blabchops *n.* a gossip; see also **blobmouth**.

black-a-top *n.* the black-cap *Curruca atricapilla* (Timmins, 1889).

black-bat *n.* a beetle or cockroach (Hilda Walker, and Palmer, 1976).

blacking *n.* stout or porter; see also **legs 'n' wings**, **pungello** and **stingo**; also used to refer to boot polish (R. Couling).

blackstare *n.* the starling (Northall, 1896).

blacksteer *n.* see **blackstare**.

blart *vi.* to cry EG "'Er's still blartin' about that doll 'er lost," "I'll swear as I wos blartin' wen I does a sneak inside" (Squiers, 1917, p.19), "I could hardly tell them that I had blarted, or that I had been sorry either, so I gave them the impression that we had negotiated amicably" (Smith, undated). If a lad or a wench came in from the orse road grizzling, their mom would say, "What's a marrer with yo?" "A big kid's 'it me, Our Mom." And the retort was, "Well goo outside and fight 'em, or I'll gie y' summat to blart about!" It seems likely that blart is derived from 'blaetan', the Old English word for the bleating of sheep, and it is still in common use; see also **blate**.

blate *vi.* to cry, from which, as Rhodes (1950) suggests, Spenser may have coined the word 'blatant'; apparently derived from the 'bleat' of lambs; see also **blart**.

blather *n.* bladder; commonly used in the expression "blether-head," meaning 'fool'; see also **blowblether** and **blowbelly**.

blather-head *n.* an idiot; someone whose head is "as empty as a bladder" (Rhodes, 1950).

bleeding heart *n.* a genus of garden flower; also common in the Worcestershire dialect.

blathering hash *n.* "a person who says much to little purpose" (Northall, 1896).

blather up *ph v.* to blow up; to inflate; often used in reference to gossip or idle talk EG "There's nothin' gain'd by being witty; fame gathers but wind to blather up a name" (old saying).

bleeder *n.* a contemptuous term for a person, often said in reference to children who play up EG "'Er's a right little bleeder, 'er is."

blench *vt.* to glimpse (Northall, 1896).

blether *n.* see **blather**.

blige me *interj.* an expression of surprise or bewilderment EG "Well, blige me! I never expected that."

blinder *n.* an excellent effort; a very good attempt EG "'E played a blinder straight into the back o' the net." Still in common use.

blindo *adj.* intoxicated; in a state of drunkenness; see also **blotto, bob-howler, canned, kaylied, lagging, market-peart, mopped, palatick** and **slaumsey.**

blinding *adj.* excellent; very good EG "The Villa played a blindin' match last wick."

blizzy *n.* a burst of light or flame; a blaze or blast; from the Anglo-Saxon 'blysa' (blaze).

blobchops *n.* a gossip; "a newsmonger or tattler" (Northall, 1896).

blobmouth *n.* see **blobchops.**

blobmouthed *adj.* talkative.

blobtales *npl.* chatterboxes.

block-ornaments *npl.* a butcher's scraps (Northall, 1896).

blood alley *n.* a marble streaked with red; see also **alley, alley taw, cat's eye, dogger, dummox, French alley, glarny, glass alley, gobbie, marley, pot alley** and **steelie.**

bloody-thumbs *n.* quaker-grass; also common in the Worcestershire dialect.

blotto *adj.* drunk; intoxicated; now in widespread use; see also **blindo, bob-howler, canned, kaylied, lagging, market-peart, mopped, palatick** and **slaumsey.**

blow *n.* the blossom of fruit trees (Rhodes, 1950); from the Anglo-Saxon 'blowan' (to bloom); also common in the Worcestershire dialect.

blowbelly *n.* see **blowblether.**

blowblether *n.* bellows; a device originally made from an animal's bladder which produces a current of air and is used to stoke an open fire (Rhodes, 1950).

Blues *n.* Birmingham City Football Club EG "Gooin' down the Blues on Saturday?"

blueing *n.* the process whereby Reckitt's Blue is put into a bucket of water during the wash. Whites would be placed in the bucket after they had been 'maided' (pounded clean with a maid or dolly) to try and give a bluey-white colour to greying whites.

bluffy *adj.* puffy; swollen; inflamed (Northall, 1896) EG "Me hands're as bluffy as bluffy, I swear" (Skeat, 1876).

blunt *n.* money; fairly common in the late 1800s, though now obsolete (Northall, 1896).

bmal *bsl.* lamb.

bob *n.* swagger, arrogance or conceit. The word is always used in the phrase "'Er's got a bob on, 'er 'as." This refers to someone who acts arrogantly. 'Bob' might be derived from the Middle English word 'bobaunce', meaning arrogance, pomp or pride.

bob-a-lantern *n.* a scooped-out turnip-head, lit by a candle, and used to make a ghost - esp. at Halloween (Rhodes, 1950, and Northall, 1894).

bob bowler *n.* see **bob-howler.**

bobby *n.* a robin (Skeat, 1876).

bobby dazzler *n.* a person dressed in colourful, striking or fashionable clothes; "a resplendent fop" (Northall, 1894).

bobby howler *n.* see **bob-howler**.

bob-howler *n.* a tiger moth; any brightly coloured butterfly (Northall, 1894); K. M. Felton, a contributor to the *Daily Mail* (26 October 2000), suggests that the term was created by the parents of the infant Bob Slade: "Moths terrified him to such an extent that he howled the house down if they were anywhere near him – hence moths became known as Bob Howlers." However, Maurice Ivor Birch proposes that, since the word is normally pronounced 'bobowler', the word comes from two underworld terms: 'bob', a shoplifter's apprentice, and 'owler', a wool smuggler. Some moths like wool and are attracted to such goods, often laying their eggs and flying away with their bellies full after a quick feed. The thin little moths which do this are believed to become fat-bellied moths as a result, and so the moths are thieves or smugglers of wool. In fact, the fat-bellied moths also suck nectar from flowers and, when they have done so, seem to fly around haphazardly as if drunk, hence the phrase 'as drunk as a bobowler'; also used as a term for a small motor car during the thirties and forties (Tennant, 1983).

bobowler *n.* see **bob-howler**.

bobtibby *n.* local variant of 'bob-howler' (A. Sealey).

boco *n.* nose.

bodge *vt.* to perforate; to puncture; to pierce holes in something EG "Our Jack's got a job bodgin' 'oles in piekelets" (Rhodes, 1950), to botch EG "With this, we charg'd again; but, out, alas! We bodg'd again" (Shakespeare, *Henry VI (Part 3)*, Act I, Sc. IV).

bodger *n.* tailor (Northall, 1894).

bodging *n.* going from house to house to sing Christmas carols; a kind of busking by children EG "We 'ad a lot o' bodgers last night".

boffle *vt.* to impede; to thwart or obstruct EG "Only done it to boffle her" (Hampson, 1936, p.196).

bog *n.* see **bog'ole**.

bog'ole *n.* lavatory EG "I'm bostin' to goo to the bog'ole."

bogs *n.* see **bog'ole**.

boiling *n.* a family; a group or social class EG "I don't much care about the Taylors, Frank's about the best of the boiling" (Northall, 1896); also applied more widely to "a quantity or number of things or persons" (Halliwell, 1855).

boisting-custard *n.* see **boistings**.

boisting-pudding *n.* see **boistings**.

boistings *n.* first milk drawn from the udder of a cow after calving (Rhodes, 1950); from the Anglo-Saxon 'bysting' (Marshall, 1796); boisting-custard and boisting-pudding are delicacies made from it (Skeat 1876); according to Jackson (1879) it is "of a peculiar richness and has the property of thickening when cooked, as ordinary milk does with the addition of eggs"; although variants such as 'beestins', 'bestnynge', 'bwoistin', and 'bystins' were heard throughout England, 'boistings' was most common in the area now known as the West Midlands.

boko *n.* see **boco**.

Boldmere *n.* area within the Sutton Coldfield borough of Birmingham; its name probably signifies a house near a lake or moor.

boldrib *n.* a joint of pork.

bollen *adj.* enlarged; bloated; swollen (Alexander, 1950) EG "Here one being throng'd bears back, all boll'n and red" (Shakespeare, *The Rape of Lucrece*, 1417).

bolten *n.* see **bolting**.

bolt *vi.* see **bolter**.

bolter *vi.* not, as Alexander (1951) suggests: "to sift," but to adhere or stick; to become congealed. According to Halliwell (1855), flakes of snow were said to 'bolter together' in the old Warwickshire dialect EG "As soft as dove's down, and as white as it, / Or Ethiopian's tooth, or the fann'd snow that's bolted" (Shakespeare, *The Winter's Tale*, Act IV, Sc. IV).

boltered *adj.* congealed; clotted or matted.

boltin *n.* see **bolting**.

bolting *n.* a bundle of straw from 12 to 14lbs in weight; "a bolting of the best and longest straw was usually tied with two bands; bolting containing the short and inferior straw with only one" (Rhodes, 1950); also common in the Worcestershire dialect. According to Palmer (1976), "If the farmer had not completely finished with a field he would leave a swathe uncut, one or two shucks uncollected, or put up a bolten of straw, as a signal that leasing might not yet begin."

bonce *n.* head.

bone orchard *n.* a graveyard or cemetery (D. Adams).

bonk *n.* a hillock or small mass of land.

bonk-eyed *adj.* cross-eyed.

bonksmen *npl.* men from the Black Country; 'banksmen' was the variant in the Derbyshire dialect for "one who superintends the business of the coal pit" (Halliwell, 1855).

bony pie *n.* a pie made with bones which had had most of the meat taken off them; see also **resurrection pie**.

boosings *npl.* cattle stalls (Marshall, 1796).

boosing-stake *n.* the post to which stall cattle are tied (Marshall, 1796).

Bordesley Green *n.* area of Birmingham referred to in the thirteenth century as 'La Grene de Bordeslie', when it was an area of common pasture on the edge of the Bordesley and Saltley manors.

Bormingham *n.* variant of Birmingham listed in Langford (1868).

Bormycham *n.* variant of Birmingham listed in Langford (1868).

Bormyngeham *n.* variant of Birmingham listed in Langford (1868).

boss-eyed *adj.* cross-eyed.

bost *pa p.* and *adj.* bust; burst; broken (Rhodes, 1950), also *vt.* to hit EG "If yer doan watch out I'll bost yer!"

bosted *adj.* see **bost**.

bostin *adj.* brilliant; fantastic; great; derived, perhaps, from the Anglo-Saxon 'bosten', meaning 'something to boast about' (Walker, undated); still in common use.

bost-up *n.* a fight; a row or argument; still in common use.

botch *vt.* to patch or mend clumsily EG "And botch the words up fit to their own thoughts" (Shakespeare, *Hamlet*, Act IV, Sc. V); now in common use throughout England.

botch-job *n.* a careless piece of work; still in common use.

boughten *adj.* purchased, as opposed to home-made EG "En't there no boughten cake?," "I can't eat boughten bread, gi'us home-made" (Northall, 1896).

Bourmyneham *n.* variant of Birmingham listed in Langford (1868).

bourn *n.* a brook EG "Come o'er the bourn, Bessy, to me" (Shakespeare, *King Lear*, Act III, Sc. VI); see also **Bournbrook** and **Bournville**.

Bournbrook *n.* area of south Birmingham near Selly Oak. The early English tended to call a stream a 'burna' (bourne) when it had gravel beds and was characterized by clear water and submerged water plants. By contrast 'broc' usually denoted muddy streams with sediment-laden water. Normally both words were used for streams of a considerable size, thus Bournbrook actually means 'brook brook'.

Bournville *n.* area of Birmingham world-renowned for its Cadburys chocolate manufactory. Because French chocolate was regarded as peerless, the Cadburys sought to show the superiority of their product by naming their factory Bournville - connecting the name of the nearby Bourn Brook to that of the French word for 'town' (ville).

brack *vt.* to damage; to tear, mark or stain.

brahma *adj.* very good; excellent; probably derived from the Indian creator God, Brahma, and brought back by former soldiers who had served in India EG "That goal was a brahma." However, C. Goodall writes that the phrase 'a right brahma' is commonly used to refer to someone who is a bit of a nuisance or hindrance to others.

Brammingham *n.* variant of Birmingham listed in Langford (1868).

Brandwood End *n.* area of Birmingham at the southernmost tip of Kings Heath; probably takes its name from the Middle English word 'brend', meaning 'burnt'.

bran-faced *adj.* freckle-faced EG "Be off, yer bran-faced madam"; according to Northall (1896), also common "near Warwick."

brass *n.* a prostitute; see also **nail**, also *n.* effrontery; audacity; impudence EG "Can any face of brass hold longer out?" (Shakespeare, *Love's Labours Lost*, Act V, Sc. II); see also the phrase **to have the brass skimmer rubbed over your face**.

brass gall *n.* commonly used to refer to someone who has got a real cheek EG "I tell y' wha', 'e inarf gorra a brass gall."

brass neck *n.* see **brass gall**.

bravery *n.* finery (Wise, 1861); bold display of clothes or feelings (Alexander, 1951) EG "With scarfs and fans and double change of brav'ry" (Shakespeare, *The Taming of the Shrew*, Act IV, Sc. III).

bread 'n' cheese *n.* young hawthorn shoots and leaves eaten by children (Northall, 1894 & 1896); also common in the Shropshire dialect.

bread 'n' scrape *n.* a slice of bread coated in a layer of dripping or margarine (Tennant, 1983) EG "But on Saturdays in Guest Street it meant getting up later, and after breakfast, a birra bread an' scrape, an' a cuppa tea, our kid and me allus used gu lookin' at trains in All Saints Road" (Smith, undated).

breed and seed *n.* birth and parentage; ancestry EG "I know the breed 'n' seed of 'im'" (Northall, 1896).

Breedon Hill *n.* an area of Cotteridge in south Birmingham; the word 'bre' is Celtic in origin and means hill, whilst 'don' is an Old English word also signifying hill. It seems likely that the early Anglian settlers in this neighbourhood heard the local British folk talking of the 'bre' and thought that this was the name of the hill. Thus Breedon Hill actually contains the word hill three times. However, Breedon may well be a name which was transferred from Bredon in Worcestershire and thus would not necessarily indicate a Celtic presence in this area.

Breemejam *n.* variant of Birmingham c.1573 (Gelling, 1991).

breese *n.* the gadfly EG "The breese upon her, like a cow in June" (Shakespeare, *Antony and Cleopatra*, Act III, Sc. X); see also **brize**.

breeze *n.* small coke used by blacksmiths (Rhodes, 1950).

breezer *n.* the fundament; the buttocks or anus (Northall, 1896).

breffus *n.* breakfast.

Bremecham *n.* variant of Birmingham listed in Langford (1868).

Bremicham *n.* variant of Birmingham listed in Langford (1868).

Bremichem *n.* variant of Birmingham listed in Langford (1868).

Bremingem *n.* variant of Birmingham listed in Langford (1868).

Bremingham *n.* variant of Birmingham listed in Langford (1868).

Bremiseham *n.* variant of Birmingham listed in Langford (1868).

Bremisham *n.* variant of Birmingham listed in Langford (1868).

Bremmencham *n.* variant of Birmingham listed in Langford (1868).

Bremygiam *n.* variant of Birmingham c.1522 (Gelling, 1991).

Bremyngham *n.* variant of Birmingham listed in Langford (1868).

Brennyngeham *n.* variant of Birmingham listed in Langford (1868).

brevet *vi.* see **brevit**.

brevit *vi.* to rummage or pry; to nose about, as a dog does (Skeat, 1876) EG "I'll 'ave to brevit through all my things for that mitten" (Northall, 1896). The alliterative poem *St Erkenwald* was written in the late 1300s or early 1400s by someone whose dialect marks him out as coming from Cheshire, a county that fell within the West Mercian dialect area. In this poem the word 'brevit' means 'reported'. It is derived from the Old English 'gebrefan'.

brewhouse *n.* a communal out-house or wash-house in the yards or courts of back-to-back houses (Tennant, 1983); originally the place where beer was brewed EG "Mr Twigg 'oo lived the other side o' the entry dain't gurra werk, cus 'e wus a 'undred years old, an' 'is missus wus a witch an' med us kids drown lickle kittens, cus she dain't wannem, in a bucket o' water in the brew 'ouse in the yard, an' she'd promise us 'a'penny, an' never paid us, the rotten sod" (Smith, undated). Shakespeare uses the same term in *The Merry Wives of Windsor*. In Scene III of Act III, Mistress Ford and Mistress Page prepare a surprise for Sir John Falstaff, who has been flirting with both these women, even though he knows they are married. Determined to show him up, the ladies devise a cunning plan to trick him at Mrs Page's house when their two husbands are out. As they prepare for Falstaff's arrival. Mrs Page tells her two servants to bring a washing basket into the room and then instructs them: "Marry, as I told you before, John and Robert, be ready hard by in the brew-house."

brew'us *n.* see **brewhouse**.

bride-ball *n.* many nineteenth century Midlands weddings were followed by a sports meeting in which all the villagers took part; the most popular activity being football. "The ball was provided by the bridegroom and known as the 'bride-ball'. The game was played through the streets by large numbers of players before they were served drinks and cake" (reported in *Metro*, 5 March 2001).

brief *adj.* widespread; rife; prevalent; according to Northall (1896), "generally applied to disorders of an epidemic description" EG "A thousand businesses are brief in hand" (Shakespeare, *King John*, Act IV, Sc. III).

Brimcham *n.* variant of Birmingham listed in Langford (1868).

Brimechame *n.* variant of Birmingham listed in Langford (1868).

Brimicham *n.* variant of Birmingham listed in Langford (1868).

Brimigham *n.* variant of Birmingham listed in Langford (1868).

Brimingeham *n.* variant of Birmingham listed in Langford (1868).

Brimingham *n.* variant of Birmingham; on Morden's (1695) *Map of Warwickshire*, the place is called "Brimingham alias Birmingham" (Gelling, 1991); also listed in Langford (1868).

Brimisham *n.* variant of Birmingham listed in Langford (1868).

Brimmidgeham *n.* variant of Birmingham listed in Langford (1868).

Brimmigham *n.* variant of Birmingham listed in Langford (1868).

Brimmingham *n.* variant of Birmingham listed in Langford (1868).

Brimyncham *n.* variant of Birmingham c.1486 (Gelling, 1991).

brinded *adj.* striped (Alexander, 1951) EG "Thrice the brinded cat hath mew'd" (Shakespeare, *Macbeth*, Act IV, Sc. I).

Brinnicham *n.* variant of Birmingham listed in Langford (1868).

Brinningham *n.* variant of Birmingham listed in Langford (1868).

brize *n.* see **breese**.

Bromicham *n.* variant of Birmingham listed in Langford (1868); according to Miege (1691), Bromicham was particularly noted "for the counterfeit groats made here, and from hence dispersed all over the kingdom." False coins were also minted in Birmingham in the nineteenth century by the notorious forger William Booth. According to a local 'factfile' in *Metro* (June 18, 2001), "his fortified farmhouse was stormed [in 1812] by the military and the authorities found £3,000 in good notes, 200 guineas in gold, £600 in counterfeit silver coins and a large pile of forged notes." He was hanged in August, 1815.

Bromidgham *n.* variant of Birmingham listed in Langford (1868), and Halliwell (1855):

"a corruption of Birmingham. A Bromidgham groat, a spurious fourpenny-piece. A person neither Whig nor Tory, but between both, was called a Bromidgham."

Bromidgome *n.* variant of Birmingham listed in Langford (1868).

Bromincham *n.* variant of Birmingham listed in Langford (1868).

Bromisham *n.* variant of Birmingham listed in Langford (1868).

Bromwichham *n.* variant of Birmingham listed in Langford (1868).

Bromwycham *n.* variant of Birmingham c.1576 (Langford, 1868); in Ogilby's road-atlas of 1675 the place is called 'Birmingham vulgo Bromwichham' (Gelling, 1991).

brown *n.* a copper coin. The word was brought into use by the well-known racecourse bookie Jim Smith, who worked tirelessly in the 1920s and 1930s to raise funds for the Birmingham Mail Christmas Tree Fund – which gave out boots to poorer kids. Jim actually wrote a song called *Can you spare a brown?*

browsy *adj.* ruddy-faced; having a reddish colour to the skin (Northall, 1896).

Brum *n.* Birmingham; abbreviated form of Brummagem, also *n.* a citizen of Birmingham EG "Some of the old Brums round here say it's a ghost, but we are paid to catch thieves, not ghosts" (Palmer, 1976). Used commonly both within and outside Birmingham. In the nineteenth century, Brummies were called Brum or Brums by outsiders. Charlie Mitchell was a renowned boxer born in Summer Lane in 1861 and in *The Life of Charlie Mitchell. (Triple Champion of the World)* compiled by A.G. Hales, Mitchell states that he was, "what is so well known in ring parlance as a 'Brum'."

Brumdriver *n.* a hammer; see also **Brummagem screwdriver**.

Brumegume *n.* variant of Birmingham listed in Langford (1868).

Brumicham *n.* variant of Birmingham listed in Langford (1868).

Brumidgham *n.* variant of Birmingham listed in Langford (1868).

Brumidgum *n.* variant of Birmingham listed in Langford (1868).

Brumigam *n.* variant of Birmingham listed in Langford (1868).

Brumigham *n.* variant of Birmingham listed in Langford (1868).

Brumingham *n.* variant of Birmingham listed in Langford (1868).

Brummagem *n.* popular variant of Birmingham; local form of the name of the city of Birmingham, as in the Brummagem street ballads *I Can't Find Brummagem* (James Dobbs, 1828); *Mary, Mary, Brummagem Mary* (sung by Mr E. W. Simmons of Stirchley, collected by Roy Palmer, 12th December 1971, unpublished), and *They're Changing Dear Old Brummagem* (G. S. Miles, 1972):

> Poor old Spiceal Street's half gone,
> And the poor Old Church stands all alone,
> And poor old I stand here to groan,
> For I can't find Brummagem.

> Mary, Mary, Brummagem Mary, how does your allotment grow?
> Yo've 'ad some shy knocks through werkin' at Kynoch's [arms factory],
> Although you don't mind, we all know.
> Yo've never seen Arizona, and Texas is not your abode,
> Yo're just Mary, Mary, Brummagem Mary, what lives up the Pairsher Road
> [Pershore Road].

> They're changing dear old Brummagem before our very eyes,
> Places that we know so well are hard to recognise;
> In Balsall Heath and Ladywood, in Aston and Newtown,
> The blocks of flats are going up, the homes are coming down.

"Generally allowed to mean the home of the [Anglo-Saxon] Beormingas, a tribe, the chief of which was named Beorm" (Kemble, 1876). An alternative spelling is suggested in Lingo's *Opinions on Men and Manners*, an entertainment written for John Edwin to speak in the character of the Irish school-master Lingo in *The Agreeable Surprise*, by Anthony Pasquin (printed in *The Eccentricities of John Edwin, Comedian*, by Anthony Pasquin, Dublin, 1791):

> I popt my ear the other day to the door of a puerile Seminary of the Female Gender - I looked, and had a full view of the Magestra, and the whole Scholia - a little Miss was spelling the word Birmingham - B, I, R, M, - Birm: I, N, G, -ing: H, A, M, -ham: Birmingham. The lady Abecarian screw'd up her face, admonished her pupil, and set her right. "My dear, the word is not Birmingham: 'tis Brumidgum -mind how I spell it: B, I, R, M, -Brum: I, N, G, -idge: H, A, M, -um. Brumidgum."

Also applied to anything made in Birmingham; often used contemptuously by outsiders with primary allusion to counterfeit groats coined in the city during the seventeenth century. In an attempt to counter prejudice against Brummagem goods, it seems likely that in the later eighteenth century leading manufacturers such as Matthew Boulton encouraged the use of the name Birmingham. This led to the belief that Brummagem was an inferior name. It is not. Its use reflects working-class loyalty to our city. As Gelling (1991) affirms, the use of Brummagem is as correct as that of Birmingham and "long may it flourish," also *adj.* relating to the city of Birmingham; made in Brummagem EG "A work table . . . inlaid with brass . . . in that peculiar taste which is vulgarly called Brummagem" (Lytton, 1853), "The vulgar dandy, strutting along, with his Brummagem jewellery" (Boyd, 1885). Older fans of Birmingham City Football Club also call the team 'Brummagem'.

Brummagem button *n.* a native Brummie; "springing from the intensive manufacture of buttons [in Birmingham] by such industrialists as John Taylor" (Tennant, 1983), as commemorated in the eighteenth century ballad slip *The Button-Maker's Complaint*:

> In Birmingham I liv'd 'tis true,
> Where many people did me know;
> A Button-maker by my trade,
> Tho' I was ruin'd by a maid.

Brummagemish *adj.* belonging to Birmingham; like Birmingham (Murray, 1888).

Brummagemism *n.* appertaining to Birmingham (Murray, 1888); a witty phrase or remark which is characteristically Brummie.

Brummagemites *npl.* citizens of Birmingham (Old Sarbot, 1869).

Brummagemize *vt.* to force someone or something to become more Birmingham-like in appearance or temperament (Murray, 1888).

Brummagem rough *n.* a hooligan; a street tough.

Brummagems *npl.* citizens of Birmingham EG "We have in view to castigate the degenerated race of Brummagems, and show them the handicraft of their forefathers" (*The Birmingham Reporter* No.1, Vol.1, 1823).

Brummagem screwdriver *n.* a hammer; "a scurrilous attack upon the standards of Birmingham craftsmen, implying as it does that they all knock their screws in with a hammer" (Tennant, 1983).

Brummejam *n.* variant of Birmingham; also applied to an article of Birmingham manufacture EG "It proved to be a Brummejam of the coarsest and clumsiest kind" (Southey, 1840).

Brummidgham *n.* variant of Birmingham listed in Langford (1868).

Brummie *n.* a person from Birmingham; a local name for a native or inhabitant of the city of Birmingham; the diminutive form of 'Brummagem' EG "He proclaims proudly, in a modulated Birmingham accent that makes him sound like a well-bred Australian: 'I'm a natural born Brummie'" (*New Statesman*, 30 April 1965), "You're a Brummy boy. I can tell by your accent" (Kersh, 1941), also *npl.* Birmingham citizens . EG "Now it tries hard to avoid being swamped by Birmingham – permanently, in the way of urban sprawl; temporarily, by the ebb and flow of the country-bound Brummies at week-ends" (*Architectural Review* CXX, 1956), and *adj.* relating to Birmingham EG "'Er's got a Brummie accent, en't 'er?" In the past, Brummies tended to be seen as and regarded themselves as white, working class and English. Now the word Brummie is much more inclusive and refers to anyone who feels that they belong to Birmingham, whether or not they were born in the city. Thus Irish Brummies, South Asian Brummies, Black Brummies and others all see themselves as Brummies and are viewed by others as such.

Brummigham *n.* variant of Birmingham listed in Langford (1868).

Brummingham *n.* variant of Birmingham listed in Langford (1868).

Brummingsham *n.* variant of Birmingham listed in Langford (1868).

brummish *adj.* "of coin: of counterfeit character, doubtfully genuine" (Murray, 1888).

Brummy *n.* and *adj.* see **Brummie**.

Brums *npl.* see **Brum**.

Brumwycham *n.* variant of Birmingham listed in Langford (1868).

Brunningham *n.* variant of Birmingham listed in Langford (1868).

brushing-hook *n.* "a sickle-shaped hook on a long handle for cutting tall hedges" (Northall, 1896).

Brymecham *n.* variant of Birmingham c.1402 (Gelling, 1991).

Brymedgham *n.* variant of Birmingham c.1537 (Gelling, 1991).

Brymicham *n.* variant of Birmingham listed in Langford (1868).

Brymingecham *n.* variant of Birmingham listed in Langford (1868).

Brymingham *n.* variant of Birmingham listed in Langford (1868).

Bryminham *n.* variant of Birmingham listed in Langford (1868).

Brymmyngeham *n.* variant of Birmingham listed in Langford (1868).

Brymmyngham *n.* variant of Birmingham listed in Langford (1868).

Brymmyngiam *n.* variant of Birmingham c.1486 (Gelling, 1991).

Brymycham *n.* variant of Birmingham common between the fourteenth and seventeenth centuries (Gelling, 1991).

Brymyecham *n.* variant of Birmingham listed in Langford (1868).

Brymygeham *n.* variant of Birmingham listed in Langford (1868).

Brymyham *n.* variant of Birmingham listed in Langford (1868).

Brymymcham *n.* variant of Birmingham listed in Langford (1868).

Brymyncham *n.* variant of Birmingham listed in Langford (1868).

Brymyngeham *n.* variant of Birmingham listed in Langford (1868).

Brymyngham *n.* variant of Birmingham listed in Langford (1868).

Brymyngiam *n.* variant of Birmingham c.1520, listed in Langford (1868).

Brymynham *n.* variant of Birmingham listed in Langford (1868).

Brymycham *n.* variant of Birmingham listed in Langford (1868).

Brymyscham *n.* variant of Birmingham listed in Langford (1868).

Brymysham *n.* variant of Birmingham listed in Langford (1868).

BSA *n.* an abbreviation of Birmingham Small Arms, a world-renowned company based in the Small Heath area of Birmingham which specialised in the manufacture of firearms, bicycles and motorcycles. BSA began its life in 1692 when William III, concerned about having to buy all of his armaments from Dutch companies, ordered his Board of Ordnance to draw up a contract with five Birmingham gunsmiths. For well over the next century, thousands upon thousands of firearms were supplied to both British and foreign governments. It was not until the Crimean War, however, that BSA was first used as a name - when fourteen gunsmiths formed the Birmingham Small Arms Trade Association. The Birmingham Small Arms Company was not officially formed until 1861, and its factory in Small Heath was opened in 1863. When the need for mass production of armaments declined sharply in the late nineteenth century, BSA began to make bicycles and tricycles using a 'piled arms' device which became known all over the world. In the early twentieth century, the company produced its first motorcycle, and others swiftly followed. Production switched back to armaments during the Great War, with over 10,000 rifles being made per week. BSA also produced 145,000 Lewis guns, countless gun locks, airplane components, shells and fuses, as well as the gearbox and engine of the world's first tank for the war effort. The company, now consisting of 67 factories, was well prepared for the huge increase in guns, shell fuses and other munitions during the Second World War, and it also produced over 126,000 M20 motorcycles. BSA continued to do a brisk trade in motorcycles throughout the post war years until Japanese and German companies began to challenge its dominance. After the failure of a rescue plan initiated by the Department of Industry in the 1970s, the factory in Small Heath was closed. The company still trades under the name of BSA, but has since relocated to Southampton.

buck up *ph v.* and *interj.* cheer up, as in, "Come on, buck up!" The phrase 'buck yerself up' can also mean to pull yourself together, and it can serve as a warning or admonition to improve yourself EG "Y'd better buck yer ideas up, ma lad, or else you'll be fetching yer cards!"

bug *n.* fright; alarm EG "The bug with which you fright me with I seek" (Shakespeare, *The Winter's Tale*, Act III, Sc. II), also *n.* a bogey; "a clot of mucus from the nose" (Northall, 1894).

bug-hutch *n.* a term used in reference to anywhere that is dirty, dingy or lousy; a place infested with fleas EG "That old cinema in Alum Rock's a right bug-'utch, 'en't it?"

bull *n.* a factory siren or 'hooter' used to summon employees to work and to signal that it is time to 'knock off' (Geoff Moore) EG "There goes the Cadburys bull" (C. Butters), "Lumme, there's the fleekin' waerks bull agooin'" (Squiers, 1916, p.11), "The 'Bulls' for the workers had already put forth their wail. 'owletts, Wheways, The Bandalasta, Swallow Raincoats, Lucas's an' God knows 'ow many more wus guin' at it, no rest for the wicked?" (Smith, undated).

bullace *n.* a wild plum (Northall, 1896).

bull-head *n.* a tadpole (Northall, 1894).

Bull Ring *n.* an area of central Birmingham famed for its shops and markets. As a name, the Bull Ring is first recorded as 'le Bulrynge' in the charter of King Edward's School in 1552. According to William Hawkes Smith writing in 1825 in *The Picture of Birmingham*, it "arose from certain privileges granted to one John Cooper, who was flourishing in the High Street about three hundred years ago, and who was a benefactor to the town. One of the remunerating privileges claimed by the said Cooper was that he should bait a bull in this part of the town whenever he pleased." It may be that this John Cooper was an ancestor of the family which came to own Cooper's Mill in Heath Mill Lane. Until the redevelopment of the area in the 1960s, a bull ring was attached to a wall in the Bull Ring itself, although bull baiting in Birmingham was effectively put down by the Street Commissioners in the late eighteenth century.

bully-head *n.* see **bull-head**.

bullyrag *vt.* to scold, chide or rebuke (Northall, 1896).

bum-bags *n.* trousers.

bum-bailey *n.* see **bum-baily**.

bum-bailiff *n.* see **bum-baily**.

bum-bailisses *npl.* bailiffs; sheriff's officers (Northall, 1896). In twentieth century Brummagem, bailiffs were regularly sent into homes when someone hadn't paid their rent. In Nechells and Ladywood there were places known as the Bum's Puzzle. According to David Rice, both were large yards of back-to-backs that ran into other large yards and which had a number of entries and double knacks. This meant it was hard for the bum-bailisses to find the house they wanted to. T. Hadley writes that families often avoided the bailiffs by moving all of their possessions in a handcart to some other part of the town: "sometimes the bailiffs were compassionate enough about the prevailing poverty to slip us a warning before the due date, so we got the midnight flit."

bum-baily *n.* a bailiff (Alexander, 1951); a sheriff's officer (Rhodes, 1950) EG "Go, Sir Andrew; scout me for him at the corner of the orchard, like a bum-baily" (Shakespeare, *Twelfth Night*, Act III, Sc. IV).

bumble-footed *adj.* heavy-footed; clumsy; "having a foot that moves without pliability" (Northall, 1896).

bumble-puppy *n.* a pitching game; "a game at ninepins" (Northall, 1896); in this game a two-pound disc, usually made of metal, is pitched rather than bowled at the pins.

bummer *n.* a works foreman; see also **ganger**.

bum's puzzle *n.* a large yard of back-to-backs that usually ran into other large yards and which had a number of entries and double knacks (David Rice). One such place was in Duddeston Mill Road; see also **bum-bailisses**.

bunce *n.* idle chatter; talk of little consequence or importance (Old Sarbot, 1866), also *n.* betting terminology for money.

bung *vt.* give (as in pay) or lend EG "Yer couldn't bung us a few quid till next wick could yer?"

bunk-eyed *adj.* squinting; as used in the following old Warwickshire street-rhyme:
> Bunk-eye, Squint-eye, went to the fair,
> Bought two horses, and one was a mare,
> One was blind, and the other couldn't see,
> Bunk-eye, Squint-eye, one, two, three!

bunt *vt.* to push, shove or jostle.

burgage *n.* a standard house plot held by yearly rent.

Buringham *n.* variant of Birmingham listed in Langford (1868).

Burmedgeham *n.* variant of Birmingham listed in Langford (1868).

Burmegam *n.* variant of Birmingham listed in Langford (1868).

Burmegham *n.* variant of Birmingham listed in Langford (1868).

Burmegum *n.* variant of Birmingham listed in Langford (1868).

Burmicham *n.* variant of Birmingham c.1317 (Gelling, 1991).

Burmicheham *n.* variant of Birmingham listed in Langford (1868).

Burmigam *n.* variant of Birmingham listed in Langford (1868).

Burmigham *n.* variant of Birmingham listed in Langford (1868).

Burmincham *n.* variant of Birmingham c.1260 (Gelling, 1991).

Burmingham *n.* variant of Birmingham listed in Langford (1868).

Burmucham *n.* variant of Birmingham listed in Langford (1868).

Burmycham *n.* variant of Birmingham listed in Langford (1868).

Burmycheham *n.* variant of Birmingham c.1550 (Gelling, 1991).

Burmygham *n.* variant of Birmingham listed in Langford (1868).

Burmyncham *n.* variant of Birmingham listed in Langford (1868).

Burmyngcham *n.* variant of Birmingham listed in Langford (1868).

Burmyngeham *n.* variant of Birmingham listed in Langford (1868).

Burmyngham *n.* variant of Birmingham listed in Langford (1868).

burrow *adj.* snug; sheltered EG "It's very burrow in 'ere in the winter" (Skeat, 1876).

Burymynham *n.* variant of Birmingham listed in Langford (1868).

buskins *n.* leggings.

bussock *n.* an ugly or generally unappealing person; according to Northall (1896) this word, peculiar to the Warwickshire dialect alone, was commonly used in reference to "a gross, fat, vulgar female."

butterfly shooter *n.* a volunteer, esp. a member of a rifle corps.

buttermilk-can *n.* the old Warwickshire dialect word for a long-tailed tit (Palmer, 1976).

butter-my-eye *n.* a butterfly (Northall, 1894).

buttie *n.* see **butty**.

butty *n.* a work colleague, comrade or assistant (Marshall, 1796); the men who contracted with the mine owner for removal of coal from the pits (Raven, 1977) EG "John's my butty" (Skeat, 1876), also *vi.* to work in company (Northall, 1896) EG "I'm buttying with Smith nex' wick"; also common in the Worcestershire dialect; see also **doggy**.

butty-collier *n.* employer in a leased colliery.

by-by *n.* see **bye-bye**.

bye-bye *n.* sleep, esp. in baby-talk (Northall, 1896) EG "Babby wanna goo bye-bye?"

Byrmegham *n.* variant of Birmingham listed in Langford (1868).

Byrmicham *n.* variant of Birmingham listed in Langford (1868).

Byrmigcham *n.* variant of Birmingham listed in Langford (1868).

Byrmincham *n.* variant of Birmingham listed in Langford (1868).

Byrmingeham *n.* variant of Birmingham listed in Langford (1868).

Byrmingham *n.* variant of Birmingham listed in Langford (1868).

Byrmycham *n.* variant of Birmingham listed in Langford (1868).

Byrmyncham *n.* variant of Birmingham listed in Langford (1868).

Byrmyngcham *n.* variant of Birmingham listed in Langford (1868).

Byrmyngeham *n.* variant of Birmingham listed in Langford (1868).

Byrmyngham *n.* variant of Birmingham listed in Langford (1868).

byslings *n.* see **boistings**.

bytte *n.* an old Warwickshire dialect word for a bottle; a flagon (Halliwell, 1855).

C

cack *vulg.* faeces; excreta; "alvum exonerae" (Halliwell, 1855); commonly used to express disapproval or dissatisfaction EG "That's a right load of old cak!". Also applied to coarse, bad food of any kind.

cackabed *vulg.* a term of contempt listed in Halliwell (1855); see also **cack**.

caddle *vt.* to mollycoddle or pamper; to spoil; probably a frequentative of 'cade' (to pet), as in the phrase 'cade and cosset' (Raven, 1978) EG "She caded 'n' cosseted all 'er children," also *vt.* to squander money (Halliwell, 1855), and *n.* a mess or muddle; a state of general confusion (Skeat, 1876).

cade *vt.* to pet or pamper (Rhodes, 1950), also *adj.* tame EG "The cade lamb is the pet lamb" (Skeat, 1876); hence also applied to a pet child (Halliwell, 1855).

cadey *n.* cap (K. Carruthers).

cadge *vi.* to beg (Northall, 1896), now in widespread use. The phrase "Watch 'im, 'e's on the cadge" relates to someone who is trying to get money from someone for doing nothing and has no intention of paying it back.

cadger *n.* a person who begs, though, as Northall (1896) points out, not so elsewhere: "in Scotland, a packman or huckster; in Cheshire, a carrier; in Herefordshire, an itinerant dealer whose wares are carried in a cart."

cagement *n.* casement; the case or frame of a window EG "Pd. Glazier for school and schoolhouse 2 doz. of Squares 2s. 0d. 2 doz. of Quarries 1s. 6d. For cutting and priming two Cagements" (*King Edward's School Records*, 17 March 1672).

cag *vi.* to argue or quarrel (Rhodes, 1950); to cank, chatter or gossip (Northall, 1896).

cag-butcher *n.* a person who deals in poor quality meat (Northall, 1896).

caggy *adj.* left-handed (Northall, 1894, and Rhodes, 1950); also used to describe someone who is awkward or ungainly (Geoff Moore); still in common use throughout Birmingham.

caggy-handed *adj.* see **caggy**.

cag-mag *n.* meat of poor or inferior quality (Rhodes, 1950); tough, worthless or unwholesome meat; the flesh of an animal that has died a natural death (Northall, 1896).

cak *vulg.* see **cack**.

cakey *adj.* foolish; stupid; witless, or, as Northall (1896) puts it, "weak of intellect"; see also the phrases **my cake's all dough** and **put in with the bread and pulled out with the cakes**.

Cain and Abel *n.* table; like Cockney, rhyming slang was also a common feature of the Birmingham dialect.

calflick *n.* "a tuft on the forehead which cannot be made to lie in the same direction with the rest of the hair" (Halliwell, 1855); see also **cowlick**.

call *n.* occasion; reason; excuse or right EG "'E 'adn't no call to mek no work about it" (Skeat, 1876).

cank *vi.* to gossip or chatter; to prate (Northall, 1896); an old street-ballad sung in Birmingham during the reign of George IV had the refrain: "They're always cankin', cankin' down our street"; a derivative, perhaps, of 'cant'.

canker *n.* anything diseased, rotten, decayed, or infected; an "ulcer-like evil or sore" (Alexander, 1951) EG "Banish the canker of ambitious thoughts!" (Shakespeare, *Henry VI (Part 2)*, Act I, Sc. II); now in widespread use.

cankered *adj.* mildewed; blighted, as wheat and other grain (Marshall, 1796).

canned *adj.* intoxicated; in a state of drunkenness; see also **blindo, blotto, bob-howler, kaylied, lagging, market-peart, mopped, palatick** and **slaumsey**.

cannock *n.* face; from the Brummagem rhyming slang 'Cannock Chase'.

cansh *n.* a small pile of faggots (Marshall, 1796).

cansh up *ph v.* to make a pile; to pile something up.

cant *vi.* to talk; to chatter. Often used with reference to someone who does nothing else but chatter EG "All 'er does all day is stand cantin'."

canting *adj.* saucy; brazen; pert (Skeat, 1876).

caper *n.* goings-on; frolicking; behaviour or activities, esp. if open to censure EG "Y'know, an' all that caper."

capers *n.* scented tea (Raven, 1977) EG "There was ninepence went for capers" (from the old Brummagem street ballad entitled *How Five & Twenty Shillings Were Expended in a Week*).

cap-it *n.* a boys' game (Northall, 1896).

card *n.* a comedian; a person who is fond of having a laugh and a joke EG "'E's a right card 'e is, en't 'e?"; often used with a heavy dose of irony when someone is decidedly not funny.

carney *vt.* and *vi.* to coax, wheedle or entice; to cheat by cajolery EG "I got no money to buy sucks: carney yer dad" (Northall, 1896).

carol-bodging *n.* see **bodging**.

caser *n.* five shillings, also *n.* a leather football.

Casey Court *n.* a noisy or riotous place (Geoff Moore).

casualty *adj.* see **casulty**.

casulty *adj.* decrepit; infirm; feeble (Northall, 1896) EG "'E's gettin' casulty now 'e's gettin' on fer seventy" (Skeat, 1876); also used in reference to uncertain or doubtful weather EG "like the martlet, Builds in the weather on the outward wall, Even in the force and road of casualty" (Shakespeare, *The Merchant of Venice*, Act II, Sc. IX).

caswy *n.* see **cawsey**.

Castle Bromwich *n.* an area of north-east Birmingham; given as Bramewice in 1168, Bromwich means the dwelling or farm where the broom grows. A shrub with yellow flowers, broom was common in the Birmingham region. By the late thirteenth century, Bramewich was known as Castelbromwic to distinguish it from a nearby Bromwich which became Little Bromwich.

cat *n.* a small piece of wood used in the game of 'bandy'; "the cat is knocked with the bandy in opposite directions by the opposing players" (Northall, 1896); also common in the Worcestershire dialect.

catch out *ph v.* to get into trouble EG "Yo wunnarf catch out, y'know." 'Catch it' has the same meaning, and is also fairly common.

catching *adj.* uncertain; changeable; said of the weather (i.e. 'showery'); Jackson (1879) states that in the Midlands "it is called catchin' time when, in a wet season, they catch every available minute of favourable weather for field work."

cat-lick *n.* a hasty wash, from which apparently comes the phrase "a lick and a promise".

cat's concerts *npl.* informal get-togethers or sing-songs round the piano (Palmer, 1976).

cat's eye *n.* a medium-sized marble; see also **alley**, **alley taw**, **blood alley**, **dogger**, **dummox**, **French alley**, **glarny**, **glass alley**, **gobbie**, **marley**, **pot alley** and **steelie**.

catterpuller *n.* pronunciation variant of catapult (Northall, 1896, and Rhodes, 1950).

causey *n.* see **cawsey**.

cawsey *n.* a raised road; a paved walk or footpath; "the older and more correct form of causeway" (Rhodes, 1950) EG "To mending the causey near the Bridge, 4d" (Town Book, 1679). A cawsey is also referred to in a deed of the Guild of the Holy Cross (1468). In 1482-3 a deed stated that John Lench of Deritend, master of the Guild of the Holy Cross, with the unanimous assent of the brothers and sisters of the guild, leased to William Wyot, a tanner of Brum, a parcel of land "lying jux le caswy" (i.e. next to the causeway, in the Digbeth area of central Birmingham).

cazulty *adj.* see **casulty**.

Celboldestone *n.* see **Edgbaston**.

centre knobs *n.* "gallery boys who used to rush the doors at the old Theatre Royal, before the establishment of queues, and secure the front rows of the gallery, selling the seats at two pence or three pence each. A brass rail, with knobs, ran along the front, and the best seats were near the centre knob. Possibly influenced by 'nobs', 'nabs', all derived from 'nob', short for 'nobleman'. A strictly local phrase, for the gallery of the old Royal, demolished 1902" (Rhodes, 1950).

cess *interj.* according to Northall (1896), this word was used in the Midlands, as well as southern parts of England, as a way of directing or inciting dogs to the scent, or, as Halliwell (1855) points out, "to call dogs to eat."

chafern *n.* see **chafforne**.

chafforne *n.* a chafing-dish, in use c.1605 (Hoddinott and Nikitas).

chance-child *n.* a bastard; an illegitimate child (Northall, 1896).

Chaney *adj.* Chinese (Northall, 1896).

Chapelmaster *n.* "the chief ruler of the meeting-house" (Northall, 1896).

charky *adj.* dry; parched; arid (Northall, 1896).

Charley *n.* slang term for a Watchman, the equivalent of today's police (Old Sarbot, 1866), latterly used to refer to a hump or fleshy protuberance on a person's back EG "Swathed in a large overcoat meant for a man three times his build, he was always hunched forward with what we kids thought of as a permanent charlie on his back" (Smith, undated), also *n.* an idiot or fool EG "'E looked a right charley, 'e did."

charlie *n.* see **Charley**.

charm *n.* bird song, esp. in the morning EG "Charm of earliest birds" (Milton, *Paradise Lost*, Bk. IV, I); also *n.* a whispering or murmuring noise; "a hum as of many voices" (Northall, 1896) EG "What a charm them children mek in school."

chats *npl.* small pieces of firewood; kindling or tinder; small sticks used for fuel EG "'E's out gatherin' chats" (Northall, 1896); see also the proverb **love of lads and fire of chats is soon in and soon out again**.

chatterwater *n.* tea; according to Northall (1894) this was a phrase coined during the latter half of the nineteenth century, though it appears to be obsolescent now.

chaun *n.* a crack or fissure either in the ground, floor or wall (Northall, 1896).

Chaunting Jemmy *n.* a blind beggar.

chaw *vt.* to chew or masticate.

chawl *n.* a pig's cheeks and jowls; pig's face, as food (Rhodes, 1950); according to Carpenter (1977), this word was known to J. R. R. Tolkien, who used it often in his correspondence; also *vi.* to chew slowly EG "'Er was sittin' there chawlin' fer ages."

cheapen *vt.* to haggle; to bargain; to negotiate; to ask the price of anything (Northall, 1896); from the Anglo-Saxon 'ceapian'.

ched *adj.* stuffed; full up; "full to the brim with eating" (Northall, 1896).

cheese-cup *n.* see **Billy Button**.

cheeses *npl.* plants of the genus *Malva*: "properly, the reference is to the unripe seed-vessels. Children often amuse themselves with gathering and eating the unripe seed-vessels, which they call cheeses; they are insipid, but not unwholesome" (Skeat, 1876, and Northall, 1896).

chelp *vi.* according to Northall (1894), 'chelping' means "replying or chattering to one's elders without much respect," but it appears to have been generally applied to any form of gossip or idle chatter EG "As if she'd got time to stand chelping with a bit of a girl," also *n.* a chat EG "You are a one for a chelp, aren't you?" (Hampson, 1936, p.3).

cherry curds *npl.* see **boistings**.

chester *n.* a penny, in use c.1870-1900; see also **coal-heaver**.

chewer *n.* a narrow passage or road between two houses (Northall, 1896); see also **tewer**.

chibbals *npl.* onions grown from bulbs; scallions (Northall, 1896).

chice *adj.* from choice; dainty; choosy EG "She won't eat this meat, she's a chice madam" (Northall, 1896).

chill *vt.* to take the chill off; to warm slightly EG "Chill that milk" (Skeat, 1876, and Northall, 1896).

chilp *vi.* see **chelp**.

chimberley *n.* pronunciation variant of 'chimney' EG "Now Mrs Morris got up to brew; there was summat the matter with the chimbley flue" (old Warwickshire folk rhyme).

chimbley *n.* see **chimberley**.

chimbly *n.* see **chimberley**.

chimdy *n.* see **chimberley**.

chin-cough *n.* whooping-cough; according to an ancient Midlands superstition, a child with chin-cough will be cured if taken out before sunrise on three mornings and passed under and over a briar bush nine times, whilst repeating:

> Under the briar, and over the briar,
> I wish to leave the chin-cough here

The briar must then be cut, made into the form of a cross, and worn on the breast. According to Palmer (1976), "In Birmingham infants were taken to Saltley gas works to smell the aroma; in other parts of north Warwickshire they were given a roasted mouse to swallow." Raven (1978) also states that 'chin-cough' appears to have once been used in a humorous sense as a relatively meaningless term.

chin-cuff *n.* see **chin-cough**.

chine *n.* a slice containing the spine cut out of the back of a pig. It is usually cut up into four or five lengths, each of which is called a 'chine', as in the Mothering Sunday folk-rhyme:

> The lad and lass on Mothering Day
> Hie home to their mother so dear;

'Tis a kiss for she and a kiss for they,
A chine of pork and a sprig of bay.
A song and dance – but never a tear.

chip *n.* one shilling.

chip out *ph v.* to fall out; to argue or quarrel EG "Jack and me 'ad a bit of a chip out last night" (Northall, 1896).

chitlings *npl.* see **chitlins**.

chitlins *npl.* boiled pig's intestines EG "There wos 'am and tongue, baacon and eggs, chitlings, and me and Gaertie sat at the top agin a big caake" (Squiers, 1916, p.10); also common in the Worcestershire dialect.

chitterling *n.* chickling.

chitterlings *npl.* see **chitlins**.

chittlins *npl.* see **chitlins**.

chiv *n.* a knife or razor; also common in the Cockney dialect.

chiv marks *npl.* scars or slashes left on the face by a knife or razor; also common in the Cockney dialect.

chivvy *n.* chin EG "Ther bloke kept givin' me a 'ankercher to mop me chivvy on" (Squiers, 1916, p.14); also common in the Cockney dialect.

chobble *vi.* to eat noisily, "frequentative of 'chop' in sense of jaw" (Rhodes, 1950); also listed in Northall (1896) and still in common use in the Birmingham dialect.

chock *vt.* to throw, chuck or cast; see also **chock-hole** and **chock-in**; used in a game called either chock o' fours, chock-in or chock-hole, which involved throwing four marbles into a hole in the ground. "Any 'remainders' - that is, marbles undeposited by one player at a cast - become the property of the other player" (Northall, 1896).

chock-a-block *adj.* overcrowded; full of people EG "The Old Crown was chock-a-block last night."

chock-full *adj.* stuffed; full up (Skeat, 1876); as full as possible (Northall 1896).

chock-hole *n.* a game of marbles; see also **chock**.

chock-in *n.* a game of marbles; see also **chock**.

chock o' fours *n.* a game of marbles; see also **chock**.

choice *adj.* particular; choosy; pernickety; finical EG "'E's very choice over 'is victual" (Skeat, 1876), "The cat won't eat this meat, 'er's a choice madam" (Northall, 1896).

chomble *vi.* see **chobble**.

chop-gos *n.* a boor; "a man rough and uncouth of manner" (Northall, 1896); from 'chop' and 'gos' (gorse); see also the phrase **as rough as chopped gos**.

chops *n.* jaw EG "I gi'im one on the chops".

chow-row *n.* noise; uproar; commotion.

chuck *n.* "A cut of beef extending from the horns to the ribs, including the shoulder piece" (Northall, 1896).

chuck-full *ph v.* (Halliwell, 1855); see **chock-full**.

chuckies *npl.* a children's word for chickens (Bob Houghton).

chuff *n.* bread; "sometimes, but not often, used broadly for food" (Northall, 1894), also *vi.* to eat EG "Jist yo wait afore yo begin to chuff" (Northall, 1896), and "They worn't 'alf chuffin' it" (Rhodes, 1950); an anonymous contributor to the *Birmingham Weekly Post* (4 Oct. 1924) stated, however, that this word was only used "when the food was tasteless or unappetising."

chuffed *adj.* happy; content EG "'Er was dead chuffed when 'er 'eard the news," "We was dead chuffed with the do they purron fer us."

chump *n.* idiot, fool (Rhodes, 1950); still in common use.

chunder *vi.* see **chunter**.

chunter *vi.* to mutter, grumble or moan quietly under one's breath (Northall, 1896).

church-clipping *n.* the practice of encircling a church; Hone (1838) describes a church-clipping that he was once taken to see as a child: "This ceremony was performed, amid crowds of people and shouts of joy, by the children of the different charity-schools, who at a certain hour flocked together for the purpose. The first comers placed themselves hand in hand with their backs against the church [St Martin's], and were joined by their companions, who gradually increased in number, till at last the chain was of sufficient length completely to surround the sacred edifice. As soon as the hand of the last of the train had grasped that of the first, the party broke up, and walked in procession to the other church [St Philip's], (for in those days Birmingham boasted but of two), where the ceremony was repeated." Church-clipping is no longer practiced in Birmingham.

clack *n.* gossip; chatter; idle talk; "a contemptuous epithet," according to Northall (1896), "for a woman's tongue."

clam *vt.* to starve EG "Clam your tongues and not a word more" (Shakespeare, *The Winter's Tale*, Act IV, Sc. IV); derived, perhaps, from the German word 'klemmen' (to pinch); see also **clemmed**.

clammed *adj.* see **clemmed**.

clap-gate *n.* "a gate which shuts on either of two posts joined with bars to a third post, so that only one person can pass through at a time" (Skeat, 1876).

clappers *npl.* "two, and sometimes three tongues of wood fitted on to a handle, used to scare birds from crops. The outer tongues work on a hinge, and the bird boy, striking them against the fixed tongue, makes a clapping sound to discomfit the birds, and utters his monotonous verse" (Northall, 1896); see also the phrase **to run like the dappers.**

clat *vi.* to natter; to tell tall tales (Skeat, 1876), also *n.* cattle droppings; cow dung EG "Mind, or you'll tread in that cow clat" (Northall, 1896).

clatter *vt.* to collide with something; to bang into something heavily EG "'E dain't arf clatter into it."

claw *vt.* to flatter EG "If a talent be a claw, look how he claws him with a talent" (Shakespeare, *Love's Labour's Lost*, Act IV, Sc. II).

clay-dabber *n.* a brickmaker's apprentice, from when bricks were hand-made, as in the old Warwickshire folk-rhyme:

Clay-dabber Dick,
Three fardins a wick,
Three lickle monkeys
To carry one brick

clean *adv.* wholly; entirely; completely EG "It is clean out of the way" (Shakespeare, *Othello*, Act I, Sc. III); still in common use.

cleas *npl.* the paws of cattle or sheep (Marshall, 1796, and Northall, 1896).

clees *npl.* see **cleas**.

cleft *n.* wood or timber, but only that deemed "fit to be cloven into coopers' ware, spokes, laths, &c." (Marshall, 1796).

clemance *vi.* to solicit gifts and money on the night of St. Clement's Day (23 November), as described in an old Tamworth folk-rhyme :

> Clemancing, clemancing, year by year,
> Apples and pears are very good cheer;
> One for Peter, two for Paul,
> And three for the man that made us all.
> Up with your stocking, and down with your shoe;
> If you've got no apples, money'll do.
> Clement was a good old man,
> For his sake pray give us some;
> None of the worst, but some of the best.
> I pray God send your soul to rest.

According to Northall (1896), in Aston and neighbouring areas of Brum, the first line ran: "Come Clement's, come Clement's, come once a year." Another variant ran thus:

> Clemeny, Clemeny, Clemeny mine!
> A good red apple and a pint of wine.
> Some of your mutton and some of your veal,
> If it is good, pray give a deal;
> If it is not, pray give some salt –
> Butler, butler, fill in your bowl.
> If thou fill'st it of the best,
> The Lord'll send your soul to rest;
> If thou fill'st it of the small,
> Down goes butler, bowl and all.
> Pray, good mistress, send to me,
> One for Peter, one for Paul,
> One for Him who made us all.
> Apple, pear, plum or cherry,
> Any good thing to make us merry;
> A browning buck or a velvet chair.
> Clement comes but once a year;
> Off with the pot, and on with the pan,
> A good red apple and I'll begin.

clem-gutted *adj.* thin and miserable-looking; emaciated; pinched in appearance (Northall, 1896).

clemmed *adj.* hungry; starving; "half starved, for want of sufficient pasture" (Marshall, 1796), but not - as in other dialects - to die of starvation EG "I'm fair clemmed" (Hampson, 1936, p.4); the variant 'clammed' was also quite commonly heard throughout Brummagem well into the twentieth century, and this is still the usual pronunciation among older Brummie speakers, 'clemmed' being more common in the Potteries EG "My main memories comprise a convocation of under-nourishment, leg-irons, impetigo, pneumonia, consumption, diets of bread and lard or fish paste sandwiches for half-clammed kids" (Smith, undated). In the Middle English poem *Patience*, the poet writes, "Al schal crye, foreclemmed, with alle oure cleare strength." In this sense, 'foreclemmed' means starving. The word is made up from the Old English words 'for' and 'clemman'. In Brummie the word is normally pronounced as 'clammed' EG "I could do with summat to eat, I'm fair clammed"; also common in the Geordie and Black Country dialects.

clevvy *n.* see **clivyes**.

cleys *npl.* see **cleas**.

click *n.* a small group or gang (Bob Houghton); a corruption, perhaps, of 'clique', also *vi.* to hit it off with someone; to become friends EG "We 'ad a mooch down the monkey run an' bumped into each other an' just clicked, sort a thing."

clicky *adj.* used to refer to people in a pub or workplace who are hostile or not welcoming to newcomers EG "They're very clicky."

clinker *n.* a punch EG "'E copt the bloke a clinker in the neck with 'is left 'oof" (Squiers, 1916, p.4).

clinking *adj.* excellent; splendid; admirable EG "En't these a clinkin' pair o' trousers?" (Northall, 1896).

clipping-the-church *n.* "an old Warwickshire custom on Easter Monday. The charity children joined hand in hand formed a circle completely round each church" (Halliwell, 1855); see also **church-dipping.**

clivyes *n.* a u-shaped piece of metal to which (by a pin or a bolt) a plough was connected to a draught animal (Marshall, 1796, and Hoddinott and Nikitas).

clock *vt.* to see or recognise EG "'As he clocked us yet?," also *vt.* to punch or strike EG "I clocked 'im one on the boko good 'n' proper," and *n.* "the ball of seeds of the dandelion: children disperse the ball by blowing off the downy seeds, and pretend to determine the time of day, each puff answering to one hour; hence the name" (Northall, 1896).

clods *npl.* betting terminology for the police.

close *n.* a field (Skeat, 1876); Northall (1896) suggests that the plural 'closen' was fairly common in the late nineteenth century, also *adj.* warm, humid weather EG "It's a bit close, ennit?"; still in common use.

clothing-boots *npl.* cloth or button boots that reach to the calf of the leg; common in the Sutton Coldfield area of Birmingham up until the late nineteenth century (Northall, 1896).

clout *n.* clothes, clothing EG "He hid behind a wench's clout" (Rhodes, 1950), also *vt.* to strike or hit EG "I'll clout y' one if y' doan packirrup."

clouter-headed *adj.* stupid; thick; "deficient in understanding" (Northall, 1896).

clozam *vt.* to appropriate; to filch (Northall, 1894).

coal-heaver *n.* one penny; see also **chester**.

coal-hod *n.* "any utensil that differs in shape from the 'scoop' or 'scuttle' for holding coal" (Northall, 1896).

cob *vt.* to defeat; to beat, actually or figuratively; to surpass EG "That cobs Dolly, and Dolly cobb'd the Devil" (Midlands folk-phrase), also *n.* a cake or bun; according to Wise (1861), cakes in which warden pears were baked ('warden-cobs') were common throughout Warwickshire up until the late nineteenth century, though the word is now only used to refer to a small, round loaf of bread, a bread roll or 'bap'.

cob-loaf *n.* a loaf with a thick crust; "in [Shakespeare's] *Troilus and Cressida*, act ii. scene 1, Ajax calls Thersites 'cob-loaf', and the allusion is to his ill-shaped head; and in act v. scene 1, the metaphor is still carried out and explained by his being called a 'crusty batch'" (Wise, 1861).

cockaiver *n.* a powerful punch which knocks the person struck off their feet (Ian Reid); from the verb 'aive' (to heave or lift) and 'cock' (man) see also **aive** and **heaving day**.

cock-eyed *adj.* cross-eyed (Upton, Sanderson and Widdowson, 1987); now in widespread use, though variants such as 'boss-eyed', 'squint-eyed', 'skend' and 'glee-eyed' are preferred in other dialect areas of England..

cockney *n.* "a useless fellow" (Alexander, 1951) EG "Vent my folly! I am afraid this great lubber, the world, will prove a cockney" (Shakespeare, *Twelfth Night*, Act IV, Sc. I).

cock of wax *n.* a familiar form of address (Palmer, 1979) EG "Indeed, said she, then list to me, my bonny cock of wax" (from the old Brummagem Street ballad *How Five and Twenty Shillings Were Expended in a Week*, c.1845-61).

cock-sure *adj.* overcertain; overconfident (Northall, 1896); now in widespread use.

cod *vi.* to joke or jest EG "'E's only coddin'," also *n.* a friend or companion; according to Northall (1896), this was often "prefixed to a surname, as Cod Bennett, Cod Jackson, &c.; and possibly may be a diminutive of *codlin*, an old term of endearment."

codderversen *adj.* out of truth, in use c.1850 (H. Hall, *Birmingham Weekly Post*, 4 Oct. 1924).

codge *vi.* to patch or cobble together roughly and in a slipshod manner; to tailor clumsily EG "Bodgin' needles, codgin' needles, all sorts of needles, oh!" (folk-rhyme, Minworth District c.1850), "'E's med a right codge of it" (Raven, 1978); frequently used in the phrase 'codge and modge' EG "'Er's codgin' an' modgin' 'er 'ole dress" (Rhodes, 1950, and Northall, 1894).

codge-modge *n.* a piece of careless sewing.

codger *n.* a miser (Skeat, 1876); now in widespread use as 'old codger'.

coffin *n.* pie-crust (Alexander, 1951) EG "And of the paste a coffin I will rear" (Shakespeare, *Titus Andronicus*, Act V, Sc. II).

cogwinder *n.* a punch.

cold-crowdings *npl.* bad times EG "There'll be cold-crowdings if bread gets much dearer" (Northall, 1896).

Cole *n.* a Birmingham river; its name appears to signify a river abounding with hazels.

collar *n.* work; labour; graft EG "It worn't arf 'ard collar in them days," also *vi.* to work

EG "'Er's bin collarin' all night on that dress," and *vi.* to receive a scolding, thrashing or other punishment EG "'Er collared it when 'er got 'ome" (Northall, 1896); see also the phrase **to catch it.**

collied *adj.* sooty; blackened (Northall, 1996) EG "Brief as the lightning in the collied night" (Shakespeare, *A Midsummer Night's Dream*, Act I, Sc. I), also overcast and troubled (Alexander, 1951) EG "And passion having my best judgment collied" (Shakespeare, *Othello*, Act II, Sc. III).

colly *n.* the soot from an open fire that has collected on the outside of pots, pans or kettles (Northall, 1896).

collywobbles *n.* the jitters; a state of nervousness or anxiety; now in widespread use.

coloured *adj.* fortunate; lucky, though more often used in negative form to denote a distinct lack of fortuity EG "'E en't coloured" (J. Woodward).

come out of *ph v.* to come from somewhere. This phrase provides an interesting analogy with childbirth. Poorer Brummies always say they come out of a particular street, showing their loyalty to this street which to them was a living thing. It came alive because the people of the street were bonded by ties of neighbourliness and kinship.

comming-gen *interj.* an expression used by waggoners to make the horses turn left (Palmer, 1976); see also **an, eet, gee-gen** and **gee-whoop.**

congreves *npl.* matches (Palmer, 1979); a type of friction match named after its inventor, Sir W. Congreve (Raven, 1977) EG "You had a penny box of congreves, and a half penny baked potato" (from the old Brummagem street ballad *How Five and Twenty Shillings Were Expended in a Week*, c.1845-61).

conk *n.* nose.

conk out *ph v.* to break down (D. Adams) EG "'Er car conked out on the expressway."

conkers *npl.* horse-chestnuts, "otherwise called 'cobblers'; apparently derived from their use in the game of 'conkers,' i.e., 'conquers'. The [two] players have their chestnuts on a string, and they hit each other's conker alternately until one breaks. Each 'conker' has a number denoting the chestnuts it has already 'conquered' or 'conquered out'" (Rhodes, 1950).

connegre *n.* a rabbit-warren (Hoddinott and Nikitas).

cop *vt.* to catch EG "Yo know, ower old mon daint 'arf cop a cold dahn at St. Andrew's awatchin Baernegum" (Squiers, 1916, p.1).

cop out *ph v.* to get into trouble EG "Y' wunnarf cop out, yo will." Like 'catch it', 'cop it' can also be used instead of 'cop out' and has the same meaning.

cordwainer *n.* a cobbler.

cordwood *n.* firewood cut into four-foot lengths.

corking *adj.* excellent; brilliant; fantastic EG "It was a corkin' match down the Blues last wick."

corkle *n.* a lump of snow, ice or mud - particularly, according to an anonymous contributor to the *Birmingham Weekly Post* (4 Oct. 1924), that which "accumulates under the boot, or hoofs of horses. (I understand at one time corks were used to put under the soles of boots and clogs, and perhaps felt bumpy, hence the 'corkle')."

Raven (1978), however, states that the same word is used in the Black Country dialect for an apple core, and Northall's (1894) definition; "the core of fruit," appears to confirm that this is indeed the correct meaning.

corning *vi.* to beg corn for frummety on St. Thomas' Day (21 December).

Corterich *n.* see **Cotteridge**.

cosh *n.* a schoolmaster's cane EG "'E dain-alf get the cosh fer waggin' it".

costrell *n.* an eared bottle or wine vessel to be hung at the waist, in use c.1615 (Hoddinott and Nikitas).

Coteriche *n.* see **Cotteridge**.

cotter *n.* an iron key to a bolt (Marshall, 1796), also *n.* association; relationship or connection, as in the phrase **to have no cotter** (with someone).

Cotteridge *n.* an area in south Birmingham; the first indication of Cotteridge is given in 1317 when the Patent Rolls mention a Hugh de Cotteruge who is likely to have taken his name from the area in which he lived. Cotteridge belonged to King's Norton and between 1494 and 1504 the Court Rolls of the manor mention Coteriche Gate, Coteriche Hall, Coteriche Lane and Corterich. It is probable that the name means Cotta's Ridge, and indeed there is a clear ridge running up from Breedon Hill. Other less likely explanations suggest that Cotteridge may have been where cottars lived - farm labourers who had a cottage; or else that it is derived from the village of Cotteridge elsewhere in Worcestershire.

Cotteruge *n.* see **Cotteridge**.

cotton on to *ph v.* to get wise to something EG "Doan worry, I've cottoned on to 'em. They 'en't gonna gerraway with that again."

couch-grass *n.* coarse, rough grass (Skeat, 1876).

couperie ware *n.* equipment for making barrels c.1603 (Hoddinott and Nikitas).

couple-a-three *adj.* an indeterminate amount; three or thereabouts EG "'Ow much you 'ad t' drink?" "Only a couple-a-three."

couple o' blow *n.* two shillings.

courted-cards *npl.* the queens, kings, jacks, and jokers in a deck of playing cards (Northall, 1896); see also **faced-cards.**

Coventry-blue *n.* a vivid indigo thread, used principally for purposes of embroidery, which was very popular during the Elizabethan period:

> I have heard say that the chiefe trade of Coventry was heretofore in making blue threde, and then the town was riche, even upon that trade, in manner only; and now our threde comes all from beyonde sea; therefore that trade is now decaied, and thereby the town like-wise. (*A Compendious and brief Examination of certayne ordinary complaynts of divers of our Country-men in these our days:* a blackletter tract, published in 1581 by W[illiam] S[tafford] - long attributed to Shakespeare).

According to Northall (1896), since Coventry-blue did not fade and could not be "discharged by washing . . . the epithets of Coventry-blue and true-blue were figuratively used to signify persons who would not change their party or principles on any consideration."

coverslut *n.* a long apron, "used to hide an untidy dress" (Northall, 1896).

cowge *vt.* and *vi* to mug; to steal something forcibly; to attack suddenly with the intention of robbing EG "Let's goo 'n' cowge their marleys" (Northall, 1896).

cow it *interj.* an expletive. The phrase is used when something has gone wrong EG "Oh, cow it!' 'Cowin' hell' is another expletive, whilst to call anyone a 'cowbag' is to insult them.

cowlady *n.* common name for the ladybird (Northall, 1896).

cowlick *n.* a lock of hair on the forehead which will not lie flat (Rhodes, 1950). A contributor to the *Birmingham Weekly Post* (Oct. 4 1924), however, argued that "this, in a woman, was called the 'widow's lock', and the 'cowlick' [presumably on a man] was where the hair grew thin or receded from the forehead on one side or the other, as if a cow had licked it off."

cow's calf *n.* half; Brummagem rhyming slang for a half pint of beer.

cow shed *n.* see **duck pen**.

cow's lick *n.* see **cowlick**.

cowty *adj.* Shaw (1930) states that this was only used in the schoolboy expression 'cowty blow'; the initial blow or punch which provokes a fight.

coxy *adj.* conceited; arrogant; supercilious (Northall, 1896); a pronunciation variant, perhaps, of 'cocky'.

crab-lantern *n.* an apple pie or pasty.

crab-shulls *n.* shoes.

crab-varjis *n.* the juice (literally 'verjuice') of crab apples, "said to be good for muscular sprains" (Northall, 1896).

cracking *adj.* excellent; very good EG "We dain't arf 'ave a crackin' time last night."

crackling *n.* pork rind; pork scratchings.

cradles *npl.* an old Warwickshire dialect word for holes left in loaves of bread after baking (Palmer, 1976).

craichy *adj.* weak; infirm; shaky EG "This is a right craichy old house, ennit?" (Northall, 1896); variants such as 'craikey' and 'creachy' were also common in the Worcestershire, Leicestershire and Gloucestershire dialects.

crake *n.* a moaning or grumbling state EG "'Er's always upon the crake, 'er is," literally 'upon the croak' (Skeat, 1876).

crammer *n.* the belly or stomach.

crane *n.* a 'sway-bar', or 'hanging-bar' on which the pot-hooks hang (Northall, 1896).

cratch *n.* a rack for cheese, in use c.1605 (Hoddinott and Nikitas); according to Palmer (1976), a cratch was a rack for meat, not dairy produce: "a piece of ropey [uneatable] bread was hung on the bacon cratch [rack] on Good Friday, and allowed to remain there for a year." Northall (1896) supports the claim that a cratch was some kind of rack "suspended from the kitchen ceiling," but suggests that this was where firearms were kept; Marshall (1798), however, states that 'cratch' was an agricultural provincialism in the late eighteenth century for a hay-rack; in the Gloucester, Worcester and Staffordshire dialects the same word also appears to have been used for "the rack-like tailboard of a cart or wagon" (Northall, 1896).

craw *n.* as in the crop or throat of a bird EG "That sticks in my craw."

create *vi.* to grumble, complain, or kick up a stink; to cause a commotion or disturbance EG "The gaffer won't 'alf create when 'e knows you've lost 'is ladder" (Rhodes, 1950); see also **create at**.

create at *ph v.* to shout at; to berate (Mary Bodfish).

creepers *npl.* head-lice (Northall, 1896).

crick *n.* a winding path running through or alongside allotments or fields (Northall, 1896).

crink *n.* a very small and sweet summer apple (Northall, 1896).

crinkling *n.* see **crink**.

criss-cross-cushion *n.* "a sort of seat made by two persons taking hold of their own and each other's wrists, thus forming a square with their hands, so as to enable them to carry a child thereon" (Northall, 1896).

croak *vi.* to die (Northall, 1896); still in common use.

crocks *npl.* dishes or plates EG "The big wenches an' our Mom 'ud wash the crocks, - crocks, that was a bloody laugh. Most on 'em warn't crocks, they wus tin plates, but we called 'em crocks any road up" (Smith, undated).

croffling *adj.* old; infirm; feeble (Northall, 1896).

croodle *vi.* to crouch over a fire; to huddle closely together, esp. for warmth (Northall, 1896, and Rhodes, 1950).

crostering *adj.* boastful; big-headed EG "'E's a crosterin' sort" (Northall, 1896).

cubble up *ph v.* to cramp, squeeze or crowd EG "We'm all cubbled up at ours" (Skeat, 1876).

cubby-hole *n.* a small closet or storeroom, an enclosed space, from the archaic 'cub' (cattle-pen).

cubby-house *n.* see **cubby-hole**.

cuck-cucks *npl.* children's sweets; see also **sucks** and **rocks**.

cuddle-daddy *n.* an overcoat (Tennant, 1983).

cullings *npl.* agricultural refuse, or 'outcasts' (Marshall, 1796).

cunnythumb *n.* a method of playing a shot in a game of marbles; according to Northall (1894), "to shoot with a 'cunnythumb' is to discharge a marble with the thumb released from far beneath the forefinger."

curnock *n.* see **kernuck**.

cut *n.* a duct, canal or channel EG "The utility of a navigable Cut from the Wolverhampton Canal to this Town having been pointed out" (*Aris's Gazette*, 26 January 1767); also used in the old Brummagem street ballad *Birmingham Lads* (c.1769):

> Since by the canal navigation,
> Of coals we've the best in the nation;
> Around the gay circle your bumpers then put,
> For the cut of all cuts is a Birmingham cut,
> Birmingham cut, fairly wrought,
> For the cut of all cuts is a Birmingham cut.

cute *adj.* clever; intelligent EG "I 'eard your young un's passed 'er 11 plus", "Ar, 'er's cute, 'er is."

cut up *ph v.* depressed; grieved; troubled (Northall, 1896) cuts EG "Ar, I sin 'im yesterday an' 'e still seemed a bit cut up about it"; still in common use.

cutlins *npl.* barley slightly bruised and cleared of the husk, used for stuffing hog's pudding.

cut o' tripe *n.* tripe was sold in portions called cuts EG "A cut of tripe, found under a seat in the gallery" (*The Theatrical Looker-On*, 21 July 1823).

D

dab *n.* a bit; a piece; a small portion (Northall, 1896).

dab-hand *n.* an adept; a 'dabster' or skilled hand (Northall, 1896), commonly used contemptuously EG "'E's a dab-hand at gettin' summat for nothin'" (Rhodes, 1950); still in general use; see also **don-hand**.

dabnette *n.* a small, usually oval, tub or wash-basin used for a small (or 'dab') wash c.1605 (Hoddinott and Nikitas).

dabwash *n.* a small wash between the main weekly washing EG "Yo'd better dabwash them towels" (Rhodes, 1950).

dadacky *adj.* see **daddicky**.

daddicky *adj.* rotten; decayed; putrid (Northall, 1896) EG "That's a daddicky log of wood."

dadduck *n.* a rotten piece of wood; also common in the Worcestershire, Gloucestershire and Shropshire dialects.

daddy-rough *n.* see **daddy-ruff**.

daddy-ruff *n.* rhyming slang for snuff (K. Carruthers); Northall (1896) suggests that this was also a common word during the late nineteenth century for the stickleback.

dag *n.* dew (Skeat, 1876) EG "There's bin a nice flop o' dag" (Northall, 1896), "We be rimmin' to Tysoe, sir. Our turn's done at Radway, un' we'm obliged to get off on the ground afore the dag's dry" (Palmer, 1976).

Dagwood sandwich *n.* a sandwich with a huge filling named after a popular cartoon character (R. Couling).

dain't *vt.* negated past tense form of the verb 'do' EG "'Ad a few Waerthingtons to keep ther naerves up, dain't 'arf know abart it neyther" (Squiers, 1917, p.3), "Ruff Mo had a lungful and dain't feel too well" (from the mid-nineteenth century Midlands street ballad, *The Darlaston Dog-Fight*). Sometimes 'dain't' can be shortened to either 'dain' or 'din' EG "I dain do it, honest!" 'Dain' is also often used with 'arf' (half) to emphasise something EG "It din arf rain larst night, din it?" "Ar, it dain arf."

damping *adj.* showery; drizzling EG "It's a dampin' day" (Skeat, 1876), and "It's dampin' weather today" (Northall, 1896).

dancers *npl.* Brummagem rhyming slang, from 'dancing bears', for stairs or staircase EG "Up the dancers" (T. Beetlestone, and Joan Burgess), "So inta the 'ouse, an' sometimes yowed gerra cuppa cocoa, if the Ole Lady 'ad eny money forrit, which worn't offen, but normally it would be straight up the dancers, throw all ya clo'es under the bed by the piddle pot, 'ceptin ya shert o' course, an' inta kip yowed jump" (Smith, undated).

dander *n.* a bad temper (Janet Broome) EG "As I started to rise, not to foight mind you, I was intent on running, he kicked me up the arse and this really got my dander up" (Smith, undated).

Dandy-Grey-Russet *n.* see **grey-russet**.

Darby-and-Joan *n.* the post-war name for an O.A.P. club.

darby-kelly *n.* stomach.

daresn't *vi.* negated form of the verb 'dare' EG "'Er daresn't go back to 'er mother's."

darling *n.* often used to refer ironically to someone who is far from angelic and a bit of a nuisance or troublemaker EG "Ar, I know the one. E's a right darlin', en't 'e? A right bramah."

dayhowse *n.* a dairy c.1612 (Hoddinott and Nikitas).

dayryhowse *n.* see **dayhowse**.

dead *adv.* extremely; very; often used for emphasis with an adjective EG "It was a dead good night out on Thursday, worn't it?"

dead-man's-shift *n.* the overnight shift in a factory, so-called because of the extremely unsociable hours; see also **back-shift**.

deaf-ears *npl.* the valves of an animal's heart (Northall, 1896).

deaf-out *n.* a person who breaks a promise; someone who lets others down EG "'E's a right bleedin' deaf-out, 'im."

deahouse *n.* see **dayhowse**.

death hunter *n.* an insurance agent.

denial *n.* an obstacle, drawback or hindrance EG "It's a great denial to 'im, bein' laid up with rheumatism" (Rhodes, 1950).

Deritend *n.* area of central Birmingham. Although it belonged for hundreds of years to the parish of Aston, Deritend has been bound inextricably to Birmingham from the beginnings of the market in 1166. When John Leland visited Brum and wrote the first description of the town, he came down Camp Hill through "as pretty a street or ever I entrd." This was Deritend High Street, or 'Dirtey' as he called. He went on:

> In it dwell smithes and cutlers, and there is a brooke that divideth this street from Birmingham, and is an Hamlett, or member of belonginge to the Parish thereby (Aston). There is at the end of Dirtey a proper chappell (St John's) and mansion house of tymber (the 'Old Crown' pub), hard on the ripe (bank), as the brooke runneth downe; and as I went through the ford by the bridge, the water ran downe on the right hande (later Floodgate Street) and a few miles lower goeth into Tame, ripa dextra (by the right bank). This brooke riseth, as some say, four or five miles above Bermingham, towards Black Hilles. The beauty of Bermingham, a good market down in the extreame (border) parts of Warwickshire, is one street,

going up alonge (Digbeth) almost from the left ripe of the brooke, up on
the meane (modest) hill by the length of a quarter of a mile.

According to McKenna (1988), the 'der' is derived from the Welsh 'dwr', meaning
water, whilst the rest of the name is from 'yet-end', signifying gate end. Thus it was
the water gate end because of its proximity to the river Rea. It seems unlikely,
however, that this interpretation is correct. Only a handful of names within modern
Birmingham are derived from the British who lived here before the Anglo-Saxons.
Because greater Birmingham lay within the Forest of Arden, it is likely that this area
did not have many Celtic inhabitants and it would seem too much to expect a Celtic
element in Deritend, a name which does not occur until the later Middle Ages and
centuries after the Anglo-Saxons had taken over this region. The most convincing
explanation is that Deritend is derived from 'der-yat-end' and means the deer gate
end. This name probably arose from the deer park which had been on the north side
of Bradford Street by Alcester Street. Thus Deritend was the end of Birmingham
near the deer gate.

Devil's Nutting Day *n.* 21st September; "Between Alcester and Stratford there is a
conical hill, called the Devil's Bag of Nuts. [According to Warwickshire folklore]
the devil was out gathering nuts – appropriately enough, on the Devil's Nutting Day
(21st September). When he had collected a big bagful he had the misfortune to meet
the Virgin Mary, who happened to be passing. The shock was so great he threw
down his bag of nuts before hurrying off, and they were turned into the hill"
(Palmer, 1976); see also the phrase **the colour of the devil's nutting bag**.

dial *n.* face EG "Kid, yo should 'ave seen 'is dial!" (Squiers, 1916, p.22).

dibs 'n' dabs *npl.* paltry portions of anything.

dich *vt.* see **ditch**.

dicker *n.* the number ten; used esp. of hides and skins c.1615 (Hoddinott and Nikitas).

dicky *adj.* sickly; unwell EG "I'm feelin' a bit dicky arter las' night" (Rhodes, 1950),
"I've got a bit of a dicky tum"; now in widespread use.

diddle *vt.* to cheat, deceive or defraud (Old Sarbot, 1869); still in common use.

didguck *n.* a boy's game played with sharpened sticks.

didlum *n.* a savings club usually consisting of women who paid a certain amount each
week to a respected member of their group. Sometimes this person 'diddled'
(cheated) them, hence 'diddle 'em' or 'didlum'. Usually, however, the saved money
was paid out at Christmas or at some other special occasion.

Digbeth *n.* an area of central Birmingham forming part of Birmingham's oldest and
most important street line; according to William Hutton (1780), 'Dygbeth' meant
Duck's Bath, recalling the pools locally where the birds were kept. Another account
states that the Duck's Bath was a spring. A less colourful but more likely
explanation for the name is that Digbeth is derived from the Old English words 'dic'
and 'paeth', indicating the dyke's path.

diggum-upper *n.* a body-snatcher or grave-robber; a person who digs up dead bodies
for dissection. Doctors didn't always find it easy to get hold of corpses for medical
experiments, and this frequently led to the practice of stealing freshly interred

bodies from cemeteries. "Even after the Anatomy Act of 1832 was passed to regulate the supply of cadavers to medical schools," writes Roy Palmer in *The Folklore of Warwickshire* (1976), "the resurrection men continued to operate for about a decade. In Birmingham they were known as diggum-uppers, and the most feared and notorious of the fraternity was Ben Crouch, who later served as a model for Charles Dickens' character, Jerry Cruncher, in *The Tale of Two Cities*. Stories of the diggum-uppers continued to circulate for many generations after the illicit trade ceased. 'About forty years ago', wrote Tom Langley in 1970, 'I was talking to a very old man who remembered as a child looking from an attic window in Icknield Street, Birmingham and watching lights in the Warstone Lane churchyard. His father told him, "the diggum-uppers bin after Jobey Didlum." Jobey had been his playmate, recently dead. The medical school was in Edmund Street a few hundred yards distant.'

dilling *n.* see **dilly**.

dilly *n.* the last of a brood or litter; the weakest in a litter of pigs; a weakling EG "I've always been sorry for him. Like a dilling he was" (Hampson, 1936, p.7).

ding-dong *n.* a party; also frequently used to refer to an argument or quarrel (Northall, 1896); still in common use.

dingfart *vt.* "to swing a person's buttocks against an obstacle, or jolt him astride the knee, &c" (Northall, 1896), as in the following old Warwickshire folk-rhyme:

> Tommy, Tommy Dingfart,
> Born in a muck-cart,
> Christen'd in a wheelbarrow,
> Gee! Wo! Wup!

dink *vt.* to bounce a baby in one's arms EG "Don't dink babby up and down so much, our Mary, you'll mek 'im sick," but most frequently in the popular rhyme sung while dancing the baby:

> Dinks a babby diddy,
> What shall your mommy do wid 'e?
> Sit on her lap,
> And give him his pap,
> And dinks a babby diddy.

dipchick *n.* the water-hen (Timmins, 1889).

dipper *n.* a piece of bread dipped in the fat of a sausage or rasher of bacon after it has been fried.

dirty-daniel *n.* treacle (Northall, 1894).

dirty dan'l *n.* see **dirty-daniel**.

dishabil *adj.* naked; undressed; in an unready state EG "Don't come in yet, I'm all dishabil" (Skeat, 1876); from the French 'deshabiller' (to undress).

dishel *n.* see **dishle**.

dishle *n.* a cup of tea; Raven (1978) suggests that the word may be derived from "pouring the tea into a dish to cool."

ditch *vt.* to dye, instil, imbue or engrain; "thus a fabric the prevailing colour of which is, say, blue, but proves on close examination to contain an occasional thread of, say,

77

dark grey, is said to be *ditched with grey*" (Northall, 1896) EG "Much good dich thy good heart, Apemantis!" (Shakespeare, *Timon of Athens*, Act I, Sc. II).

dither *vi.* to shake or tremble with cold; according to Northall (1896), the word was also "substantively used as *all of a dither.*"

ditless *n.* "a portable wooden stopper for the mouth of an oven" (Halliwell, 1855); see also **oven stopliss**.

div *n.* an idiot or simpleton; still in common use, esp. among schoolchildren.

doan *vt.* don't; negated form of the verb 'do' EG "Doan bother t' goo, it en't up ter much." A shortened form, 'do' (pronounced the same as 'go'), is also fairly common EG "I do wanna goo."

dobbies *npl.* lazy, but not particularly mischievous or malevolent spirits, who, according to Palmer (1976), "would attach themselves to a particular farm. In times of trouble they sometimes exerted themselves on behalf of the family"; see also **flibbertigibbet, hob,** and **knops**.

docker me *interj.* "As, 'Docker me if I do!' Vulg." (Northall, 1896); similar in sentiment to the current expressions, "Bugger me!," or "I'll be blowed!"

do-dally-tap *adj.* see **do-lally-tap**.

dodderel *n.* a pollard tree (Northall, 1896).

doddering *adj.* tottering, pottering; wandering about aimlessly; vacant, bewildered or senile (Northall, 1896) EG "'E's a dodderin' old get, en'e?" Still in common use.

doddle *n.* a cinch; an easy task; a certainty EG "'Ow'd it goo?" "It was a doddle."

Dodestone *n.* see **Duddeston**.

dodment *n.* grease from the axle of a wheel, etc.; dodment from the axle of a church bell was supposedly a cure for shingles (Northall, 1894); see also **bowment.**

dogger *n.* a clay marble; see also **alley, alley taw, blood alley, cat's eye, dummox, French alley, glarny, glass alley, gobbie, marley, pot alley** and **steelie**; Northall (1894) states that this word was also used in the old Warwickshire dialect to refer to "a mallet or bat, comprising a handle fitted to a heavy cylindrical end, used in a game differing from *knur and spell* in that a one-nosed tipcat is used instead of a ball."

doggie *n.* see **doggy**.

doggo *adj.* dog-rough; out of sorts; really bad.

doggy *n.* an overman; a works foreman or supervisor (Palmer, 1979); the name given to the butty's underground manager in a mine (Raven, 1977) EG "Albert he was doggy, 'cause he's of higher rank" (from the old Brummagem street ballad *The Collier Lad's Lament*, c.1846-52).

dog-out *n.* betting terminology for a person who looks out for the police.

dog's holler *adv.* thoroughly; comprehensively EG "I licked 'im dog's 'oller"; apparently derived from an area (i.e., 'Dog's Hollow') local to either Nechells or Selly Oak (R. Couling).

doings *npl.* faeces; excreta; also applied indiscriminately to anything or things; often used when the exact name of an object is unknown or has been forgotten EG "Pass them doings, will yer?"

do-lally-tap *adj.* mad; crazy; insane. The word is derived from a place in India called Deolali near Bombay where time-expired soldiers were sent before going home. The wait was long and boring and some men acted strangely and seemed to have nervous problems. The 'tap' part of the word is of East Indian origin and means 'fever'.

dollar *n.* money (Rhodes, 1950); "English name for German thaler, a large silver coin" (Alexander, 1951) EG "Ten thousand dollars to our general use" (Shakespeare, *Macbeth*, Act I, Sc. II). Later dollar meant five shillings, as for many years there were approximately four American dollars to the pound or 20 shillings; see also **oxford scholar**.

dolledge *vt.* to beat or buffet (Northall, 1896).

dolledger *n.* a beating or thrashing EG "I gin 'im such a dolledger" (Rhodes, 1950).

dolly *n.* a round piece of wood with a long stem and cross handle used for pounding clothes in a tub when washing, also *vt.* to wash EG "Yo'd best dolly them sheets" (Rhodes, 1950).

dolly-doucy *n.* a doll (Northall, 1896).

dolly mixtures *n.* cinema; Brummagem rhyming slang for 'pictures' (K. Carruthers). On *Any Road Up*, the album of songs about Brum by Laurie Hornsby and Carl Chinn, there is a song from Laurie Hornsby called *Let's go to the pictures* which includes the term 'dolly mixtures'.

dolly-peg *n.* "a 'maid' or washing implement which has pegs or lengthy projections at its base, instead of the common clublike end. It is used with a twisting motion, in order to cleanse the clothes effectually" (Northall, 1896).

domber *vi.* to smoulder or burn slowly.

don-hand *n.* an expert or skilled craftsperson; see also **dab-hand**.

donkey *n.* hair falling over the brow; an old-fashioned term for a fringe; also *n.* a wooden block on which marbles are positioned to be shot at, "the term is also applied to a board pierced at intervals, each hole having a number above it, at which marbles are discharged in the hope of their passing through some hole of high value. The numbers represent the marbles that the holder of the donkey must pay if the shooter be successful. The shooter loses his marbles that strike the donkey without passing through a hole" (Northall , 1894).

donkey-bite *n.* a small patch of rough grazing ground (Northall, 1896).

donky *adj.* damp; dank (Marshall, 1796).

donnies *npl.* hands; "When we were kids, my mom used to refer to hands as 'donnies', as in "Put your gloves on, your donnies will get cold." I still refer to my hands as donnies" (S. Chapman). The word 'donnies' is probably derived from the French phrase 'donnez les mains' (give me your hands) and may well have been brought back by veterans of the First World War.

donnuck *n.* fun EG "Nevertheless, we would dawdle along Bridge Street West to Great King Street by Lucas's, there we would turn right, taking our time and have some donnuck along the way up to Hockley Hill" (Smith, undated).

donny *n.* hand (Rhodes, 1950).

donnykin *n.* see **dunnekin.**

dook *n.* nose; a mysterious contributor to the *Birmingham Weekly Post* (4 Oct. 1924) named 'EXILE' commented that this was perhaps a compliment to the Duke (i.e. 'Dook') of Wellington.

dooks *npl.* fists EG "Shove yer dooks up" (Rhodes, 1950).

doolally *adj.* see **do-lally-tap.**

doorstop *n.* a thick crust of bread.

dosh *n.* money (Geoff Moore); still in common use.

dosser *n.* a lazy person; also used to refer to a tramp or vagrant.

dot *vt.* to hit, punch or strike EG "If yo want ter dot anybody one, go and dot ther Kayser a couple" (Squiers, 1916, p.14), "Don't yo drop 'im, or I'll dot yer one" (Squiers, 1917, p.22).

dot-and-carry-one *n.* see **hoppety-kick.**

dot-and-go-one *n.* see **hoppety-kick.**

double-header *n.* betting terminology for a coin melted down so as to have a head on either side.

double-knack *n.* a back yard with two exits (Tennant, 1983); back-to-back courtyards normally had one entrance via an entry between two front houses (fronting on to the street). These yards, as a result, were 'pudding bags' (cul-de-sacs) – some bigger yards, however, had two entries and these were known as 'double-knacks'.

dout *vt.* to extinguish; to put out; "a corruption of do out: very commonly used of putting out the candle" (Wise, 1861) EG "I have a speech of fire, that fain would blaze, but that this folly [viz., my tears] douts it" (Shakespeare, *Hamlet*, Act IV, Sc. VII), "That their hot blood may spin in English eyes, and dout them" (Shakespeare, *Henry V*, Act IV, Sc. II). Beat Sherlock writes that her father often said to her older brother whenever he caught him smoking, "Dout that or I'll dout you," and the word is still in common use – particularly among older generations of Brummie speakers.

douter *n.* a person who extinguishes a fire or flame (Wise, 1861).

dowk *vi.* to bow, esp. the head (Northall, 1896).

dowl *n.* down; "any fluff-like substance" (Northall, 1896); soft hair on the chin or face EG "One dowle that's in my plume" (Shakespeare, *The Tempest*, Act III, Sc. III).

dowle *n.* see **dowl.**

dowment *n.* the black grease from church bells; used as a remedy for shingles (Palmer, 1976); see also **dodment.**

downy *adj.* cunning; sly; crafty (Northall, 1896).

dowt *vt.* see **dout.**

draft *n.* a quarter of a ton.

dratchell *n.* "a slattern" (Northall, 1896); a dirty or unkempt woman.

drawed *pa t.* and *pa p.* drew; drawn EG "'E drawed a picture of an 'orse for the competition, but it never won," "'Er's drawed it about seven times now." Dialect words and grammar are often conservative in that they preserve older speech forms;

however, in the case of 'drawed' this is a newer grammatical development in Birmingham and elsewhere. If a verb is regular, the past tense and past participle have an *–ed* ending EG "I clean*ed* the windows," "I have clean*ed* the windows." When the past tense and past participle do not end in *–ed*, the verb is irregular EG "I *spoke* to her yesterday," "I have *spoken* to her." In standard English, the transitive verb 'draw' is irregular EG "I *drew* a picture for him," "I have *drawn* several pictures for him," but in the Brummagem dialect (as is the case with many other verbs) 'draw' is given a regular *–ed* ending; see also **knowed, learned** and **throwed**.

dripping cake *n.* "a doughy currant cake with a sweet, sticky bottom" (Tennant, 1983).

drop off *ph v.* to fall asleep (Northall, 1896); now in widespread use.

drough *prep.* through; by way of; from beginning to end of (Northall, 1896).

drownded *vi.* past tense of the verb 'drown', as in the old rhyme "Adam an' Eve an' Pinch-me went down the river to bathe, Adam an' Eve got drownded, and who do you think was saved?" (Anonymous).

drummil *adj.* see **dummill**.

dry-skinned *adj.* droll EG "'E's a dry-skinned bloke, en' 'e?"

dub *vt.* to make blunt EG "You'll dub the point o' that knife against them bricks" (Northall, 1896).

dubbed *adj.* see **dubbid**.

dubbid *adj.* blunt; unsharpened; having a dull edge or point.

dubersome *adj.* dubious or doubtful (Skeat, 1876).

duck *n.* a game, or "a stone used in a game" (Northall, 1896) played thus: one boy places his 'duck' or 'quack' on a larger stone called the 'mother', and the other players attempt to knock it off with their ducks. According to Northall, "should any player miss, he must be careful in picking up his stone again, lest the guardian of the stationary stone 'tick' (touch) him before he can return to the mark from which the stones are thrown." Any player touched by the guardian must place his duck on the mother and become the guardian himself. If, at any point, the duck is knocked off the mother, all players may quickly retrieve their ducks before the stone is replaced by the guardian and the game recommences. Northall states that "another game is played by two companions when on a walk. Each one chooses a stone, and *A* casts his ahead. *B* throws at it, endeavouring to split it. If he is not successful, *A* then picks up his own duck, and casts it at that of *B*: and so on, *ad lib.*" Smith (undated) uses the variant 'ducker' to refer to any large stone used for throwing: ". . . this time the rotten sod picked up a big smooth ducker and, before we had time to stop him, had taken aim and thrown it."Duck, as in the phrase "I'll knock your bleedin' duck off", was also commonly used to refer to a person's head (Rhodes, 1950).

duck egg *n.* an Irish person. Many Irish Brummies come from the country and used to eat duck eggs. The term is not used in a derogatory or insulting sense and is mostly used jocularly. However, some Irish Brummies do take offence at its use. Carl's Great Uncle George used to say to his wife Kay, who is from Dublin, 'You're the best Duck Egg to come out of Ireland since me mother'. His Great Grandmother, Lilian Wood, was born on the Curragh Camp in the later nineteenth century, the daughter of a British soldier and a colleen.

ducker *n.* see **duck**.

duckfoot *vt.* to measure a distance by placing the feet side by side, one after the other (Northall, 1896).

duckfrost *n.* a slight frost, but also, according to Northall (1896), "jocularly used to refer to a wet night."

duck pen *n.* in Sparkbrook in the late nineteenth and early twentieth centuries this was the part of the bar in a pub where the older married or widowed women sat and had a drink. In Aston this area was known as 'the cow shed'. In this period it was not usual for women to go into pubs except in poorer neighbourhoods and then only if they were older women.

duckstone *n.* see **duck**.

Duddeston *n.* area of Birmingham; Duddeston is recorded as Duddestone in a deed of King Ethelred dated 963, and is therefore one of the oldest recorded place names in Birmingham. It appears in the Curia Regis Rolls of 1204 as Dodeston, and it is likely that the name means the farmstead ('tun') of a settler called Dudda.

Duddestone *n.* see **Duddeston**.

duff *n.* possible pronunciation variant of 'dough' (Northall, 1896).

duffer *n.* an idiot or fool; often used in the past by teachers to refer to a youngster who has great difficulty in answering a question.

duff up *ph v.* to beat up EG "'E was duffed up by the Summer Lane ruffs larst wick."

dumb-cake *n.* a cake baked by unmarried Birmingham girls in the eighteenth century, which - according to an age-old superstition - had the power to produce a vision of their future husbands: "Three girls would bake the cake and eat it at midnight before walking backwards to bed. It was said they would then see their husbands. The whole process was carried out in silence - hence the term 'dumb cake'" (reported in *Metro*, 27 Feb 2001).

dumble *n.* "a small wood in a valley or hollow" (Halliwell, 1855).

dummil *adj.* see **dummill**.

dummill *adj.* stupid; half-baked, also *n.* a dullard (Northall, 1896); a dim-witted person or 'useless article'; see also the phrase **as dummle as a donkey**.

dummle *adj.* see **dummill**.

dummocks *n.* see **dummox**.

dummox *n.* a clay marble of inferior quality; see also **alley**, **alley taw**, **blood alley**, **cat's eye**, **dogger**, **French alley**, **glarny**, **glass alley**, **gobbie**, **marley**, **pot alley** and **steelie**.

dummy *n.* betting terminology for a person who stood in to be arrested for the bookie; Northall (1894) also states that this was an old Warwickshire word for a candle.

dunch *vt.* to administer a sharp blow, usually in the ribs, with the elbow (Northall, 1896).

dunch-dumpling *n.* a dumpling made of plain flour, water and salt (Halliwell, 1855).

dunderhead *n.* an idiot or simpleton.

dungil *n.* the 18th century dungeon or lock-up in Peck Lane, as in the song *I Can't Find Brummagem*:

> Down Peck Lane I walked alone,
> To find out Brummagem;
> There was the dungil down and gone,
> What, no rogues in Brummagem?"

dunnekin *n.* a toilet (Northall, 1894).

dunny-dumpling *n.* see **dunch-dumpling**.

dup *vt.* to open up (Alexander, 1951); formed, according to Wise (1861), from 'do up' EG "And dupp'd the chamber-door" (Shakespeare, *Hamlet*, Act IV, Sc. V).

durgey *n.* a dwarf, also *adj.* small; diminutive; Lilliputian EG "'E's a durgey bloke, en't 'e?" (Northall, 1894); from the Anglo-Saxon 'dweorg' (dwarf).

dust-up *n.* a fight.

Dygbath *n.* see **Digbeth**.

Dygbeth *n.* see **Digbeth**.

Dyghbath *n.* see **Digbeth**.

dynchfork *n.* a fork used for removing animal manure c.1614 (Hoddinott and Nikitas).

E

eager *adj.* sharp; cutting; piercing – "physically or mentally" (Alexander, 1951) EG "The bitter clamour of two eager tongues" (Shakespeare, *Richard II*, Act I, Sc. I).

eames *npl.* the hames; "the iron pieces that go round the collar of a horse" (Skeat, 1876).

earlings *npl.* young lambs just 'eaned' or 'dropped' (Wise, 1861).

earhole *n.* a creep; a brown-nose; someone who sucks up to a teacher or a boss EG "'E's a proper ear'ole, 'e is."

earth *vi.* to turn up the ground (Skeat, 1876).

easens *npl.* see **easings**.

easings *npl.* the eaves of a house (Northall, 1896) EG "The swallows are buildin' under our easin's" (Marshall, 1796).

easins *npl.* see **easings**.

ecky *n.* a game which, according to Northall (1896), was played thus: "a flat, smooth stone, called the 'ecky-stone' or 'duck', is placed on the foot of a player, and he kicks it as far as he can. He and his companions run and hide, whilst the guardian of the stone goes - without looking behind him - to fetch it and place it in a small shallow hole made for the purpose. He then seeks the hidden players. Should he see one he calls 'I ecky ____' mentioning the boy's name - and rushes to place his foot on the stone: for, should the one discovered reach the place before him, and kick away the stone, he must begin over again. Any player may steal the stone, and kick it away during the absence of the guardian, and so release any players previously taken. Should the guardian succeed in finding and outrunning all the other players, a new game is started, the first lad taken becoming the guardian. The guardian must not take his stone with him when searching. I am informed that this game is not of twenty years' standing in Warwickshire."

Edgbaston *n.* area of Birmingham; meaning the farmstead ('tun') of a person called Ecgbald, Edgbaston was first recorded as Celboldestone in the Domesday Book of 1086 when it was worth 30 shillings – ten shillings more than Birmingham. Written as Egbaldestone in 1184, by the thirteenth century the manor was held by the Eggebaston family.

eet *interj.* an expression used by waggoners to make the horses move towards the right (Palmer, 1976) see also **an, comming-gen, gee-gen** and **gee-whoop**.

eeyar *interj.* contracted form of 'here you are'; often used in an exclamatory tone when making some kind of offer, or attempting to draw attention to something; still in widespread use throughout the West Midlands.

Egbaldestone *n.* see **Edgbaston**.

egg *vt.* to incite or instigate EG "Ill eggin' meks ill beggin'" (Northall, 1896); now in widespread use.

Eggebaston *n.* see **Edgbaston**.

elevlin *bsl.* 11d in old money (Harris).

elne *n.* a measure of length (originally taken from the arm) roughly equal to forty-five inches, in use c.1632 (Hoddinott and Nikitas).

end *n.* a squatters' settlement EG Ward End and Shard End; see also **green**.

enew *adv.* enough (Skeat, 1876).

entails *npl.* the ends of lands EG "When reapers come near to the finish, they cut off each other's entails: the whole finishing together" (Marshall, 1796).

er *nom.* she; the feminine pronoun of the third person EG "'Er don't 'alf fancy 'erself, 'er does!" (Ainsworth, 1989). Rhodes (1950) states: "not her, as is generally supposed, but a corruption of the Anglo-Saxon 'heo' (she)" EG "He hire hand nam and heo sona aras: *he took her hand and she at once arose*" (Bosworth and Toller, 1898). In *Sir Gawain and the Green Knight* 'hir' or 'her' is the accusative, dative and genitive of 'she'. According to Upton, Sanderson and Widdowson (1987), the dominant form now considered to be 'standard' did not emerge until medieval times.

erden *n.* hessian, as in an 'erden bag' and an 'erden aprond'.

Erdington *n.* area of Birmingham. At the time of the Norman Conquest in 1066, Erdington was part of the huge estates of Earl Edwin of Mercia. He lost his lands following the unsuccessful Anglo-Saxon rebellions of 1067-71, and in the Domesday Book of 1086 the manor is given as Hardintone and described as belonging to William FitzAnsculf, a powerful Norman lord. Hutton (1780) felt that Hardintone was a mis-spelling and that it should have been Ardenton – meaning the settlement in the Forest of Arden; whilst Fowler (1885) believed that the name was derived from 'geard ing ton' and meant the hamlet in the enclosed pastures. It is more likely that Erdington means the settlement of a man called Earda, as it is given by Mills (1995). There is also an Eardington in Shropshire which was also recorded at one stage as Ardintone. The same name has become Ardington in Berkshire and Yarnton in Oxfordshire. Whatever the case, Hardintone in Warwickshire had become Erdintone by 1260 and Erdyngtone by 1461. In this year the name was also given as Yerdington and on a map of Warwickshire dated 1610 the area is shown as Yenton. Indeed, as late as the 1830s Erdington was commonly known as Yarnton.

Erdintone *n.* see **Erdington.**

Erdyngtone *n.* see **Erdington.**

erif yennups *bsl.* 5d in old money (Harris).

erin gen *bsl.* 9/- in old money (Harris).

erin yennups *bsl.* 9d in old money (Harris).

ern *poss pron.* hers; possessive of 'she'.

erth 'n' yennups *bsl.* 3d in old money (Harris).

es *n.* ash; from the Old English 'asce' (Northall, 1896).

Escelie *n.* see **Selly Oak** and **Weoley.**

es-hole *n.* ash hole; space below the fire basket in a lead grate where the ash accumulates; usually spoken of as 'thessole' (J. Alldritt).

es-miskin *n.* an ash pit; place for dumping ashes.

ess *n.* see **es.**

ess-hole *n.* see **es-hole.**

etherins *npl.* "rods or pliant boughs twisted on the top of a newly cut hedge, to keep the stakes firm" (Halliwell, 1855); from the Anglo-Saxon 'ether' (a hedge) or 'edor' (what bounds or defends) (Northall, 1896).

execution day *n.* wash day; see also **Saint Monday.**

extry *adj.* extra; an additional amount.

eyeable *adj.* attractive; pleasing to the eye (Marshall, 1796).

eyepiece *vt.* to analyse or scrutinise EG "Just eyepiece this sewin' over 'n' see if the stitchin's done well, will yer?" (Northall, 1896).

F

faced-cards *npl.* the 'court' or 'picture cards' in a deck of playing cards (Northall, 1896); see also **courted cards.**

fad *n.* a whim, vagary or fancy EG "'Er's always so full of 'er fads, I've no patience with 'er" (Skeat, 1876); now broadly applied to any fleeting fashion, also *n.* a fastidious person EG "'E's such a fad" (Northall, 1896).

faddle *vi.* to bother with or be concerned about something or someone EG "I can't faddle with teapots" (Hampson, 1936, p.207), also *n.* "a person who is overcareful about trifles" EG "What a faddle you are!" (Northall, 1896).

fadge *n.* farthing; see also **fardin.**

fainty-bag *n.* a lady's handbag.

fall *n.* a woman's short veil, a head covering; according to Skeat (1876), this word was also used in the old Warwickshire dialect, as it is in American English today, to refer to autumn, and 'fall o' the leaf' was once a common phrase throughout the Midlands.

famelled *adj.* famished; starving (Skeat, 1876).

fancy *n.* a sporting fraternity (Palmer, 1979) EG "Yesterday morning (Tuesday October 15ᵗʰ 1816) the attention of the milling amateurs and fancy of this town and neighbourhood was directed to the field of sport, at Sutton Coldfield, to witness a contest between two young men, named Griffiths and Bayliss, the former an inhabitant of this Town, and the latter from Wednesbury, for a purse of £40" (from *Famous Boxing Match; Three New Songs, Written on the Boxing Match, between Griffiths and Baylis*, 1816).

fanteague *n.* a fit of passion or desire (Northall, 1896).

fardel *n.* not – as Alexander (1951) postulates – a "pack or burden," but "a faggot, or 'kid'" (Wise, 1861), as used metaphorically by Shakespeare in *Hamlet*: "Who would these fardels bear, to grunt and sweat under a weary life" (Act III, Sc. I).

fardin *n.* see **farden**.

fardin *n.* pronunciation variant of 'farthing'(Northall, 1896), as in the old Warwickshire folk-rhyme:

> A bow behind, and a bow before,
> And a *beau* be [booby?] in the garden,
> I wouldn't part with my sweetheart
> Fer tuppence ha'p'ny farden.

fash *vt.* to trouble, stress or vex EG "Stop yer fashin', will yer?" (Skeat, 1876).

fat-bottle *n.* a bottle of pasteurised milk; pasteurised milk is delivered in fat bottles in Birmingham, whereas sterilised milk comes in thin bottles; Birmingham is still a stronghold of pasteurised milk and this term is used predominantly by working-class Brummies.

favour *vt.* to resemble; to be "like in feature" (Skeat, 1876) EG "'E favours 'is old chocker, an' 'er favours 'er old-Dutch," "The boy is fair, of female favour" (Shakespeare, *As You Like It*, Act IV, Sc. III). Rhodes (1950) states that "the old meaning of face is preserved in the proverb, 'Kissing goes by favour', and in 'ill-favoured' meaning ugly."

feeb *bsl.* beef.

feeders *npl.* idle, good-for-nothing servants (Wise, 1861) EG "By one that looks on feeders?" (Shakespeare, *Antony and Cleopatra*, Act III, Sc. XIII).

feelth *n.* feeling; sensation EG "I en't got no feelth in me 'ands, they'm froz" (Northall, 1896).

fenaged *adj.* tired; fatigued.

ferrott *n.* tape used for bindin c.1636 (Hoddinott and Nikitas).

festilo *n.* a fistula or pipe.

fetch *vt.* in *Cleanness*, the Middle English poem written in the dialect of the North West Midlands in the late 1300s, fetch is used in the sense of dealing a blow, as in the

Brummie "'E fetched 'im such a wallop." *Patience* was written in the same speech and in the same period and in this poem, fetch means to bring upon yourself.

fettle *vi.* to tidy, clean or organise; "to put in order" (Marshall, 1796); to set to rights; to prepare or arrange (Northall, 1896) EG "This room's all of a mullock, it wants fettlin' up a bit," and "Fettle your fine joints 'gainst Thursday next" (Shakespeare, *Romeo and Juliet*, Act III, Sc. VI); the phrase 'in fine fettle' appears to have been derived from this.

fidgety *adj.* active; lively, esp. when used to refer to a child's behaviour (Upton, Sanderson and Widdowson, 1987); now in widespread use.

fierce *adj.* bright; sharp; healthy, esp. applied to babies (Skeat, 1876).

figaries *npl.* small items of clothing EG "Ribbins and bibbins and fa-la-la figaries" (John Free Jnr., *Birmingham Weekly Post*, 1930) Northall (1896), on the other hand, states that this word was only applied to "showy or fantastic ornaments" EG "A bow under 'er chin, another atop uv 'er bonit, an' a 'ankicher all th' colours o' the rainbow, with a big 'air brooch stuck in it - she was in fine figaries, I can tell yer"; probably a corruption of 'frippery'.

file *n.* a cunning, deceitful person (Skeat, 1876); a cheat or deceiver (Northall, 1896).

findless *n.* anything found by chance (Northall, 1896).

finger-stall *n.* a bandage - usually a finger cut from a glove - for a sore finger or thumb (Northall, 1896).

fish *interj.* expressive of contempt or disparagement (Northall, 1896).

fissle *vi.* to fidget, "as in 'fissle and scawt' = to fidget and kick, as a restless bedfellow" (Northall, 1896).

fitchetty pie *n.* "a pie made with meat, apples, onions and other odds and ends" (H. Hall, *Birmingham Weekly Post*, 4 Oct. 1924).

fither *vi.* "to scratch or fidget with the fingers" (Northall, 1896).

fits 'n' girds *n.* fits and starts; irregularly or intermittently.

fittle *n.* food, victuals, provisions (Northall, 1896).

fittler *n.* a victualler; a purveyor of provisions. Rhodes (1950) states that "the earlier pronunciation is suggested by a deed of 1330 concerning the foundation of Clodsdale's Chantry; one of the jurymen being John le Fyvchelere."

fives *n.* an alcoholic beverage consisting of a mixture of ale and mild; the name for this drink appears to have been derived from its price: tuppence ha'penny for a half pint and five pence for a pint, often served with a label stuck on the top of the jar or pot if taken away to be consumed off the premises.

fizgig *n.* any temporary plaything of little lasting interest (Northall, 1896).

fizzog *n.* face; derived from 'physiognomy', meaning the cast or form of a person's features.

flacky *adj.* sloppy; shabby; unkempt (Skeat, 1876).

flannen *n.* pronunciation variant of 'flannel'; according to Northall (1896), "said to be from the Welsh 'gwlanen' (wool).

flasket *n.* a shallow basket c.1605 (Hoddinott and Nikitas).

flatch *n.* a halfpenny; see also **meg**.

flaze *vi.* to blaze or flare, "as straw or shavings do when ignited" (Northall, 1896).

flea-pit *n.* the local cinema (R. Phipp).

fleek *vulg.* to have sexual intercourse with; to mess about EG "Hay, yo don't wear it on yer neck; shove it round yer fleekin' waist" (Squiers, 1916, p.2); used as a euphemism for the more vulgar form.

fleeked *pa t.* and *pa p.* see **fleek**.

fleeking *pr p.* see **fleek**.

flibbertigibbet *n.* "a night demon who 'mopped and mowed' between the ringing of the curfew bell and the crowing of the first cock, with the object of terrifying young women" (Palmer, 1976); see also **dobbies, hob**, and **knops**.

flit *vt.* to move; to change abode EG "'Er flits backards and forrards all the time, 'er does." Normally used in the phrase 'moonlight flit', when a family moved from their home at night because they owed too much on the rent. The move was usually accomplished with a hand cart. It also refers to someone who is always going from one thing to another as in the term 'flitting and flatting'. In *The York Play of the Crucifixion* written in the Northern dialect in the late 1300s or early 1400s, flitte is used as move. It is derived from the Old Norse 'flytja'.

flitchen *n.* a side of bacon; also common in the Black Country dialect (Shaw, 1930).

flob *vi.* to spit; to eject saliva from the mouth EG "Every time 'e opens 'is gob 'e flobs all over the shop."

flommack *vi.* to slouch, lounge or loll about.

flommacks *n.* an ill-dressed or untidy person.

flommacky *adj.* untidy; unkempt; messy (Northall, 1896).

flommax *n.* see **flommacks**.

flothery *adj.* nonsensical; meaningless; unintelligible (Northall, 1896) EG "'Im 'n' 'is flothery talk - I can't mek sense of it."

flummuxed *adj.* bewildered; confounded EG "I was completely flummoxed - 'adn't gorra clue what wuz gooin' on."

fode *n.* a yard; the area of land immediately in front of a dwelling; also common in the Black Country dialect, though in rapidly declining use.

food garage *n.* mouth EG "I points ter my food garage like this - and lumme, 'e went and brought me a fleekin' toothbrush" (Squiers, 1917, p.4).

fooley-addlum *n.* a fool; a stupid person (Northall, 1896).

foot-ale *n.* "a fine spent in beer on a workman's first entering a new place of employment" (Northall, 1896).

footstitch *n.* footstep (Northall, 1896) EG "I wun't tek another footstitch."

forby *prep.* nearby; close at hand.

fordrough *n.* a narrow lane or driveway leading to a farm EG Fordrough Lane, Stirchley; also used to refer to a green trackway between two hedges (T. Jones); Northall (1896) suggests that both 'fordrough' and 'foredraft' were common in the Birmingham area, but, since 'drough' means through, the former variant "is probably the better."

foreby *prep.* see **forby**.

foredraft *n.* see **fordrough**.

forjitting *n.* a mixture of mortar and cow-dung used for plastering the inside of chimneys.

form *n.* a first-rate manner; a perfect or faultless fashion EG "If you let 'er play the accompaniment, we'll sing it in a form." According to Skeat (1876), the Cockney equivalent is 'in form'.

forrad *adj.* pronunciation variant of 'forward' (Northall, 1896).

fossit *n.* see **Spiggit 'n' Fossit**.

fother *vt.* to feed or nourish, esp. cattle or other livestock (Skeat, 1876).

Fox Hollies *n.* area of Birmingham. Hollies is derived from the Old English word 'holegn', meaning holly and this part of Acocks Green and Hall Green must have been noted for this tree. By the early fifteenth century, the Fox family had settled locally, 'atte' (at) the Hollies. Gradually the 'atte' was dropped and the name Fox Hollies evolved.

frail *n.* a workman's satchel made of 'rush' or some similar material (Northall, 1896).

frailbasket *n.* see **frail**.

Franchelie *n.* see **Frankley**.

Franckleye *n.* see **Frankley**.

Frankley *n.* area of south Birmingham. The Domesday Book of 1086 indicates that the overlord of Frankley was the great William FitzAnsculf and that it was worth 30 shillings. The name was written as Franchelie, and by the twelfth century it was given both as Frankley and Franckleye. It means the woodland clearing made by a person called Franca, although some believe that it is derived from the Old French word 'frank', meaning free. In the later Middle Ages a franklin was a landowner who was of free birth but not of noble descent. Accordingly, it is proposed that Frankley means a free or privileged place and that in Anglo-Saxon times it was granted by a lord to tenants who did not have to perform base services. In his *Ballads of Old Birmingham* (1911), E. M. Rudland includes a ballad on 'Franchelie' with the lines: "When men shall ask where men are free, O proudly tell of Franchelie."

franzy *adj.* enthusiastic; fervent EG "The master's such a terrible franzy man" (Skeat, 1876); interestingly, both Shaw (1930) and Walker (undated) claim that this word means 'irritable' in the Black Country dialect, whereas Tomkinson (1893) lists it as an adjective meaning 'passionate' in the Worcestershire dialect.

fratch *vt.* to argue or dispute (Raven, 1977) EG "While we are fratchin' wi' gaffer for snatchin', we know to his brass he will cling" (from *Poverty Knock*, a nineteenth century Brummagem street ballad).

free-and-easy *n.* a Saturday night out on the town; "After World War 1, Solihull pubs tried to boost morale with weekly concerts. The Saturday night events, 'free and easies', attracted hundreds of young people from outlying villages. They were soon banned by local police following complaints of fights and rowdiness at the train station as they waited for trains home" (reported in *Metro*, 30 March 2001).

frem *adj.* flourishing; vigorous; hardy, esp. when applied to plants EG "Your plants do look frem" (Skeat, 1876)..

French alley *n.* a marble made of china, probably kaolin; see also **alley, alley taw, blood alley, cat's eye, dogger, dummox, glarny, glass alley, gobbie, marley, pot alley** and **steelie**.

fresh-liquor *n.* unsalted hog's lard.

fretchet *adj.* irritable; peevish; fretful (Northall, 1896).

fretting-frock *n.* Northall (1896) defines this as "a figurative garment which is supposed to clothe a troubled female" EG "'Er's got 'er frettin' frock on". Similar, in many ways, to 'thinking-cap'.

frigabob *n.* see **frigumbob**.

friggling *adj.* trifling; insignificant (Northall, 1896) EG "Dun't waste no more time frigglin' at that knot."

frighted *pa p.* see **frit**.

frigmajig *n.* a toy (Northall, 1896).

frigumbob *n.* "anything dancing up and down; jerking from side to side; moving about rapidly" (Northall, 1896).

frit *pa p.* frightened (Skeat, 1876) EG "Summat frit the 'orses last night."

fritch *adj.* conceited; vain; big-headed.

frizzle *n.* a meal of anything fried EG "Let's 'ave a frizzle for dinner" (Northall, 1896).

frock *n.* dress; taken from the Middle English 'frok', meaning 'garment' EG "It was a lovely frock 'er was a-wearin'."

frogging *interj.* faring; doing EG "How're you froggin'?" Northall (1896) states that this was the usual form of greeting in and around the Sutton Coldfield area of Birmingham.

frowsty *adj.*, dirty or dishevelled in appearance.

froz *vi.* past participle of the verb 'freeze' EG "The cut's froz" (D. Jones).

frum *n.* lustful; lascivious; concupiscent; according to Northall (1894), this is "the exact Warwickshire meaning," though it has "other meanings in other counties."

frumenty *n.* see **frummety**.

frummety *n.* "a delicacy composed of baked creed wheat, sugar, dried currants, &c., boiled in milk, and sometimes thickened with flour and eggs. It used to be customary in Warwickshire on St Thomas' Day, Dec. 21st, for the poor people to go *a-corning*, i.e. to visit the farmhouses, to beg corn to make this compound, frummety being a traditional delicacy for that day" (Northall, 1896); variants of this, such as 'frumenty' (from the Latin *frumentum*, meaning 'corn'), 'furmety', 'furmatty', and 'thrummety' were also common throughout England in the nineteenth century.

Fuddling Day *n.* see **Saint Monday**.

fudge *vi.* to attempt to gain an advantage by unfair means; to cheat (Rhodes, 1950); Northall (1894) implies that this term was only used to refer to ungentlemanly conduct in a game of marbles, whereas 'hodge' was "the word near Tamworth."

fuggles *npl.* large hops; according to a report in *Metro* (21 May 2001), the picking of hops "was popular with Midlands women and children in the 19th century when hundreds would travel into fields each September to look for employment to supplement their wages. They slept in barns and rough shelters and earned around one shilling and three pence for a bushel of the bigger hops called *fuggles*."

fullock *n.* a heavy fall or bad trip EG "He came such a fullock over that step," also *vt.* to hit or punch EG "Fullock 'im one in the jaw" (Northall, 1896).

fundless *n.* see **findless**.

fust *adj.* pronunciation variant of 'first' common up until the nineteenth century, as in the Midlands folk-rhyme:

> Billy, Billy Bust,
> Who speaks fust (for a gift)?

G

gack *n.* Blue Coat School slang for a schoolmaster's cane (F. M. A. Wright, *Birmingham Weekly Post*, Oct. 4 1924).

gaffer *n.* both Rhodes (1950) and Northall (1896) claim that this word was used, as indeed it is today, to refer to a boss, master or "the overlooker or foreman of a gang of labourers," whereas Skeat (1876) suggests that it may have formerly been used to refer to a grandfather EG "Our old gaffer's dog killed a fox hisself." A contraction, perhaps, of 'godfather'.

gaig *vt.* see **geg**.

gain *adj.* handy; skilful; apparently the opposite of 'ungainly' EG "'E's a gain bloke" (Northall, 1896).

gainly *adj.* see **gain**.

gale-hook *n.* a hook for hanging a pot over a fire.

galeny *n.* guinea-fowl.

gall *n.* a vacant or bald place in a crop (Marshall, 1796).

galland *n.* a vessel for holding liquids c.1619 (Hoddinott and Nikitas).

gallit *n.* a left-handed person (Northall, 1896).

gallus *adj.* evil; wicked; impudent; a corruption of 'gallows' EG "'E's a gallus young rascal" (Northall, 1896), "Ay, and a shrewd unhappy gallows too" (Shakespeare, *Love's Labour's Lost*, Act V, Sc. II).

gally *adj.* scattered with bald spots (Marshall, 1796); an agricultural term.

gambrel *n.* a bar of wood used by butchers to hang up the carcasses of sheep, pigs, etc., as in the old proverb "Soon crooks the tree that good gambrel would be."

game *adj.* crooked or wavering (Northall, 1896).

gammit *n.* a practical joke or trick.

gammy *adj.* disabled; lame (Northall, 1896); now in widespread use.

gamp *n.* umbrella (R. Reay).

ganger *n.* a foreman; see also **bummer**.

gansey *n.* an undervest; a woollen jersey, pullover or sweater EG "I shoved me boots on, an' if it wus cold, an' I 'appened ta 'ave one, I'd stick me ganzi on as well" (Smith, undated); could either be derived from the Irish word for jumper, or a corruption of 'guernsey'.

gansy *n.* see **gansey**.

ganzi *n.* see **gansey**.

ganzy *n.* see **gansey**.

gardener *n.* a store for grain c.1625 (Hoddinott and Nikitas).

garner *n.* a bin in a mill or granary (Marshall, 1796).

gasunder *n.* see **gazunder**.

gaubshite *vulg.* "a filthy boor" EG "Yer jolter-yeded (headed) gaubshite" (Northall, 1894); now in widespread use as 'gobshite'.

gaum *vi.* to purposefully handle objects in a way which will damage or ruin them; to mar the appearance of something with malice of forethought; to dirty or make filthy (Northall, 1896).

gaumless *adj.* see **gawmless**.

gaun *n.* a gallon measure (Marshall, 1796).

gaup *vi.* see **gawp**.

gawby *n.* an idiot, fool or simpleton.

gawk *n.* a badly dressed person, also *vi.* to stare; to glare; to look with a fixed gaze EG "What you gawkin' at, mate?" (Northall, 1896); see also **gawp**.

gawmless *adj.* dim-witted; slow on the uptake (Northall, 1896); now in widespread use.

gawn *n.* a tub holding approximately one gallon and usually having a handle projecting upwards on one side; a corruption, perhaps, of 'gallon'.

gawp *vi.* to stare or gaze; see also **gawk**.

gazunda *n.* see **gazunder**.

gazunder *n.* a chamberpot; contracted form of 'goes under' (i.e., the bed), as used in Laurie Hornsby's song *The Old Crock Po* on the album *Any Road Up*.

gear *vt.* to harness or fetter; to equip for work (Skeat, 1876), also *n.* belongings; equipment; accoutrements as in "'Ave y' gorrall yer gear?" The word is more than likely derived from the Middle English word 'gere' meaning to dress or clothe, and it is used in this sense in *Sir Gawain and the Green Knight*.

gee-gen *interj.* an expression used by waggoners to make the horses turn right (Palmer, 1976); see also **an**, **eet**, **comming-gen** and **gee-whoop**.

geering *n.* the ladders and side-rails of a waggon (Marshall, 1796).

gee-whoop *interj.* "an expression used by waggoners to make the horses come to the near or off sides" (Skeat, 1876); see also **an**, **eet**, **comming-gen** and **gee-gen**.

geg *vt.* to swing (Skeat, 1876).

gen *bsl.* 1/- in old money (Harris).

Gerlei *n.* see **Yardley**.

gerrout *interj.* literally 'get out'; commonly used to express surprise, stupefaction or wonderment EG "'Er's a-gerrin' married again." "Gerrout! 'Er only got married larst year, dain't 'er?"

ghasse *n.* furze or whin, used as fuel for heating bread ovens c.1634 (Hoddinott and Nikitas).

gib *n.* see **gib-cat.**

gib-cat *n.* a male cat (Alexander, 1951); an old Warwickshire dialect word for a tom-cat; according to Wise (1861), the phrase 'as melancholy as a gib-cat', as spoken by Falstaff in the first part of Shakespeare's *Henry IV* (Act I, Sc. II), "probably arose because, as Linnaeus observes of the animal, *misere amat.*"

gibber *vi.* to sweat or perspire (Skeat, 1876).

giddling *adj.* giddy; thoughtless; unsteady (Skeat, 1876).

gifts *npl.* white specks on the fingernails, as in the old Warwickshire saying:
> Gift on your finger - sure to linger,
> Gift on your thumb - sure to come.

gifty-day *n.* "a boon-day, as a day's work given, by neighbour to neighbour" (Marshall, 1796).

gindge *vt.* to join c.1625 (Hoddinott and Nikitas), also *adj.* EG "A gindge chest."

ginnel *n.* an entry, alleyway or passage between terraced houses; see also **gulley.**

gip *n.* pain EG "My tooth en't arf givin' us gip."

gippo *n.* gypsy (Upton, Sanderson and Widdowson, 1987); now in widespread use, though variants such as 'pikey' and 'didikoy' are preferred in other dialect areas of England. Gippo is now regarded as a derogatory term.

girt *adj.* great (Skeat, 1876).

glad-iron *n.* a smoothing iron; also common in the Black Country dialect.

glad-rags *npl.* best clothes EG "'Er must be gooin' somewhere special 'cos 'er's got 'er glad-rags on."

glarney *n.* see **glarny.**

glarny *n.* a glass marble; Tennant (1983) states that glarneys were often acquired by "purchasing a bottle of lemonade for one penny in old money . . . no charge was made on the bottle, which could be broken to obtain the 'glarney' in the top"; see also **alley, alley taw, blood alley, cat's eye, dogger, dummox, French alley, glass alley, gobbie, marley, pot alley** and **steelie.**

glass alley *n.* a glass marble with coloured streaks running through it; see also **alley, alley taw, blood alley, cat's eye, dogger, dummox, French alley, glarny, gobbie, marley, pot alley** and **steelie.**

Glebe Farm *n.* area of Birmingham; a glebe is a piece of land serving as part of a clergyman's benefice and providing him with an income.

glede *n.* a lump of burnt-out coal; also used to refer to a glowing ember or red-hot cinder (J. Alldritt). Referring to burning embers, the word was and is more common in the Black Country, although many Brummies have written in to inform us that the term was also used by their parents or grandparents. In Chaucer's *The Reeve's Tale* is the line "Foure gleedes have we, which I shall devyse," and the word is Old English in origin; see also the phrases **like a glede under the door** and **to riddle the gledes.**

gleed *n.* see **glede.**

glir *vi.* to slide, esp. on ice (Skeat, 1876).

glorry *adj.* fat, greasy or corpulent (Northall, 1896).

glozzer *n.* "a perfect cast or throw of a spinning top" (Northall, 1894).

glue pot *n.* a slang term for a local pub; see also **rub-a-dub**.

gob *n.* mouth EG "'E en' arf gorra a big gob on 'im."

gob off *ph v.* to mouth off EG "'E was gobbin' off left right and centre."

gob *vt.* to spit; to eject saliva from the mouth EG "It was vile, they was gobbin' at everyone."

gobbie *adj.* mouthy; EG "'Er's a gobbie wench, 'er is," also *n.* a large glass marble; see also **alley**, **alley taw**, **blood alley**, **cat's eye**, **dogger**, **dummox**, **French alley**, **glarny**, **glass alley**, **marley**, **pot alley** and **steelie**.

gobbinshire *vulg.* see **gaubshite**.

gobby *n.* see **gobbie**.

go-by-the-ground *n.* a dwarf; according to Northall (1896), another Midlands term for a dwarf in the nineteenth century was 'John-above-ground'.

godcake *n.* a cake which it was customary on New Year's Day for godfathers and godmothers to send to their godchildren; Northall (1896) states that these triangular-shaped cakes filled with mincemeat were about an inch thick and varied in price from a halfpenny to one pound.

gods *n.* the gallery upper circle at the cinema or 'picture house' EG "We'm in the gods tonight."

gods bobs *npl.* gallery patrons in the upper circle at a picture house EG "There was another exit door just on the left inside the passage, but that was for the exclusive use of the patrons in the Stalls, the 'ninepennies', as was the front foyer the exclusive exit for the gallery patrons, the 'gods bobs'. We could not use either of these exits to force our illegal entry, but had to be satisfied with the pits, or the 'tanna mana'" (Smith, undated).

golden chain *n.* the flowers of the laburnum (Northall, 1896).

gomeril *n.* a fool - "usually a female fool" (Northall, 1896).

gommock *n.* a coarse or uncouth person; a lout.

gondud *n.* a gander; the male of the goose.

gone of *ph v.* become of EG "What's gone of me coat?" (Northall, 1896).

goose-gog *n.* gooseberry; see also **sog**.

gorbellied *adj.* fat; obese; overfed (Alexander, 1951) EG "Hang ye, gorbellied knaves, are ye undone?" (Shakespeare, *Henry IV (Part 1)*, Act II, Sc. II).

gorby *n.* see **gawby**.

gormless *adj.* see **gawmless**.

gorn *n.* an old brewing term for a gallon, as in the old rhyme: "Two gorns of very good, Two gorns of Robin Hood, Two gorns of Tip Tat, Two gorns of wuss than that, And two gorns of Thip Thin, Just to dip the children's bread in"; see also **ladegorn**.

goss *vt.* to spit; to eject saliva from the mouth, also *n.* pronunciation variant of gorse EG "Tooth'd briers, sharp furzes, pricking goss, and thorns" (Shakespeare, *The Tempest*, Act IV, Sc. I); see also **Gosta Green**.

Gosta Green *n.* area of Birmingham. The Assize Roll of 1306 mentions a William de Gorsty, and as late as 1758, J. Tomlinson's *Plan of Duddeston and Nechells Manors* indicates both an Upper Gorsty Green and a Lower Gorsty Green. By this date the two places were also called Gostie Green. Langford (1868) explained this spelling change; in a number of old deeds he had found reference to Gosty Green, Upper Gosty Green, Gosty Piece and Gosty Field in different parts of Birmingham, and noted that gorse was still pronounced 'goss' by local country folk. Tomlinson also records fields with names such as Upper Gorsty Close, and it is apparent that once the spiny, yellow flowered shrub called gorse had been common locally.

gownd *n.* gown.

gowt *n.* a short drain.

graff *n.* "the quantity of earth turned up by a spade at once; a spade-graff deep is the extent to which the implement can be in digging thrust into the ground" (Northall, 1896); from the Anglo-Saxon 'grafan' (to dig).

graft *n.* work; labour of any kind (Northall, 1896); now in widespread use.

grainch *vi.* to grind; to make a grating or grinding sound.

granny-reared *adj.* brought up by a grandmother rather than a mother or father; according to Northall (1896), this could also mean pampered or spoilt.

grass nail *n.* the hook which supports the scythe in its attachment to the **sned**.

graunch *vi.* see **grainch**.

grauncher *n.* a huge, heavy person (Northall, 1896).

gravel *vt.* to upset or dismay; to vex, mortify or perplex (Northall, 1896) EG "This I'm told seemed to gravel the company, and made them so glum" (Job Nott, Jun. His Second Address), and "Nay, you were better speak first, and when you were gravelled for lack of matter, you might take occasion to kiss" (Shakespeare, *As You Like It*, Act IV, Sc. I).

grawt *n.* groats; hulled and crushed grain (usually oats).

grawty dick *n.* a stewed mixture of groats [dried oats stripped of their husks], onions and meat [usually shins of beef] well seasoned with salt and pepper and sold in pennyworths at small eating houses where dinners were provided for workers, common c.1850-60 (Northall, 1896); "a very common article of sale at Birmingham" (Halliwell, 1855). Also written as 'grorty dick', this food is still eaten in the Black Country.

grawty pudding *n.* see **grawty dick**.

Great Barr *n.* area of Birmingham; recorded as Bearre in 957 and as Barre in the Domesday Book of 1086; 'barr' is a Celtic word meaning hill top.

greaty pudding *n.* see **grawty dick**.

grecian *n.* the yellow-hammer; this name "owes its origin to Greek characters, which, it is said, are to be found in the marks on its eggs" (*B'ham and Mid. Instit. Archaeolog. Trans.*, 24 Nov. 1875).

green *n.* squatters' settlement EG Acock's Green and Bordesley Green; see also **end**.

greengages *npl.* Brummagem rhyming slang for wages (K. Carruthers, Hall Green).

green Sal *n.* the edible leaves of a sorrel plant; see also **green sauce**.

green sauce *n.* "sour dock or sorrel mixed with vinegar and sugar" (Halliwell, 1855).

Greet *n.* area of Birmingham; from the Anglo-Saxon 'greot', meaning a gravelly place.

grey-russet *n.* "a coarse kind of grey, woollen cloth, to which the epithet 'dandy' was often prefixed, as *Dandy-Grey-Russet*. The name and the material have both fallen into disuse" (Northall, 1896).

griskin *n.* "a lean piece out of the loin of a bacon pig, lying between the ham and the flitch" (Northall, 1896).

grit *n.* piece-work (Skeat, 1876); see also the phrase **to work by the grit**.

grizzle *vi.* to cry or blart EG "Stop yer grizzlin' or yo'll get no suck," "Yo cun gu on grizzlin' cus it ain't gunna 'elp ya, now bloody tell me what yo've bin up to, cum on out with it ya little bleeder" (Smith, undated); still in common use.

groaning-cheese *n.* "a cheese provided on the occasion of an accouchement. A sage cheese is generally had for the purpose, which is frequently a present . . . it was the practice to cut the cheese in the middle, and by degrees to form it into a large kind of ring, through which the child was passed on the day of its christening" (Halliwell, 1855); not restricted to the Midlands.

groaty pudding *n.* see **grawty dick**.

grudging *n.* fine bran; pollard (Marshall, 1796).

guggle *n.* throat; gullet; the windpipe or trachea (Northall, 1896).

Guilder *n.* a Dutch coin, but – like dollar – often used for money generally in the old Warwickshire dialect (Alexander, 1951) EG "Who, wanting guilders to redeem their lives" (Shakespeare, *The Comedy of Errors*, Act I, Sc. I).

gulley *n.* an entry, alleyway or passage between terraced houses EG "The next shop was the second of the Higgs' shops situated on the corner of the passage leading to Hunters Road, or 'The Gulley' to give it its local name" (Smith, undated); see also **ginnel**; still in common use.

gully *n.* see **gulley**.

gunner *n.* a one-eyed person; "the allusion is to the closing of one eye when taking aim with a firearm" (Northall, 1896).

gurgeons *npl.* coarse refuse from flour, produced from the inner skin of the grain (Northall, 1896).

gurt *adj.* see **girt**.

guss *vt.* to bind tightly EG "Don't guss the babby like that" (Halliwell, 1855).

gusunder *n.* see **gazunder**.

guttle *vt.* to eat; consume; to bite, chew and swallow EG "Ah know ah can guttle when ah hear me shuttle" (from the nineteenth century street ballad, *Poverty Knock*).

Gyrdleah *n.* see **Yardley**.

H

hack *vi.* to cough feebly and frequently (Skeat, 1876); still in common use. Like all words beginning with an aitch in the Brummagem dialect, hack is usually pronounced as 'ack. Large numbers of dialects have dropped the 'h', probably because, as sociolinguist Peter Trudgill postulates, it is relatively unimportant. It occurs only at the beginning of a word or in front of a stressed syllable, as in the word 'behind'. English has no words in which 'h' is pronounced before a consonant or at the end of the word. To this end, the loss of 'h' in most traditional dialects is similar to the dropping of the 'h' sound in French and Italian.

hackamore *n.* see **huggermaw.**

hackle *vt.* to hew, cut or chop; to pull crops up with a two-pronged hack (Marshall, 1796).

hag *vt.* to cut; a lumberjack's term; according to Halliwell (1855), in Warwickshire the rods which mark the boundary of a fall of timber are called haggstaffs; and the separate parts so divided are called each man's hagg."

haiver *n.* a fat, obese or generally overweight person EG "'Er's a right haiver" (S. Kay); a corruption, perhaps, of 'heaver'.

half-saved *adj.* demented; stupid (Northall, 1896).

Hall Green *n.* area of Birmingham. Once within the manor and parish of Yardley, Hall Green is derived from Hawes Green – itself named after the Hawes family which was mentioned as living locally in the fourteenth century.

hame *n.* one of two curved bars of a draught horse's collar c.1615 (Hoddinott and Nikitas).

hammer *vt.* to hit or strike someone; to beat (somebody) up EG "Them roughs 'ammered 'im down our gulley larst night." To 'gie it some hammer' means to get stuck in. In this ammer is pronounced as ommer, as in *Sir Gawain and the Green Knight*: "he homered (struck) heterly (fiercely)"; see also **omber** and the phrase **to get hammered.**

hamper-logged *adj.* according to Halliwell (1855), "a witness at a late assize at Warwick used this word in the sense of being overborne or persuaded by his wife." Shakespeare appears to use the word 'hamper' in a similar sense EG "She'll hamper thee and dandle thee like a baby" (*Henry VI (Part 2)*, Act I, Sc. III).

Hamstead *n.* area of Birmingham; meaning the homestead, and first noted in 1227.

Handsworth *n.* area of Birmingham. Given as Honesworde in the Domesdsay Book of 1086, and recorded as Hunnesworth in the twelfth century, it is believed that in old English the name means the enclosure or enclosed settlement ('worth') of a settler called Hun. A hundred years later, Alice the late wife of John de Bruera granted to her son William a tenement in Honesworth, indicating the development of the name.

happen *adv.* perhaps EG "'Appen I'll goo down the Old Crown tonight; I en't med me mind up yet" (Skeat, 1876).

haprond *n.* see **aprond.**

Harborne *n.* area of Birmingham. McKenna (1988) believes that the name of this district is made up of the Old English words 'har', meaning boundary, and 'borne', signifying brook. The stream in question is the Bourn Brook – after which the district of Bournbrook is named – and which formed part of the old dividing line between Harborne, Staffordshire, Weoley, and Worcestershire. McKenna's interpretation appears strong given that the Bourn Brook cuts Harborne off along its whole southern length, whilst the Chad Brook provides the dividing line with Edgbaston in the north-east. However, contrary to a widely-held belief, 'har' does not mean boundary. Early spellings, moreover, give Horborne, not Harborne. It therefore seems wise to accept the explanation of Mills (1995), who states that the name is derived from the word 'horu', meaning dirty.

Hardintone *n.* see **Erdington**.

hare-shore *n.* a hare-lip.

hare-shorn *adj.* having a cleft lip (Northall, 1896).

hark *vi.* to listen EG "'Ark at 'er moanin'" (R. Couling); often used sarcastically EG "'Ark at 'er, who does 'er think 'er is?" The word is derived from the Middle English 'herk', meaning to listen (to something), to hear.

Harry-long-legs *n.* the daddy-long-legs, or crane-fly, as in the Midlands folk-rhyme:

'Arry, 'Arry-lung legs,
Couldn't say 'is pray'rs,
Ketch 'im by the left leg
An' throw 'im down the stairs.

hastener *n.* a contrivance of metal placed before an open fire to hasten the roasting of meat by reflecting the heat (F. Jones, *The Birmingham Post*, 22 August, 1956).

hatchell *n.* an instrument for combing flax or hemp c.1603 (Hoddinott and Nikitas).

hatredans *npl.* tantrums EG "Don't let me 'ave no more of yer 'atredanz" (Northall, 1896).

Hauckslowe *n.* see **Hawkesley**.

haulm *n.* a tuft of grass; a cluster or clump of plant stalks (Raven, 1977) EG "For its black sour haulm covered over the blood of a murdered man" (from the mid-nineteenth century Brummagem street ballad, *The Bad Squire*).

haunty *adj.* lecherous; lustful; prurient, "equal to the Scotch *fidgin-fain*" (Northall, 1894).

Hawkesley *n.* area of Birmingham. First mentioned in the Subsidy Rolls of 1275 as Hauckslowe, this estate in King's Norton had become Hawkslow in 1565 when a bond was recorded between John Middlemore of Hawkeslow, gentleman, in favour of Richard Hawkes. The name itself may signify the tumulus (ancient burial mound) belonging to a family called Hawks, or that it was a place where hawks gathered.

Hay Mills *n.* area of Birmingham; in Old English a 'gehaeg' meant a woodland enclosure - over time, the 'ge' part of the word was dropped and haeg developed into hay.

headland *n.* see **adlan**.

head-sir-rag *n.* "an ironical term for a petty leader" (Northall, 1896) EG "Bob Walker's taken up with the ranters, an' 'e's 'ead-sir-rag, I can tell yer."

heafer *n.* see **heckeforde**.

heaving-days *npl.* Easter Monday and Tuesday; on Easter Monday it appears to have been customary up until the twentieth century for men to lift and then kiss women, and on Easter Tuesday for women to lift and kiss men. The person lifted would usually pay a fine which would later be spent on alcohol. All were involved, regardless of social status, and the 'women's day', according to a Birmingham observer, was by far the most amusing: "Many a time have I passed along the streets inhabited by the lower orders of people, and seen parties of jolly matrons assembled round tables on which stood a foaming tankard of ale. There they sat in all the pride of absolute sovereignty, and woe the luckless man that dared to invade their prerogatives! As sure as he was seen he was pursued – as sure as he was pursued he was taken – and as sure as he was taken he was heaved and kissed, and compelled to pay sixpence for 'leave and licence' to depart." Northall (1896) suggests that 'lifting', or 'aiving' as it was commonly known in the Midlands, was a national custom, and so may have been common in other dialects; see also **aive**.

heck *n.* a rack for animal fodder c.1613 (Hoddinott and Nikitas).

heckeforde *n.* a young cow, in use c.1603 (Hoddinott and Nikitas).

heckfor *n.* see **heckeforde**.

heel rake *n.* a large rake with curved teeth used for collecting hay or loose corn.

heighfor *n.* see **heckeforde**.

hell rake *n.* see **heel rake**.

help *vt.* to send; to return; to give or take something back EG "Cheers, I'll 'elp it back when I've done" (Skeat, 1876).

helve *n.* the handle of an axe or hatchet, as in the nursery rhyme *One, two, buckle my shoe*: "Eleven, twelve, a hatchet helve."

hen-scratlings *npl.* streaming clouds (Marshall, 1796).

hern *pron.* hers; belonging to her; genitive (or *poss adj.*) of 'she' (Skeat, 1876).

hewsick *n.* the fly-catcher (Timmins, 1889).

heyfare *n.* see **heckeforde**.

hickle *n.* the woodpecker (Northall, 1896, and Timmins, 1889).

higgler *n.* a travelling dealer in farm produce (Northall, 1896).

Highter's Heath *n.* area of Birmingham; the Patent Rolls of 1549 give this district as Halers Heth, but by 1650 it had become Hayter's Heath. It would seem to be called after someone named Hayter – from which the word Hayter developed.

hike *vt.* and *vi.* to beckon, signal or call EG "I iked 'im over". Northall (1896) suggests that in the Midlands, "the sense seems to be allied to that of 'hook'. 'Hike him in' may mean 'beckon him in' (with a hooked finger), or 'haul (as with a hook) him in'; whilst 'to hike a thing up' means to raise anything, as a cow does with its horns." This word, as Northall goes on to point out, was also applied in Warwickshire to the practice of 'hikeing [sic] a toad', which involved placing a toad on a plank of wood and striking the other end so that it would fly into the air: "It was customary to inflate the wretched creature at the vent, through a hollow stalk, so that it should 'bost' on falling. About Stratford-on-Avon this is called 'filliping the toad', which naturally brings to mind the Shakespearian phrase, 'Fillip me with a three-man beetle'."

hillings *npl.* "the upper bedclothes" (Northall, 1896); no longer in common use.

hill up *ph v.* according to Northall (1894), this meant to cover up, or "to tuck or round up a child in bed," from the Anglo-Saxon 'helan'; "*hilling* or *heeling* the round back of a book seems to be formed from this verb."

hind-post *n.* a gatepost; a post from which a gate is hung or against which it shuts (Northall, 1896).

his'n *pron.* his; belonging to him; literally 'his one'; genitive (or *poss adj.*) of 'he' (Skeat, 1876, and Upton, Sanderson and Widdowson, 1987), as in the old rhyme:

> Him wot steals isn't his'n,
> When he's cotch'd will go to prison.

Ian Glaze points out that 'in medieval times the possessive was indicated by adding an 'n' sound to the end of the pronoun EG thy book - that book is thine. This is continued today in conventional English but only in the first person EG my book - that book is mine. In the second and third person singular in standard English the 'n' sound has for some reason been dropped and we get your book - that book is yours, and his book - that book is his. But come into the West Midlands and we hear your book - that book is yourn, and his book - that book is his'n. Thus we have retained the 'n' possessive ending and are obeying the rules of language. Mine, hisn, hern, ourn, yourn and theirn are also common in many other traditional dialects.

hisself *pron.* himself; the emphatic form for 'he' or 'him' (Upton, Sanderson and Widdowson, 1987) EG "'E took it on hisself to get it sorted out."

hit *n.* "an abundant crop" (Northall, 1896) EG "There's a good hit o' taters this turn."

hivering and hovering *vi.* see **ivvering and ovvering**.

Hoarstone *n.* according to Halliwell (1855), hoarstones are "stones of memorial; stones marking divisions between estates and parishes." At least one such ancient boundary marker exists in the Hockley area of Birmingham; see also **Warstock**.

hob *n.* an imp or demon; contracted form of 'hobgoblin'; compared to other areas of England, there do not seem to be many references to the devil in Warwickshire folklore, yet there are goblins, ghouls and spectres aplenty, as is evident in the following list of place names from all over Birmingham and the Midlands; Hob Acre, First Hob Ridge, Far Hob Ridge, Hob Redding, and Hob Croft (in Northfield); Hob Lane (in Yardley); Hob's Moat, Hob Moor, and Hoberdy's Lantern (in Solihull); Hob Lane (in Sheldon); Little Hob's Hole (in Willington); Great Hobbs' and Lower Hobbs' Meadow (in Tredington); Hobbin's Close (in Great Alne and Copt Heath); Hob's Hole (in Barcheston), and also Hobgoblin's Lane (in Fillongley); see also **dobbies, flibbertigibbet**, and **knops**.

hobany's lantern *n.* see **hobbady-lantern**.

hobbady-hoy *n.* see **hobble-de-hoy**.

hobbit *n.* one of a race of imaginary elfish underground dwellers invented by the Birmingham author J. R. R. Tolkien in his novels *The Hobbit* (1937) and *Lord of the Rings* (1955).

hobble-de-hoy *n.* a youth; a person "too young for a man and too old for a boy" (H. Hall, *Birmingham Weekly Post*, 4 Oct. 1924).

hobble-de-lantern *n.* see **hobbady-lantern**.

hobbady-lantern *n.* the ignis fatuus or will-o'-the-wisp; the light generated by ignited marsh gas; the word is preserved in place-names such as Hob's Moat in Solihull, and Hob Lane in Yardley (Timmins, 1889).

hob-gobs *npl.* small heaps of dirt or rubbish from the gutters, which were "scraped together by roadmen at regular intervals" (Northall, 1896).

hocketimaw *n.* see **huggermaw**.

hocketimow *n.* "an instrument for cutting the sides of ricks, generally formed of a scythe blade fixed to a pole or staff" (Halliwell, 1855); see also **huggermaw**.

hockle *vi.* to shuffle, scuffle or walk heavily and with great difficulty (Northall 1896) EG "I sin 'im 'ocklin' along up the fordrough last wick" (Skeat, 1876).

Hockley *n.* area of Birmingham. Because Hockley is first recorded in 1529, McKenna (1988) feels that it was a name which was first used in Birmingham during the Tudor period by someone from another Hockley. He strengthens his argument by pointing out that there are five other places in Warwickshire with the same name. The absence of a mention before the early sixteenth century, however, does not rule out the possibility that Hockley is of an older date and that it recalls someone called Hocca who may have made a clearing locally.

Hocks-Tuesday *n.* an ancient play peculiar to Warwickshire which commemorated the massacre of the Danes on St. Brice's Day in 1001 (Timmins, 1889).

hod-bow-lud *n.* a large moth.

hodge *n.* the belly or stomach, as in the phrase 'to stuff your hodge' (Northall, 1894) EG "'Ere ya' are son, get this down yar odge" (Smith, undated); still in common use.

Hodge Hill *n.* area of Birmingham; noted in a rental from 1569 as Hidgehyll, it is likely that this district was named after someone called Hodge. This was a common nickname for anybody named Roger, and it later came to be used as the general term for English agricultural labourers.

hoggeram-i *n.* see **huggermaw**.

hoggerdemow *n.* see **huggermaw**.

hoggermaw *n.* "an instrument used for cutting hedges" (Halliwell, 1855); see also **huggermaw**.

hoggery-maw *n.* see **huggermaw**.

hog's pudding *n.* chitterlings stuffed with cutlins and seasoned with herbs; according to Palmer (1976), hog's puddings were prone to burst during cooking, "but this could be avoided by hanging an old clergyman's wig in the chimney."

holy-falls *npl.* trousers; "buttoned breeches, having the flap, not the fly front" (Northall, 1894).

hommacking *adj.* awkward; clumsy EG "'E's a great 'ommockin' thing" (Northall, 1896).

hommocking *adj.* see **hommacking**.

onesworde *n.* see **Handsworth**.

Honesworth *n.* see **Handsworth**.

honey-stalks *npl.* white clover; "so called because it is so full of honey" (Wise, 1861).

hoof *n.* fist, commonly pronounced without the 'h' EG "'E copt the bloke a clinker in the neck with 'is 'oof" (Squiers, 1916, p.4).

hoogy *adj.* bulky; ill-fitting; too big EG "These are 'ougy boots" (Northall, 1896).

hooter *n.* "an ale-warmer; an extinguisher-shaped utensil of metal for thrusting deep into the fire" (Northall, 1896).

hop-o'-my-thumb a dwarf, gnome or midget; also the title of a well-known nursery rhyme in the nineteenth century (Northall, 1896).

hoppety-kick *n.* applied to a person with an irregular gait or limp; according to Northall (1896), 'dot-and-go-one', 'dot-and-carry-one', and 'step-and-fetch-it' were similar terms used in the Midlands; see also **bandylegs**, **knock-knees** and the phrase **Walsall whoffler**.

Horestock *n.* see **Warstock**.

horserake *n.* a wooden platform (Old Sarbot, 1866).

hose *n.* "the vagina, or *sheath* of corn" (Marshall, 1796).

hougy *adj.* see **hoogy**.

housen *npl.* houses; according to Skeat (1876), "this old Anglo-Saxon plural" was still commonly used in the West Midlands area up until the late nineteenth century: "Many Anglo-Saxon plurals end in -*an*. Oddly enough, the word *hus* (house) was originally unchanged in the plural," also *vt.* to muffle, impede or encumber EG "Don't 'ousen yer neck wi' that great comforter" (Northall, 1896).

hove *vt.* and *vi.* to hoe (Skeat, 1876).

howgy *adj.* see **hoogy**.

howk *vi.* to yelp or howl (Northall, 1894).

howsumdever *adv.* nevertheless; moreover; however (Skeat, 1876).

huckster *n.* see **huxter**.

huckster's *n.* a cornershop; in some areas of Birmingham this word was used to refer to a sweetshop or confectioner's only. More usually, however, a huckster's was a shop that sold everything. It is an old word for a pedlar, who did indeed sell everything. In some Middle English dialects the word 'huck' meant to bargain, which is what a pedlar would do; see also **huxter**.

hudge *vt.* to crease or crumple.

hudged *adj.* rumpled; crinkled or creased, as in clothing (Northall, 1896).

huggerillhaugh *n.* see **huggermaw**.

huggerimaw *n.* see **huggermaw**.

huggermaugh *n.* see **huggermaw**.

huggermaw *n.* a type of hay knife; tool used to produce an 'Eton crop' on hay ricks. Accounts of the exact size and shape of this tool appear to differ considerably, as do accounts of its name; one contributor to the *Birmingham Weekly Post* (4 October 1924) states that it was "of the same shape of a normal hay knife in the blade, but less than half the width, with a straight haft let into a stick seven or eight feet long," whereas another in the same edition claims that it was "similar to a short scythe-blade". Rhodes (1950) suggests the origin of the word "may be sought in some corruption of a word meaning a hedge-bill or bill-hook" and that it may be derived from the Middle English word ('heg') for hedge.

hugger-mugger *n.* confusion; disorder (Skeat, 1876); "secretly and without due form" (Alexander, 1951) EG ". . . and we have done but greenly in hugger-mugger to inter him" (Shakespeare, *Hamlet*, Act IV, Sc. V); now in widespread use.

humstrum *vi.* to lounge around idly; to slouch or loaf about (Northall, 1896); Halliwell (1855) suggests, however, that this was a common Warwickshire dialect term for "the female pudendum."

Hunnesworth *n.* see **Handsworth**.

hurden *adj.* windy; drying EG "It's hurden weather now" (Skeat, 1876), also *n.* "coarse cloth made of hurds or herds" (Northall, 1896), as in the old Warwickshire riddle:

> Flour of England, fruit of Spain,
> Met together in a storm of rain,
> A hempen shirt, and a hurden cravat,
> If you're a wise man, tell me that.
> *Ans.* A plum pudding.

A hurden gown was made out of a hurden sack and was wrapped round a woman's waist and legs to protect her when she was working or washing in the brewus.

hurds *n.* coarse or refuse flax or hemp; from the Anglo-Saxon 'heordas'.

Hurst Street *n.* street in the centre of Birmingham which takes its name from the Old English word 'hyrst', meaning wooded hill.

hussif *n.* see **hussy**.

hussy *n.* a case for holding sewing materials, such as needles, thread and buttons; "It is made of a strip of some suitable material, and is fitted up with longitudinal 'casings' for the thread, and with pockets for the buttons, &c. It rolls up when not in use, and fastens with a loop and a button" (Northall, 1896).

huswife *n.* see **hussy**.

huxter *n.* a shopkeeper; a person who owns and works in a cornershop EG "May others join in the good cause and well support his valour, against a phalanx of base rogues, or Cobler, Huxter, Tailor" (from *A New Song Called 'Opposite a Playhouse'*, reprinted in Palmer, 1979).

I

I-acky *n.* a game, similar to hide-and-seek EG "We would play I ackey with the seeker standing under the gas lamp outside Donnie Harbridges house, half way down Guest Street" (Smith, undated), also *interj.* the cry when the searcher discovered the hider EG "I-acky Jack in the ash-pit!" (Rhodes, 1950); see also **ecky**. There was a similar game called acky-one-two-three. One person was on and the others hid. The youngster who was on had to find the hiders before they could run back to the den and shout, "acky-one-two-three!"

Icknield Street *n.* a Roman road which passed through Birmingham, also known as Ryknield Street; it started in Alcester, went through King's Norton and crossed the Rea at Lifford, struck along the Pershore Road at Stirchley, headed across Edgbaston and by the Roman camp at Metchley, followed the line of Monument Road and Icknield Street, hit Great Hampton Street, went on to Wellhead Lane and then crossed the Tame at Holford, and eventually passed through Streetly; see also **Metchley**.

iffing and offing *vi.* hesitating or dallying; taking a long time to decide EG "'E can never mek up 'is mind, 'e's allus iffin' 'n' offin'" (Northall, 1896); see also **ivvering and ovvering** and **umming and arring**.

ill-conditioned *adj.* naughty; badly-behaved (Skeat, 1876).

ill-favoured *adj.* ugly; unattractive; see also **favour**.

in-and-in *adv.* from the same line of parentage; the practice of breeding livestock, "not from the same *line* only, but the same *family*; the phrase *breeding in-and-in* is as familiar in the conversation of Midland breeders, as *crossing* is in that of other districts" (Marshall, 1796).

in'arf *adv.* very; extremely; contracted form of 'isn't half' EG "It in'arf a good film."

inchy-pinchy *n.* a game similar to 'leap-frog' common in parts of Birmingham which were once in the county of Warwickshire (Northall, 1894); "the formula is 'Inchy-pinchy, last lie down'. The player who first cries this is entitled to wait until all the other players are 'down' before he leaps" (Northall, 1896).

inkle *n.* coarse tape or thread; "the poorest and cheapest kind being called 'beggar's inkle'" (Wise, 1861) EG "He hath ribbons of all the colours I' the rainbow . . . inkles, caddisses, cambrics, lawns" (Shakespeare, *The Winter's Tale*, Act IV, Sc. III). According to Northall (1896), "As thick as inkleweavers" was a "common local proverb" up until the nineteenth century.

Inkleys *n.* named after the Hinckleys – a prominent Brummie family, the Inkleys was once an area of gardens adjoined by fields in the John Bright Street neighbourhood of Birmingham. By the early nineteenth century all traces of gardens had disappeared and the district had gained a frightening reputation as a rookery – a place filled with tottering, decrepit dwellings in which lived criminals, rogues, roughs and through which the police only ventured in pairs. This terrible image was apparently vindicated by the Navigation Street Riots of 1875. Seven years later, a writer in the *Town Crier* exclaimed:

> Where are the peaceful Inkleys fair?
> Where I did roost at night,
> And murder and manslaughter were
> Among its pleasant sights.

Such a negative view of the district was exaggerated by outsiders. There were fights and rowdiness, and the Inkleys was a place of bad housing, overflowing suffs, dirty water supplies and reeking miskins. Not surprisingly, those who packed into the area were mostly poor, many coming from Ireland. Yet the great majority of the local people struggled daily to survive as best they could. They were not vile folk, and their struggles to maintain decency were largely ignored by the better-off.

innards *npl.* see **inwards**.

incense *vt.* to inform; to appraise, instruct or inform (Northall, 1896) EG "I think I have incens'd the lords o' the council that he is a most arch heretic" (Shakespeare, *Henry VIII*, Act V, Sc. I).

insense *vt.* see **incense**.

in't *vt.* literally 'have not'; negated form of the verb 'have' in the present tense EG "I in't done nothing, wrong, honest!" Also commonly pronounced as 'en't', and obviously a variant of 'ain't'. In't and en't can also act as the negated form of the verb 'be' in the present tense, as in "I in't doin' it" for "I am not doing it."

inwards *npl.* insides; entrails; the interior of the body (Skeat, 1876); bowels of man or beast (Northall, 1896) EG "But the sherris warms it and makes it course from the inwards to the parts extreme" (Shakespeare, *Henry IV (Part 2)*, Act IV, Sc. III); still in common use.

itching-berries *npl.* dogrose berries, the prickly seeds of which children used to "put down their playmates' backs, to induce irritation" (Northall, 1894).

ivell *vt.* to steal; to pilfer; to take by theft (Northall, 1896).

ivvering and ovvering *vi.* hesitating or dallying; taking a long time to decide EG "They was ivvering and ovvering and just couldn't mek their minds up"; see also **hivering and hovering**, **iffing and offing** and **umming and arring**.

J

jack-at-a-pinch *n.* a person who is always ready in an emergency; according to Northall (1896), the expression was also often used "to indicate a person who is ignored at ordinary times, but made to serve a purpose on occasion."

jack-bannel *n.* see **jack bannil**.

jack-bannial *n.* see **jack bannil**.

jack-bannil *n.* a tadpole, minnow or tiddler (Skeat, 1876); a stickleback or any small freshwater fish caught in the cut (Northall, 1894) EG "They've filled up poor old Pudding Brook, Where in the mud I've often stuck, Catching jack-bannils near Brummagem" (James Dobbs, *I Can't Find Brummagem*, 1828); the same term also appears to have been applied to hair lice or nits, but is no longer in common use.

jack-bannock *n.* see **jack bannil**. Jack bannock was the term that was used more regularly in the twentieth century. In Laurie Hornsby's song *A face as long as Livery Street* on the album *The Brummagem Air*, there is a line including the phrase 'Jumping Jack Bannock'.

jacks alive *n.* betting terminology for £5; the term was often shortened to 'jacks'.

jack-sharpling *n.* the stickle-back (*Gasterosteus aculeatus*) (Timmins, 1889).

jack-squealer *n.* the swift (*Hirundo apus*) (Timmins, 1889, Palmer, 1976, and Mary Bodfish).

jackstones *n.* a popular boys' game, also known as 'fivestones' (Tennant, 1983).

jack up *ph v.* to finish or end; to throw up or relinquish EG "Let's jack up this game," "I'm tired, an' gooin' to jack up" (Northall, 1896).

jacky-squealer *n.* see **jack-squealer**.

jangling *adj.* disputing; quarrelling; arguing (Northall, 1896).

jank *n.* excrement; waste matter (Northall, 1896).

jankhole *n.* lavatory; toilet; cess pit.

jannock *adj.* see **jonnock**.

jarvy *n.* a Hackney coachman (Raven, 1977) EG "Tara for jarvies, whales for horses" (from the late eighteenth century Brummagem street ballad *When Birmingham is a Seaport Town*).

jed *adj.* pronunciation variant of dead; deceased (Northall, 1896). Although Northall gives jed as a word used in Birmingham, and Steve remembers his grandfather, Joe Reynolds – a born and bred Brummie – using it on occasion, it was rarely heard in the twentieth century outside the Black Country.

jee *adj.* crooked; awry; not straight (Timmins, 1889).

jerry-house *n.* a public house frequented by the working or lower classes; according to Northall (1896), "Tom-and-Jerry-house" was also common in some districts in the late nineteenth century.

Jerusalem-cuckoo *n.* see **Jerusalem-pony**.

Jerusalem-pony *n.* a donkey or ass (Northall, 1896).

jessup *n.* juice or syrup; "as of fruit pies, puddings, &c." (Northall, 1896).

jet *vi.* to walk or strut proudly, "like a crow in a gutter, as the common Warwickshire saying that accompanies it runs" (Wise, 1861); to parade or swagger around EG "Contemplation makes a rare turkey-cock of him; how he jets under his advanced plumes" (Shakespeare, *Twelfth Night*, Act II, Sc. V).

jibber and jumbles *npl.* sweetmeats; lollipops (Northall, 1894); more common, perhaps, in the Stratford-upon-Avon dialect.

jiffy *n.* a moment; a short amount of time EG "I'll be with you in a jiffy, our kid."

jimmie *n.* a sovereign.

jimmy *n.* see **jimmie**.

jimrags *npl.* shreds; tatters EG "Me ankercher's all to jimrags" (Northall, 1896).

joal *n.* a deep round earthenware vessel, wider at the top than the bottom, holding four to five gallons.

joanna *n.* piano; also common in other dialects.

job *n.* a stab, thrust, poke or perforation (Northall, 1896); see also the phrase **handy bandy, sugar-candy**.

jobber *n.* a dealer in live-stock (Northall, 1896).

joey *n.* a fourpenny piece, also *n.* an old Warwickshire word for the green linnet (Northall, 1894), and *n.* "a small glass for containing a victualler's three-pennyworth of brandy" (Northall, 1896).

John-above-ground *n.* see **go-by-the-ground**.

Johnny-raw *n.* a country bumpkin or rustic; a farm labourer (Northall, 1894).

Johnny Whipstraw *n.* see **Johnny-raw**.

Johnny Wopstraw *n.* see **Johnny-raw**.

jole *vt.* see **joul**.

joll *vt.* see **joul**.

jollop *n.* a medicinal drug used as a purgative; Davis (1841) gives an alternative spelling, 'jalap', and states that "the pronunciation of this word (as if written 'jollop')" is, in his opinion, "now confined to the vulgar and illiterate." Also widely used within the Birmingham area as a word for beer.

jonnock *adj.* fair and just; honourable (Northall, 1896); "one who always pays his full share in a reckoning for beer" (Tomkinson, 1893) EG "'E's a jonnock sort," "That en't jannocks" (S. Thomas); also common in the Worcestershire, Staffordshire and Shropshire dialects.

jonnuck *adj.* see **jonnock**.

jimmie *n.* sovereign.

joul *vt.* to knock two things together; to cause two objects to come into contact with each other EG "They may joul horns together like any deer I' the herd" (Shakespeare, *All's Well That Ends Well*, Act I, Sc. III), "Jowl, jowl and listen lad, and hear the coal face workin'" (from the old Midlands street ballad *Disaster: Jowl, jowl and listen*).

jowl *vt.* see **joul**.

jumpers *npl.* chesse-maggots or mites; the larvae of *Musca putris* (Northall, 1896).

jumping-stock *n.* see **jump-jack**.

jump-jack *n.* two vertical sticks protruding from the ground with a horizontal cross-piece between them for children to jump over.

jussly *adv.* exactly; precisely; strictly; a corruption of 'justly' (Skeat, 1876) EG "I don't justly know" (Northall, 1896).

just-nows *adv.* soon; in a short time; immediately (Geoff Moore).

K

kaggy *adj.* see **caggy**.

kaggy-handed *adj.* see **caggy**.

kag-handed *adj.* see **caggy**.

kayli *n.* sugar crystals bought from sweet shops; children eat kayli by wetting a finger, dipping it into the bag and then licking it.

kaylied *adj.* drunk; inebriated; also fairly common in the Black Country dialect; see also

blindo, blotto, bob-howler, canned, lagging, market-peart, mopped, palatick and **slaumsey**.

keck *n.* see **kex**.

keech *n.* "a cake of consolidated fat from the slaughterhouse, rolled up to go to the chandler's for tallow. Shakespeare makes an appropriate surname of the word: "Did not goodwife Keech, the butcher's wife, come in then and call me gossip Quickly?" (*Henry IV (Part 2)*, Act II, Sc. I), and applies it figuratively to Wolsey, 'the butcher's son', in *Henry VIII* (Act I, Sc. I):

> I wonder
> That such a keech can with his very bulk
> Take up the rays o' th' beneficial sun,
> And keep it from the earth.

Prince Henry also calls Falstaff a "greasy tallow-keech" in *Henry IV (Part 1)*, Act II, Sc. IV."

keel *vt.* to scrape - not, as is commonly thought, to simmer, cool or 'to keep the pot from boiling over' (Alexander, 1951) EG "Tu-who; Tu-whit, Tu-who - A merry note, While greasy Joan doth keel the pot" (Shakespeare, *Love's Labour's Lost*, Act V, Sc. II); still in use among older generations of Birmingham speakers.

keen *vt.* to sharpen EG "Theym keenin' the kitchen knives."

keffil *n.* see **keffle**.

keffile *n.* see **keffle**.

keffle *n.* a lumbering, awkward or clumsy person EG "'You great keffle". Derived, perhaps, from the Welsh word ('ceffyl') for horse, and meant to imply that a person is as clumsy as a cart-horse; also common in the Black Country dialect. In the Worcestershire dialect the same word is also applied to "anything of bad or inferior quality" (Tomkinson, 1893).

kench *vt.* to injure or strain by overworking; to wist or wrench (Northall, 1896) EG "I've kenched my back" (Rhodes, 1950).

kernuck *n.* four bushels of barley.

ketched *adj.* partially burnt; stuck to the pan, in boiling; esp. said of milk (Northall, 1896); literally 'catched'.

ketchpit *n.* a cesspit; a pool for collecting sewage.

kettledrum *n.* "music-hall performers' cant, being rhyming-slang for 'Brum'. Now obsolete, but common c.1870-90" (Rhodes, 1950).

kettle wedges *npl.* pieces of wood for fuel (K. Carruthers).

kex *n.* "used in Warwickshire and the midland counties, generally of the various species of the umbelliferous plants which grow in the ditches and hedges" (Wise, 1861); "the hemlock; but liberally used for umbelliferous plants of similar appearance, such as cow-parsnip, wild-carrot, hedge-parsley, &c." (Northall, 1896):

> nothing teems
> But hateful docks, rough thistles, kexes, burs
> (Shakespeare, *Henry V*, Act V, Sc. II)

kexes *npl.* see **kex**.

kibble *vt.* to crush or grind (Marshall, 1796).

kibbles *npl.* small pieces of coal.

kick *vt.* see **shell**.

kid *n.* a faggot of sticks.

kiddle *n.* a child's spittle; drool; saliva.

kidneys *npl.* small stones for paving.

kindle *vi.* to give birth; to bring forth young (Tomkinson, 1893), also *n.* "a kindle is sometimes used of a litter" (Wise, 1861).

King's Heath *n.* area of south Birmingham; the earliest reference to Kyngesheath is from 1511, and eight years later Humfrey Stafford granted John Middilmore the annual rent of a messuage (dwelling house with out buildings) and land on the heath called Kingsheth in the parish of Kings Norton. Another deed from 1541 also mentions Kyngisheith as lying close to the lands of Bartholomew More.

Kingsheth *n.* see **King's Heath**.

King's Norton *n.* area of south Birmingham; Nortune (north settlement) is mentioned as a berewick (dependent settlement) in the Domesday Book of 1086, and by 1286 it had become Northone Regis. The suffix 'of the king' came about to differentiate the place from another Norton in Worcestershire, which itself became Bredon Norton.

Kingstanding *n.* area of Birmingham; according to Mills (1995), the name is derived from a standing – a hunter's station from which to shoot game, but a popular local story has it that the district got its name from the fact that Charles I, on his way to Aston Hall during the civil war in 1642, stood here in order to review his troops.

kip *n.* sleep EG "So inta the 'ouse, an' sometimes yowed gerra cuppa cocoa, if the Ole Lady 'ad eny money forrit, which worn't offen, but normally it would be straight up the dancers, throw all ya clo'es under the bed by the piddle pot, 'ceptin ya shert o' course, an' inta kip yowed jump" (Smith, undated).

kipe *n.* "a coarse kind of osier basket, wider at the top than at the bottom, with a short handle on each side" (Northall, 1896).

kippered *adj.* tired; exhausted EG "I've bin on the dead man's shift all wick 'n' I'm bleedin' kippered, I can tell yer."

kisser *n.* mouth EG "The bloke that caught me dain't talk, he just thumped me in the kisser, and the stars I saw wus just like a firework show as I landed on my arse in the grass" (Smith, undated).

kissing-bush *n.* a sprig of mistletoe, beneath which a kiss "may be lawfully taken at Christmas-tide. A berry should be plucked from it each time a kiss is taken" (Northall, 1896).

kit *n.* an old Warwickshire word for a flock of pigeons (Northall, 1894).

kitha *interj.* used to attract attention EG "Kitha! Tek a dekko at this, our kid."

kiver *n.* a tub that butter, whey or dough is made up in, hence 'butter-kiver', 'whey-kiver' and 'dough-kiver'; thought to be a corruption of 'cover' (Northall, 1896).

knab *vt.* to nibble; to bite gently or playfully (Northall, 1896).

knabs *n.* a youth; a young man; from the German 'knabe' (boy; knave); according to Northall (1896), the word was often used to imply that a person was deceitful or dishonest in some way: "It is always preceded, too, by a possessive pronoun; and spoken of one guilty of some offence" EG "I saw 'is knabs this mornin', but 'e kept 'is distance: 'e knows I'm aware of 'is tricks."

knack-and-span *n.* a game of marbles, played thus: "One player casts a marble ahead. His fellow casts another marble after it. Should he knack (knock) it, or bring his own within a hand's-span, he is lawfully entitled to that of his opponent. The second player then casts his own marble ahead, &c." (Northall, 1896).

knacker *vt.* to steal; to pilfer EG "I vividly remember one dare I had to carry out. That was to knacker a loaf of bread off a George Baines van, whose driver was taking goods into one of their shops on the corner of Farm Street and Hunters Road . . . Knackerin' from sweet shops was a crime committed by most kids, and some adults too" (Smith, undated).

knerly *adj.* knotted, esp. applied to timber; Rhodes (1950) suggests that this word was a corruption of 'gnarly' and implied that something or someone was old or decrepit, whereas Northall (1894) suggests that, when applied to a person, this meant "one hard, compact and sturdy of make," also *n.* the ball of hard wood used in the game of bandy.

knock-down-brick-and-carry-one *n.* a boy's game, played thus: "One brick is placed upon another to form a T-shape, and guarded by a band of players. Another band stand at taw, and throw duckstones at it; and, should it be knocked from its position, they run backwards as far as possible, followed by the guardians of the brick. Each guardian, on catching a runner, must carry him on his back till the brick be reached. The order of the game is then reversed" (Northall, 1896).

knock-kneed *adj.* said of a person with an irregular gait or who seems unsteady on their feet (Showell, 1885); see also **knock-knees**.

knock-knees *n.* a person with an irregular gait, or shaky legs; someone who seems unsteady on their feet (Showell, 1885); see also **bandylegs**, **hoppety-kick** and the phrase **Walsall whoffler**.

knoll *vi.* to toll; to sound, as a large bell does EG "Remember'd knolling after a departing friend" (Shakespeare, *Henry IV (Part 2)*, Act I, Sc. I).

knops *npl.* hobgoblins which, according to Palmer (1976), were much feared: "They were originally demon horses, and it is clear that belief in them remained strong in Warwickshire, for in parts of the country on All Souls' Day (2nd November) those brave enough went out carrying a simulated horse's head covered with a sheet to frighten the timid"; see also **dobbies**, **flibbertigibbet**, and **hob**.

knowed *pa p.* and *pa t.* knew; known EG "Ar, I knowed 'im once," "I've knowed 'er since 'er was a nipper." If a verb is regular, the past tense and past participle have an *–ed* ending EG "I clean*ed* the windows," "I have clean*ed* the windows." When the past tense and past participle do not end in *–ed*, the verb is irregular EG "I *spoke* to her yesterday," "I have *spoken* to her." In standard English, the transitive verb 'know' is irregular EG "I *knew* him when I was young," "I have *known* him all my life," but in the Brummagem dialect (as is the case with many other verbs) 'know' is given a regular *–ed* ending; see also **drawed**, **learned** and **throwed**.

knowledge *n.* range; remembrance; view EG "Gardener's gel's wum agen; 'er's quite growed out o' my knowledge," "Look at this poor dog, 'e's got out of 'is knowledge" (Northall, 1896).

know-nothing *n.* an ignoramus; an idiot or fool (Northall, 1896).

knubblings *npl.* small cobbles of coal (Northall, 1896).

knur and spell *n.* a ball-game; although Northall (1894) suggests that this game was played in Birmingham, both the term and the game originated in Yorkshire; see also **dogger** and **tip-cat.**

knurly *n.* a small wooden ball used in the game of bandy (Northall, 1896); see also **knerly.**

krop *bsl.* pork.

kuk-kuks *npl.* see **cuck-cucks.**

kyind *adj.* favourable; agreeable.

kyipe *n.* a basket..

Kyngesheath *n.* see **King's Heath.**

Kyngisheith *n.* see **King's Heath.**

L

lade-gaun *n.* see **ladegorn.**

lade-gawn *n.* see **ladegorn.**

ladegorn *n.* an old brewing term for a small round tub, "with one stave much longer than the others for a handle, used for lifting the liquid from one vessel to another" (H. Hall, *Birmingham Weekly Post*, 4 Oct 1924). Tomkinson (1893) states that this term was also used in the Worcestershire dialect for "a ladle or long-handled gawn, for serving out pigs' wash from the cistern."

Ladies'-Needlework *n.* London Pride, *Saxifraga umbrosa* (Northall, 1896).

lady-cow *n.* "the 'lady-bird,' a name appled to all the coccinella" (Northall, 1896).

lady-smock *npl.* the cuckoo-flower, *Cardamine pratensis* (Northall, 1896).

lafe *n.* the fatty lining extracted from the inside of a pig's carcass.

lagger *n.* litter; rubbish; a mess (Skeat, 1876).

lagging *adj.* intoxicated; in a state of drunkenness; see also **blindo, blotto, bob-howler, canned, kaylied, market-peart, mopped, palatick** and **slaumsey.**

laggy *adj.* cracked or warped wood; a defect of timber; having a natural crack inside, frequently with a portion of bark (then called 'bark-lag'); "it is a cleft or rift, reaching sometimes from the top to the bottom of the stem, and, perhaps, to near its center" (Marshall, 1796); also common in the Worcestershire dialect (Tomkinson, 1893).

lamb's tails *npl.* the male catkins of hazel and filbert trees (Northall, 1896).

lamp *vt.* to hit, beat or thrash EG "'E lamped that ball for four"; see also **larrup, tank** and **thrape.**

lanty *n.* a balancing pole used by tightrope walkers EG "While watching Blondin cross the Edgbaston Reservoir I heard a woman say: 'Look at his LANTY pole'" (F. Lamb, *Birmingham Weekly Post*, Oct. 4 1924).

lap-love *n.* climbing buck-weed (Marshall, 1796).

la pom *n.* toilet; lavatory.

larpom *n.* see **la pom**.

larrup *vt.* to hit, beat or thrash; see also **lamp, tank** and **thrape**.

lated *adj.* belated; benighted (Wise, 1861) EG "Now spurs the lated traveller" (Shakespeare, *Macbeth*, Act III, Sc. III).

lather *n.* pronunciation variant of ladder common up until the late nineteenth century (Northall, 1896).

lattermath *n.* a second crop of grass (Skeat, 1876).

laund *n.* see **lawnd**.

lawnd *n.* lawn; area of ground covered with grass EG "Henry the Eighth of England by his indenture bearing the thirty third year of his Reign (1541) delivered to Edward and Elizabeth Ludford one meadow called le Launde in Byrmingham" (Letters Patent of Philip and Mary to Thomas Marrow, 1557).

lawter *n.* the number of eggs laid by a chicken before incubation (Northall, 1896); known in slightly varied forms throughout England and Scotland.

laylands *npl.* grass ridges in common fields; "arable lands which have been suffered to lay down to grass: hence, *lay*, as above, and hence, probably, *ley* and *leigh*" (Marshall, 1796).

lazy-back *n.* an iron frame hung over an open fire upon which to rest pots and pans.

lazy backs *npl.* small, hard lumps of dough left in loaves of bread after baking; "an indication that the kneading had not been done properly" (Palmer, 1976); see also **slut farthings**.

leam *vt.* see **leem**.

leamer *n.* see **leemer**.

lean-to *n.* a shed leaning against another building (Skeat, 1876); still in common use.

learn *vt.* to teach (Skeat, 1876) EG "whether Tinkers or Tailors or Omnibus cads, we can learn them a tune called the Warwickshire lads" (from the street ballad *The Cockney's Trip to Brummagem*, c.1876); Shakespeare uses it in *The Tempest* when Caliban says: "The red plague rid you for learning me your language." Disraeli also used it when he said: "Learn to know the House; learn the House to know you," and it is still quite commonly used in Birmingham, though many look upon it incorrectly as 'sub-standard' English.

learned *pa t.* and *pa p.* learnt EG "I learned 'im 'ow to set the machine." If a verb is regular, the past tense and past participle have an *–ed* ending EG "I clean*ed* the windows," "I have clean*ed* the windows." When the past tense and past participle do not end in *–ed*, the verb is irregular EG "I *spoke* to her yesterday," "I have *spoken* to her." In standard (British) English, the transitive verb 'learn' is irregular EG "I *learnt* how to speak Chinese," "I have *learnt* how to speak Chinese over the last few months," but in the Brummagem dialect (as is the case with many other verbs) 'learn' is given a regular *–ed* ending; see also **drawed, knowed** and **throwed**.

lease *vt.* to glean, esp. corn after the harvest has finished (Skeat, 1876); from the Anglo-Saxon 'lesan'.

leasowe *n.* meadow; pasture; grassland; a name retained in a few Birmingham street names. In parts of the Black Country people still say they are 'gooin across the lezzer' (the field).

leastways *adv.* at least (Skeat, 1876).

leatheren-bat *n.* the common bat (Northall, 1896).

leatherhead *n.* "a numskull, dolt" (Northall, 1896).

leathern *adj.* made of leather EG "No shoes or stockings they had on, or hat had they to wear, but a leathern frock and linsey drawers, their feet and hands were bare" (from *Young Henry the Poacher*, old song reprinted in Palmer, 1979).

lection *n.* chance; possibility or probability EG "There's no lections of rain is there?"

leem *vt.* to separate nuts from their husks (Northall, 1896); also in use in various Scottish dialects.

leemer *n.* a nut sufficiently ripe to fall out of its husk (Northall, 1896).

leese *vt.* see **lease**.

lef *n.* see **lafe**.

leg-o'-mutton *adj.* a style of sleeve on dresses common in the early twentieth century.

legs-and-wings *n.* beer; see also **blacking**, **pungello** and **stingo**.

leman *n.* loved one (Rhodes, 1950); sweetheart (Alexander, 1951) EG "I sent thee sixpence for thy leman" (Shakespeare, *Twelfth Night*, Act II, Sc. III).

lewbelling *n.* a public outcry; an organised protest; according to Palmer (1976), "Adultery was strongly disapproved of, and local feeling towards the offender was expressed by playing rough music or 'lewbelling', as it was called in parts of Warwickshire." The following report on lewbelling appeared in *The Illustrated London News* in 1909:

> PUNISHMENT BY EFFIGY: A LEWBELLING BAND AND THE DUMMIES OF AN ERRING PAIR
>
> Lewbelling is a custom which, although it has almost died out, is occasionally observed, and such an observation took place recently. The word 'lewbelling' seems to be derived from 'lewd' and 'belling', roaring or bellowing. A 'lewbelling' occurs when the morals of a married man or a married woman have left something to be desired, and neighbours wish to show their disapproval. In the case illustrated, the effigy of the man was made first, and exposed for three days: the effigy of the woman was exposed for two days. The figures were placed side by side, the woman's arm upon her lover's shoulder. A band of thirty or more youths and boys, beating all kinds of utensils, paraded the village for three nights. On the third night, after dark, the effigies were taken down and burnt. The dummies were set up opposite the woman's house. The fear of this form of public exposure is said to act as a great deterrent.

lezzer *n.* see **leasowe**.

lezzow *n.* see **leasowe**.

lick *vt.* to beat (as in a fight) EG "I licked 'im," also *n.* EG "I gave him a right lickin'" (R. Couling).

licker *n.* "special officials who checked the dogs [at a dog fight] for concealed spikes, poisons, etc. Sometimes they used a milk wash but often a licker used his tongue" (Raven, 1977) EG "The lickers licked hard and they licked very well, they dain't miss a hair on them dogs – you can tell" (from the mid-nineteenth century Midlands street ballad, *The Darlaston Dog-Fight*).

lief *adv.* gladly; willingly (Skeat, 1876); soon (Wise, 1861) EG "I had as lief the town-crier spoke my lines" (Shakespeare, *Hamlet*, Act III, Sc.II).

lif *adv.* see **lief**.

lifter *n.* a thief; hence, as Wise (1861) remarks, "our modern phrase of *shoplifter*" EG "Is he so young a man and so old a lifter?" (Shakespeare, *Troilus and Cressida*, Act I, Sc. II).

lig *vi.* to lie; to deceive; to tell a falsehood; from the Anglo-Saxon 'leogan' (Northall, 1896).

ligger *n.* a liar.

limb *n.* a rascal; a hooligan; an unruly or troublesome person; Northall (1896) states that 'limb of the devil' is probably meant, and that the term was also commonly applied "to a termagant."

limber *adj.* pliant; supple; flexible EG "How limber your tongue is" (Skeat, 1876); now in widespread use.

limmel *adv.* torn in pieces; shredded; destroyed EG "'E tore 'im limmel, 'e did." A corruption, perhaps, of 'limb-from-limb'.

Linde *n.* see **Lyndon**.

litterment *n.* a general state of confusion or untidiness EG "What a litterment this kitchen's in!" (Northall, 1896).

little'un *n.* a younger brother or sister EG "We allus 'ad to look after the little'uns of a Saturday mornin' whilst our Mom got the shoppin' in"; see also **big'un** and **babby**.

liv *adv.* see **lief**.

livener *n.* the first alcoholic drink in the morning.

liver-pin *n.* "the instrument which, by way of jocular hypothesis, is said to support, sustain, fasten, or secure the human liver" (Northall, 1896) EG "'Ave a drop more soup; it'll oil yer liver-pin."

liver-wing *n.* "the wing through which the liver is inserted on a dressed fowl. The 'gizzard-wing' is that through which the gizzard is passed" (Northall, 1896).

living *n.* an old agricultural provincialism for a tenement or farm; according to Marshall (1796), "the common field townships were divided into a certain number of livings."

lobbat *vi.* to loiter, idle or loll (Northall, 1896) EG "'E's lobbatin' around outside again."

locks-and-keys *npl.* leaves or wisps of ash in a fire-grate.

lodge *vt.* "spoken of corn or any cereal, or even grass, being *laid*, as the more common phrase is, by wind or rain. Thus, in [Shakespeare's] *Macbeth*, act iv. scene 1, we find 'though bladed corn be lodged'" (Wise,1861).

loggats *n.* a game played in various parts of England which involved throwing small logs of wood at a mark (Alexander, 1951) EG "Did these bones cost no more the breeding but to play at loggats with them?" (Shakespeare, *Hamlet*, Act V, Sc. I);

according to Wise (1861), however, the word was most widely used in Warwickshire in the late nineteenth century to refer to any short length of wood.

logger *n.* a piece of wood fastened to a horse's leg in order to prevent it straying (Wise, 1861).

lollock *vi.* to loaf or lounge about lazily (Rhodes, 1950).

lollop *vi.* "to lounge, lean, loll . . . the word is used substantively, too; as 'You are sich a lollop'" (Northall, 1896).

lommock *n.* a clumsy person; a fool or idiot EG "You great lommock" (S. Kay).

longful *adj.* desirous; anxious EG "I've bin longful to see you again" (Skeat, 1876).

long hundred *n.* "six score . . . oranges are sold by the long hundred at most markets" (Northall, 1896).

Lorres Hill *n.* see **Lozells**.

louse-kiver *n.* a hat.

louse-pasture *n.* the scalp; the external layer of the cranium.

louse-trap *n.* a tooth-comb (Palmer, 1979) EG "At the Old Wharf I did sell coal, in Suffolk-st. made louse-traps" (from an old Brummagem ballad entitled *Birmingham Jack of All Trades*, c.1830)

lovering *vt.* "courting, wooing, sweethearting" (Northall, 1896).

low *n.* a hill; "hence the names of various hills [in the Midlands], and hence 'the low-country' i.e. the hills of Staffordshire &c." (Marshall, 1796).

Lowcells *n.* see **Lozells**.

Lowsill *n.* see **Lozells**.

lowk *n.* a blow (Northall, 1896).

Lozells *n.* area of Birmingham; according to some accounts, Lozells is named after Mr Lowe who farmed hereabouts in the late eighteenth or nineteenth centuries. This is an incorrect assumption, for the name Lowsill was first recorded in 1546, and Lowcells Farm was offered for sale in 1793. McKenna (1988) believes that the name may mean the hill of Lor since a deed of 1546 refers to "Lorres Hill, otherwise Lowsill". Contrarily, another interpretation is that it means the cold hill, arising from the Old English words 'ceald' and 'hlaw' (later low). Gelling (1992) does not support these claims, and suggests that the name might be derived from 'losel', meaning scoundrel.

lumbersome *adj.* heavy; ponderous; cumbersome.

lummock *n.* see **lommock**.

lungeous *adj.* "violent, rough, malicious, spiteful, cruel" (Northall, 1896); someone (esp. a child) who is lungeous is boisterous, exuberant and rough in play EG "I don't play with Dick Carter; 'e's such a lungeous beggar."

lye *n.* water in which the ashes from burnt wood have been infused.

Lyndene *n.* see **Lyndon**.

Lyndon *n.* area of Birmingham; there is also a Lyndon in Leicestershire and its meaning is usually given as the hill ('dun') where either lime trees or flax ('lin' or 'lind') is grown; the word therefore appears to have a Germanic root (the German for lime is

Linde). Lyndon, Warwickshire was first recorded as Linde in 1221, as Lyndene in 1262 and Lyndone by 1317. The 1262 spelling complicates matters for whilst 'Lynd' still means either flax or lime tree, 'dene' signifies a valley. This latter interpretation is preferred by McKenna (1988), however Gelling (1992) feels that Lyndon means 'at the lime tree'. This interpretation would seem more likely as Lyndon is not a hilly area.

Lyndone *n.* see **Lyndon**.

M

ma *possessive adj.* my; of or belonging to me EG "'Ow are y' ma wench?'

mable *vt.* to corrupt; to taint or debase; to come under the influence of an evil spirit; Palmer (1976) writes that 'to be mabled' in Warwickshire once meant "to be led astray by the Will o' the Wisp."

Machitona *n.* see **Sheldon**.

Mackadown *n.* see **Sheldon**.

mag *n.* a halfpenny (Palmer, 1979) EG "call when you will my husband swears you shall not have a mag" (from *Tallyman!*, an old Birmingham street ballad, c.1845-61).

magic *adj.* commonly used in the 1970s to signify something good EG "Did yo' 'ave a good time last night?" "Ar, it was magic!"

maid *n.* "a wooden beetle used to pound clothes in the washing, or maiding-tub, a dolly" (Northall, 1894); "a washing implement with a cross-handle for pounding dirty clothes. It is worked with an up-and-down-motion. It differs from the dolly-peg in that its base is circular and solid, save for two deep intersecting fissures from the opposite diameters: thus exhibiting four massive staves, instead of slender pegs" (Northall, 1896); see also **batler**.

maiden (Wise, 1861) *n.* see **maid**.

maiding tub *n.* a washing tub; "the large, deep tub into which dirty clothes are placed to be maided" (Northall, 1896).

mail-cart *n.* pram; 'bassinet' and 'push-chair' were also commonly used in the late 1800s and early 1900s, since the word 'perambulator' (or 'pram') did not come into widespread use until 1914 (Phyllis Eastgate).

make-weight *n.* "that which is thrown upon the scale to make up the due weight of bread, meat, &c." (Northall, 1896).

malkin *n.* see **mawkin**.

mammer *vi.* to stammer; to falter in speaking; to hesitate (Alexander, 1951) EG "Or stand so mamm'ring on" (Shakespeare, *Othello*, Act III, Sc. III).

mammet *n.* a doll, manikin or puppet EG "This is no world to play with mammets" (Shakespeare, *Henry IV (Part 1)*, Act II, Sc III), "A whining mammet, in her fortune's tender" (Shakespeare, *Romeo and Juliet*, Act III, Sc. V); according to Wise

(1861), by the nineteenth century the word was "only used by crow-boys of their scarecrows."

mammock *vt.* to mangle; to smash or break into pieces (Northall, 1896); to pull in pieces (Alexander, 1951) EG "O, I warrant how he mammocked it" (Shakespeare, *Coriolanus*, Act I, Sc. III).

Maney *n.* area in the Sutton Coldfield borough of Birmingham; its name probably means 'dry ground in the marsh'.

manky *adj.* dirty; untidy and smelly EG "The 'ouse was dead manky."

mardy *adj.* petulant; still in common use.

mare *n.* a term of disdain for a woman EG "'Er's a right mare, 'er is." Also used more jocularly as "'Y' silly mare," when a person (usually a woman) has done something daft and the other person laughs lightheartedly.

mares-tails *npl.* white streaky clouds believed to portend high winds (Skeat, 1876).

market-fresh *adj.* see **market-peart**.

market-merry *adj.* see **market-peart**.

market-peart *adj.* half-drunk; half-intoxicated; "about as drunk as the average farmer of the old school, by the time he returned from market" (Northall, 1896); see also **blindo, blotto, bob-howler, canned, kaylied, lagging, mopped, palatick** and **slaumsey**.

marley *n.* marble, from 'marl'; see also **alley, alley taw, blood alley, cat's eye, dogger, dummox, French alley, glarny, glass alley, gobbie, pot alley** and **steelie**.

marleys *n.* any of several different children's games played with marbles.

marley-stopper *n.* "a splay-footed person; a term suggested by the habit of turning out the toes in order to check the career of a marley" (Northall, 1896).

marlies *n.* see **marleys**.

Mary Ellen *n.* a right Mary Ellen is a woman who is known for causing ructions.

masenter *n.* see **masonter**.

mash *vt.* to draw; to infuse, said esp. of tea (Northall, 1896) EG "Put the tea to mash, while I cut the cake."

maslin-kettle *n.* a brass or tinned-copper preserving kettle, either shallow or deep, for boiling milk in (Northall, 1896); from the Anglo-Saxon 'maestling' (a kind of brass or mixed metal).

masonter *n.* a stonemason (Skeat, 1876); from the Old German 'meizan' (to hew).

matrimony *n.* cake and bread and butter eaten together (Northall, 1894).

mawkin *n.* a guy; a scarecrow; "a figure on a hockey-cart at harvest homes" (Rhodes, 1950); often used disparagingly EG "You look a proper mawkin." Children in both Birmingham and the Black Country used to play a game called 'Ode monny mawkin' in which one player dressed up as an old man and the others called after him (Shaw, 1930); now obsolete. Tomkinson (1893) claims that this word was also used in the Worcestershire dialect for a bundle of rags tied to a stick for the cleaning of ovens: "to prevent its setting on fire, the mawkin was first dipped in water." Although more than likely pronounced the same, Palmer (1976) suggests that a

117

differently spelled variant was more common in the Warwickshire dialect for the same type of cleaning utensil: "Bread was baked by burning firing in the oven, removing it, and allowing the loaf to bake as the oven cooled. First, the oven was cleaned with a piece of wet sacking attached by a chain to a pole. This was called a malkin."

mawlers *npl.* hands EG "Get yer maulers off!"

mawsey *adj.* over-ripe (esp. fruit or vegetables); soft; also used as a derogatory term for a fool or idiot EG "Yer great mawsey."

mawskin *n.* the stomach of a calf used in cheese-making (Marshall, 1796).

may-of-the-meadow *n.* Meadow-sweet, *Spiraea ulmaria*; esp. common in Sutton Coldfield (Northall, 1896).

mecklekeckle *adj.* of poor or inferior quality EG "'E's a mecklekeckle bloke, en't 'e?" According to Northall (1894), 'keckle-meckle' was the "Derbyshire miner's term for poor ore."

meg *n.* a halfpenny, in use c.1880; see also **mag** and **flatch**.

meg-flying *n.* a game of pitch-and-toss (Northall, 1896).

messengers *n.* small particles of mould which appear when a barrel or vat of beer is nearly empty.

messuage *n.* a dwelling house with out-buildings.

Metchley *n.* a Roman camp erected in Birmingham as one of the bases for the legionaries as they pushed westwards in the conquest of Britain (c.48 AD). It is likely that the camp was abandoned approximately a decade later, coming back into use about 75 AD. Half a century afterwards the troops moved out for the last time. Unlike in Alcester and Wall, a civilian settlement had not grown up around the camp and although some Roman coins have been found elsewhere in greater Birmingham there is little to suggest a significant Roman presence.

metheglin *n.* mead; an alcoholic drink made from honey.

midden *n.* a rubbish heap.

middle-earth *n.* from the Anglo-Saxon 'middan-eard', an ancient word for the world, as used by Tolkien in *Lord of the Rings* (1955). "The middle region, the earth as distinguished from heaven above and hell beneath" (Palmer, 1882).

middling *adj.* neither healthy nor ill; according to Skeat (1876), the meaning alters slightly when preceded by either 'pretty' or 'very' EG "'I'm pretty middling, we gets on pretty middling,' means 'I am tolerably well, we are doing well.' But 'I'm very middling, he's going on very middling,' means 'I am very unwell, he is doing very badly', or he is conducting himself very badly." The phrase 'fair to middling' means 'not too bad'.

miller's dog *n.* a caterpillar; "in other dialects, caterpillars are known as *cats and kittens*" (Northall, 1894); see also **woolly-bear**.

miller's eye *n.* "a small kernel in bread, where the water has not mixed with the flour, when the dough was making" (Northall, 1896); see also the phrase **don't drown the miller's eye**.

118

milling *n.* boxing (Palmer, 1979) EG "Yesterday morning (Tuesday October 15th 1816) the attention of the milling amateurs and fancy of this town and neighbourhood was directed to the field of sport, at Sutton Coldfield, to witness a contest between two young men, named Griffiths and Bayliss, the former an inhabitant of this Town, and the latter from Wednesbury, for a purse of £40" (from *Famous Boxing Match; Three New Songs, Written on the Boxing Match, between Griffiths and Baylis*, 1816).

millud *n.* a miller EG "The millud, the mollud, the ten o'clock scollud" (derisive song in use amongst schoolboys, date unknown).

milpun *n.* a bread pan.

mimmocking *adj.* see **mimmucking**.

mimmocky *adj.* see **mimmucking**.

mimmucking *adj.* prissy; fussy; precious EG "'E's a mimmucking feller, en't 'e?'"

mimmucky *adj.* see **mimmucking**.

mimping *adj.* dainty (Northall, 1896).

Minworth *n.* area in the north of Birmingham; its name probably means 'enclosed farmstead' of a settler called Myna.

misken *n.* see **miskin**.

miskin *n.* a pit for refuse; "a compost pit" (Northall, 1896) EG "pd Henry Cookes Mason for worke on the wall he built about the misken and pigsty" (Bailiff's Account, March 1671); latterly applied to both terrace jakes and dustbins. C. C. Green writes that a miskin was a row of brick cubicles which each had bench seats inside with a hole in them: "At the back were doors at ground level. Furnishing was complete with a three gallon bucket. Once a week the miskinman went along the back emptying the buckets. A loud yell indicated occupation – this was around the 1890s. The miskinman would also make a bit on the side selling his harvest to allotment holders. I recall one afternoon in the 1930s when Villa lost and we were all getting up to go outside to the scores of trams waiting in rows to take us all back to town; one man commented *Well, if yer cor win on yer own miskin yer cor win no road.*" Used widely in early twentieth century Brummagem, miskin is actually derived from the Old English 'mixen', meaning 'dung', and which developed into signifying 'dung heap', and so dates back hundreds of years. Although C.C. Green gives the above definition, the miskins were originally the area in a yard of back-to-backs where rubbish was put. Then when Councillor Percy Shurmer forced landlords to put in dustbins, the dustbins became known as miskins. For his efforts, Percy Shurmer was celebrated by working-class Brummies as The Miskin King.

miskinmen *npl.* dustbinmen; refuse collectors (B. King).

misle *n.* drizzle; thin mist.

misly *adj.* drizzly.

missis *n.* a female boss, supervisor or proprietor EG "The missis of the place wanted us to open up of a mornin'" (Mrs Smith, née Hands); now commonly used as an alternative form of 'wife' EG "Mr Twigg 'oo lived the other side o' the entry dain't gurra werk, cus 'e wus a 'undred years old, an' 'is missus wus a witch an' med us kids drown lickle kittens, cus she dain't wannem, in a bucket o' water in the brew 'ouse in the yard, an' she'd promise us 'a'penny, an' never paid us, the rotten sod" (Smith, undated).

mississing *adj.* "assuming the authority, without having the claims, of a mistress" (Northall, 1896) EG "The mississing hussy, I won't 'ave 'er mississing over me."

misword *n.* "a word of censure or blame" (Northall, 1896) EG "'E never gave us a misword all 'is life."

mither *vt.* to annoy, pester or perplex (Rhodes, 1950) EG "I wish 'e'd stop mitherin' us an' gerron with 'is work."

mixen *n.* see **miskin**.

mizzerling *n.* an unhappy or miserable child, esp. one desperate for attention (O. Brown).

mizzle *n.* see **misle**.

moche *vi.* see **mooch**.

modge *vi.* see **codge**.

mog *vi.* to breast-feed; to give milk from the breasts EG "Time to mog the babby" (H. Taylor).

moggins *n.* a mother who breast-feeds her baby (Hilary Taylor); see also **mog** and **tittymog**.

moikin *n.* see **mawkin**.

moil *vi.* to work hard; to graft EG "I've bin moilin' all wick" (Skeat, 1876); "to labour, drudge; with a sense of 'to soil'" (Northall, 1896); mostly used in conjunction with the word 'toil', as in "We toiled and moiled."

moither *vt.* see **mither**.

moke *n.* a child's soap-box cart (R. Powderhill); a go-kart made from odd bits of wood and discarded wheels.

mollicrush *vt.* to bruise; to beat, pound or mangle (Northall, 1896).

molly-ragging *n.* "a coarse, abusive scolding" (Northall, 1896).

mom *n.* the diminutive of mother and used overwhelmingly by working-class and lower middle-class folk in Birmingham and the Black Country. On the 'Births, Deaths and Marriages' page of the *Birmingham Evening Mail* it is rare to find the word 'mum'. In Wales, Ireland and much of northern England, the diminutive is 'mam', but in the West Midlands the 'a' vowel is often changed to an 'o' sound after an 'm' or 'n'; see also **mon**.

momble *vt.* to bungle; to botch or mess up EG "I know'd 'e'd mek a momble on it" (Northall, 1896).

mommet *n.* scarecrow; corruption of 'Mahomet', the Great Turk in medieval Mummers' plays, also *n.* an untidily or shabbily dressed person.

mommit *n.* see **mommet**.

mommock *vt.* see **mammock**.

mon *n.* man; as with 'mam' and 'mom', so too with man and mon EG "Well then axe the mon into the parlour" (from the Brummagem street ballad *Christening the Wench*

Ben, published anonymously in the 1870s), "Looking back I can see me queuing for the Tupp'nny crush on a Sat'day arternoon arter a look at ole mon Blackwell's, an' scroungin' some specks (fruit turning bad) ta stuff while we wus watchin' Buck Jones, Johnnie Mack Brown, or the Whisperin' Shadder" (Smith, undated). There is also a much earlier record of this variant; when an awesome fellow enters King Arthur's hall early in the anonymous fourteenth century epic *Sir Gawain and the Green Knight*, he is stared at hard, "for each mon had marvelled at what it might mean." In the Black Country it is still common for a chap to greet another with the phrase "'Ow are y' ma mon?" and in Birmingham, too, older folk continue to say 'our old mon' for father. The pronunciation is derived from the Old English word 'mon' which meant man. In the Anglo-Saxon period, a short sounding 'a' as in hand became a long 'o' where the vowel came before the letter 'n'. In this manner, land became lond, hand became hond and man became mon. A similar process occurred whereby words ending with -ang came to be pronounced as -ong; for example, lang turning into long and wrang into wrong. This latter development became accepted as standard English outside Scotland and the North of England, but the 'on' sound was not as successful. Instead it was restricted to the west of England, in an area from just to the north of Lancaster and down to just below Hereford. The eastern boundary ran through the Penines and along to north-east Warwickshire. This pronunciation is still retained by Brummagem speakers in the term 'the old mon' which is used to refer to a person's father EG "'Ow's yer old mon, our kid?"

moniker *n.* name or pseudonym; originally tramp's slang, moniker was used in Brummagem by punters and bookies when betting for cash away from the race-course was illegal. Each punter would identify themselves by putting a nickname or made up name on the bottom of their bet.

monkey *n.* betting terminology for £500.

monkey run *n.* a place where youths met to flirt with each other; a kind of 'lover's lane', this was a term given to a main road up and down which teenage boys and girls would parade with their pals in the hope that they might click with someone from the opposite sex EG "Later on there was always the monkey runs, one in the Hockley area along the Lozells Road, and the other in the nobs area along Soho Road. These were the places we would show ourselves off like prize cockerels, and the girls would be shy, telling us to clear off, an' don't be cheeky, but liking the attention any road up. If you were lucky you'd get to hold hands, and if you were really blessed there would be a kiss in some dark entry, before she scurried off with her mates and you went back to yours to relate some fantastic story, which was naturally all lies" (Smith, undated). The youngsters got done up in their glad rags (best clothes), and would usually go along the monkey run on a Saturday and Sunday night. In other parts of the country the monkey was known as the 'monkey parade'.

mon't *au v.* negated form of the auxiliary verb 'must'.

mooch *vi.* to nose about; to pry; to rummage "to loiter or skulk about; usually for pilfering purposes" (Northall, 1896) EG "We dain't know wot ter do till we mooched rahnd and distaerbed an old bloke undressin' 'isself" (Squiers, 1916, p.2); now in widespread use. Today, moching means wandering around just having a look around without any real purpose in mind.

moocher *n.* "a skulker; a hedge robber" (Northall, 1896).

moonraker *n.* an uneducated or illiterate person; commonly applied to "many districts whose inhabitants are considered illiterate" (Northall, 1894).

mop *n.* a fair, or, more precisely, a trade fair combined with a hiring fair; according to Palmer (1976), in Warwickshire "they were held in late September or early October, during the slack period after the harvest. Farm labourers and maid-servants wanting to hire out for the coming year assembled on the day, wearing the badge of their trade [EG. a cowherd would wear cow-hair, a shepherd would wear wool, and a waggoner would wear a piece of whipcord]. 'Mop' is said to derive from the maids' practice of holding miniature mops." The following description of the annual Kings Norton Mop is taken from an article used in a campaign which eventually led to its suppression:

> The King's Norton Saturnalia is growing worse. Hardly a man or woman with any pretension to self-respect could be seen at the Mop last Monday, and the thousands were composed of shouting hobbledehoys, screaming girls, drunken men, and shouting women. they swarmed from the station in hundreds during the day, and as night drew on the crushing, the swearing, created indescribable confusion. A great mass of people stood round the roasting ox, which had been frizzling all night before a huge fire and then was cut up for the delectation of the crowd. A basket of slices of bread stood near, and two or three hot red-faced men with carving knives, sliced away at the haunches, the ribs, and the shoulders, putting a slice of meat between two slices of bread and selling the tasty morsels at four pence each. The public houses were packed and customers had to fight their way in and out, treading on floors wet with slopped beer. Some disgraceful scenes took place in one part or another of the vicinity during the day and night. The general proceedings offered a spectacle of debauchery, drunkenness, noise and blasphemy, in strong contrast to the ordinary quiet life of King's Norton.

Thankfully, the Kings Norton Mop has now been revived and takes place successfully each year.

mopped *adj.* intoxicated; in a state of drunkenness; see also **blindo, blotto, bob-howler, canned, kaylied, lagging, market-peart, palatick** and **slaumsey**.

mopstale *n.* see **mopstick**.

mopstick *n.* a boy's game in which players in one team bend over and allow players from the opposing team to climb on to their backs. Shaw (1930) states that "when the last is mounted, he puts a finger up for the team bending down to guess. The names used, beginning with the thumb, are: Dick, Stick, Ivory, Berry, Cherry." This game was also widely known in Brummagem as 'polly on the mopstick'.

mopuses *n.* money; coins; sometimes used for bad money c.1900 (F. Jones, *The Birmingham Post*, 22 August, 1956); Northall (1896) suggests that the word may have originated from "the name of Sir Giles Mompesson, the notorious monopolist in James the First's time."

morris *interj.* go away; be off (Northall, 1894); common in both the Warwickshire and Worcestershire dialects.

morum *n.* a brilliant or ingenious idea; a blinding flash of inspiration.

Moseley *n.* area of south Birmingham; in the Domesday Book of 1086, Moseley was recorded as Museleie, whilst in 1221 it was noted as Moselege. It has three possible meanings; A. D. Mills and other place-name experts believe that it derives from 'mus' and 'leah' and signifies the woodland clearing infested with mice. However, Skipp (1980) suggests that a mouse clearing could mean a small clearing, and points out that as late as 1847 one of the smallest fields in neighbouring Yardley was called Mouse Park. The spelling of Moselege also appears to indicate a moss or bog clearing, but, as Fairn (1973) states, this interpretation can be discounted since it comes after the entry for Museleie.

mot *n.* see **motty**.

mott *n.* a moat, as in the old song *I Can't Find Brummagem*:

> But 'mongst the changes we have got
> In good old Brummagem.
> They've made a market of the Mott,
> To sell the pigs in Brummagem.

motty *n.* a mark to shoot at as a target in marbles; "anciently the peg at which quoits were thrown" (Northall, 1896).

mouch *vi.* see **mooch**.

mouche *vi.* see **mooch**.

mouter *n.* a kiss on the mouth EG "Come his little ways, and give papa a mouter" (Northall, 1896).

moze *vi.* to smoulder; "to burn slowly and dull, without any flame" (Northall, 1896).

mozey *adj.* "natureless, sapless, woolly . . . as applied to weather, warm and damp; also as applied to meat, fruit, &c., tainted, musty, beginning to decay" (Northall, 1896).

muckbird *n.* a toilet attendant or cleaner; "a jakesman, a man whose profession is not calculated to inspire lively melody" (Northall, 1896); see also the phrase **to sing like a muckbird**.

mucker *n.* friend EG "'Ow y' doin' me old mucker?"

mudgin *n.* the fat from a pig's chitlins.

mullen *n.* the head-gear or bridle of a cart-horse (Skeat, 1876).

mullin *n.* see **mullen**.

mullock *n.* a mess; a tizzy or fluster A nice old mullock I shall be in" (Hampson, 1936, p.196); Rhodes (1950) suggests that mullock may be derived from the name of the Semitic god Moloch, but this seems unlikely. In Chaucer's *Reeve's Tale*, he writes, "That ilke fruit is ever lenger the wers, Til it be rotten in mollock or in stree." Here mullock means rubbish, and it is easy to see how this word eventually came to be used in reference to any kind of mess or muddle. Its derivation, however, is unknown.

mumchance *adj.* silent; speechless or mute EG "An' theer 'er sat mumchance" (Rhodes, 1950).

mummock *vt.* to fret, pester or worry; to pull about; to pull to pieces, either physically or mentally EG "The kids don't 'alf mummock me" (Skeat, 1876); see also **mammock**.

munch *n.* a coward (Rhodes, 1950); according to Northall (1894), a 'munch' was commonly used in the Warwickshire dialect to refer to a person who maltreats his or her children EG "'E's a cruel munch to 'is kids.".

mungelling *adj.* dark; obscure; tortuous EG "A mungelling cellar wheer yo can't feel and can't find" (Northall, 1896).

muzzy *adj.* stupefied with liquor (Northall, 1896).

mynche *n.* daughter (K. Jenks).

myther *vt.* see **mither**.

N

naggle *vt.* to nag or scold.

nail *n.* a prostitute; see also **brass**.

nalls *npl.* belongings; possessions EG "Pick up yer nalls and cut."

namer *n.* an early term amongst trainspotters for engines which were named as well as numbered (Tennant, 1983).

nammus *interj.* go away; be off (Northall, 1894).

napper *n.* head (J. Alldritt); Jones (*The Birmingham Post*, 22 August 1956) states that this term was used in a game called 'pitch-back' when the boy 'down' was frequently exhorted to "keep your napper down" or "tuck your napper in."

nare *adv.* never; not ever EG "Nare-a one of 'em was any good" (Ainsworth, 1989).

narker *n.* betting terminology for a person who watches out for the police; see also **dog-out**.

narner *adj.* fool, but used in an affectionate way EG "Come 'ere y' narner and I'll do it for y'.".

nash *adj.* see **neish**.

nauger *n.* an auger; a boring tool; 'auger' appears to have been derived from 'nauger' by aphesis (Hoddinott and Nikitas).

nayward *adj.* contrary to; diametrically opposed; opposite belief (Alexander, 1951) EG "Howe'er you lean to th' nayward" (Shakespeare, *The Winter's Tale*, Act II, Sc. I).

Nechells *n.* area of Birmingham near Aston; the first notice of this name is in a deed from 1339 whereby William Holdon granted lands in Echeles to Henry, son of Robert Jordan of Erdyngton. McKenna (1988) feels that the meaning of the name is open to speculation, although it might derive from the Old English 'ecels', signifying cleared land added to an existing farm. His hunch is supported by compelling evidence from place-name expert Kenneth Cameron. He explains that originally Nechells was known as 'atten Eccheles' (at the land added to a village). As time went on, and in a process called metanalysis, the 'n' from 'atten' was taken as belonging to the word Eccheles, thus giving atte Neccheles, and at some point during the Middle English period the word 'atte' was dropped completely.

needle *n.* anger; wrath; fury; rage, esp. in the phrase 'to get the needle' EG "But oh, lumme, when I 'ad to parker up thaerteen and fower pence fer two fish and chips and two bottles of Waerthington, I daint 'arf git the needle" (Squiers, 1916, p.14).

ne'er *adv.* see **nare**.

neish *adj.* frail; fragile; weak or susceptible to cold EG "Mrs Gordon is that neish these days" (Hampson, 1936, p.4); derived from the Anglo-Saxon 'hnesce' meaning soft or tender (Walker, undated); this word is more common in the North Midlands.

nerker *n.* see **nirker**.

nerrun *adv.* not one; nare one.

nesh *adj.* see **neish**.

net gen *bsl.* 10/- in old money (Harris).

nevice *bsl.* 7/- in old money (Harris).

nextway *adv.* directly (Northall, 1896) EG "Ar, I'm a-comin' nextway"; no longer in common use.

nicker *n.* £1.

nick-and-brick *n.* a variation of chuck-farthing, "the dividing line between two bricks in a pavement affording the mark" (Northall, 1894).

nicklas *interj.* "this very common exclamation in this county amongst boys at play is evidently of great antiquity, and had its origin in times before the Reformation when St. Nicholas was considered the tutelar saint or patron of children, and is now used without the remote idea if its primitive meaning. When a boy is hard pressed in any game depending on activity, and perceives his antagonist gaining ground upon him, he cries out *Nicklas!*, upon which he is entitled to a suspension of the play for the moment; and on any occasion of not being ready, wanting, for instance, to fasten his shoe, or remedy any accidental inconvenience, the cry of *Nicklas!* entitles him to protection or safeguard. This was often expressed in the words *I cry Nicklas!*" (Northall, 1896).

nifle *vi.* to wander aimlessly from one job to another making little progress or improvement EG "'Er's niflin' about, not knowin' what er's doin'."

nifle-pin *n.* an easy job; an excuse for being idle or doing very little.

night-cap *n.* a pig's stomach.

nine-men's-morris *n.* an old Warwickshire game, similar to draughts; "a game played on squares cut into the turf" (Alexander, 1951) EG "The nine men's morris is fill'd up with mud" (Shakespeare, *A Midsummer Night's Dream*, Act II, Sc. I); according to Wise (1861), the nine-men's-morris board was "cut on the corn-bins of the stables at the Warwickshire farm-houses" and played by ploughmen who used "white and black beans to distinguish their men; the great object being to get three of them in a row, or, as it is called , to have a 'click-clack and an open row'. In order to do this, you are allowed to take up your adversary's pieces as at draughts, or else to hem them up till they cannot move." Brand (1849) describes the game thus: "In that part of Warwickshire where Shakespeare was educated . . . the shepherds and other boys dig up the turf with their knives to represent a sort of imperfect chess-board. It consists of a square, sometimes only a foot diameter, sometimes three or four yards. Within this is another square, every side of which is parallel to the external square; and these squares are joined by lines drawn from from each corner of both squares and in the middle of each line.

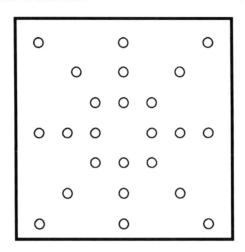

One party or player has wooden pegs, the other stones, which they move in such a manner as to take up each other's men, as they are called, and the area of the inner square is called the pound, in which the men taken up are impounded. These figures are by the country people called *nine men's morris* . . .; and are so called because each party has nine men. These figures are always cut upon the green turf or leys as they are called, or upon the grass at the end of ploughed lands, and in rainy seasons never fail to be choked up with mud." A much simpler version known as three-men's-morris was also played throughout Warwickshire.

ninepennies *npl.* the stalls in a picture house EG "There was another exit door just on the left inside the passage, but that was for the exclusive use of the patrons in the Stalls, the 'ninepennies', as was the front foyer the exclusive exit for the gallery patrons, the 'gods bobs'. We could not use either of these exits to force our illegal entry, but had to be satisfied with the pits, or the 'tanna mana'" (Smith, undated).

nineted *adj.* mischievous; badly behaved; wicked; "thought, by some glossarists, to be a corruption of 'anointed by the devil'" (Northall, 1894) EG "'E's a nineted un, 'e is."

nineter *n.* a mischievous or disobedient boy; anyone given to bad ways; a 'tartar' (Rhodes, 1950).

ninety-bird *n.* see **nineter**.

nipper *n.* a child; a youngster EG "The nipper's med it into the first team"; now in widespread use.

nirker *n.* an unmanageable or unruly person (Rhodes, 1950); "anyone or any thing difficult to master, overcome, or outmatch" (Northall, 1896); a corruption, perhaps of 'an irker'.

nisgull *n.* the smallest of a breed; the runt of a litter.

nithering *vi.* freezing; shivering with cold.

nocab *bsl.* bacon.

noggen *adj.* thick; unintelligent, as in the phrase "Yer noggen 'eaded gawk."

noggin *n.* a thick slice of bread; see also **doorstop**.

nogman *n.* "a simpleton or numbskull" (Northall, 1894).

nointed *adj.* see **nineted**.

nointer *n.* see **nineter**.

Northfield *n.* area of Birmingham first referred to in the Domesday Book of 1086 as Nordfeld; meaning the open land lying to the north, it is likely that Northfield gained its name because it was north of the royal manor of Bromsgrove whence its Saxon settlers had come in the seventh century. In this respect Northfield had much in common with nearby King's Norton: both had belonged to the kingdom of the Hwicce, which was absorbed into Mercia, and both remained in Worcestershire until joining Birmingham in 1911.

Northone Regis *n.* see **King's Norton**.

Nortune *n.* see **King's Norton**.

nothing's-nest *n.* a nonentity EG "'E's found a nothing's nest" (Northall, 1896).

noul *n.* a head; "in [Shakespeare's] *Midsummer Night's Dream*, act iii. scene 2, Puck talks about "the ass's noul" he has fixed on Bottom's head. And the word is still so used, both of animals and men, but always implying stupidity" (Wise, 1861).

nun *n.* the small disc or puck used in the game of hockey; see also **bandy**.

nunk *n.* nothing; nought.

O

oak-ball-day *n.* "May 29 was the birthday of Charles II, and also the day of his public entry into London, 1660, after his arrival at Dover on the 25th from Holland. It was in the September of 1651, after the battle of Worcester, that he concealed himself in the oak at Boscobel, Shropshire. In Warwickshire it is the custom to wear an oak-ball in the hat or button-hole on May 29, and to decorate horses with the same, as an emblem of the Restoration" (Northall, 1896).

oat 'n' erth *bsl.* 2/3d in old money (Harris).

oat yennups *bsl.* 2d in old money (Harris).

obedience *n.* obeisance; bow or curtsy EG "Now, mek yer obedience to the lady!" (Skeat, 1876).

o-braves *npl.* "acts of impudence or effrontery" (Northall, 1896) EG "Don't let's 'ave any o' yer o-braves, my lad, or you'll get a tannin' when yer dad gets in."

ochimy *n.* see **ockermy**.

ockerdocker *n.* "a greasy-looking black pebble, striped with some other colour, regarded as a lucky stone" (Northall, 1894).

ockermy *n.* alloy, amalgam or mixed metal; usually used to designate pewter or spelter. Appears to have been derived from the word 'alchemy': "Spoons and other kitchen utensils are frequently made of a mixed metal called alchemy, or, as it is vulgarly pronounced, ochimy" (Farley, 1800).

ockey-indey-berries *npl.* "a corruption of *Cocculus Indicus*, or grains of paradise; used to adulterate beer or to stupefy or destroy pigeons, &c." (Northall, 1896).

ode *adj.* aged; mature; pronunciation variant of 'old'.

Ode Monny Mawkin *n.* a game played by children (Northall, 1896, and Rhodes, 1950); see also **mawkin**.

odge *vi.* to move, as in the *phrasal verb* **odge up** (move up; edge up) EG "I asked 'im to 'odge up."

odgick *vi.* to fidget; to move about restlessly EG "Stop yer 'odgicking."

offal-work *n.* drudgery; dirty, menial work (Northall, 1896).

ogen *bsl.* 2/- in old money (Harris).

old chocker *n.* father.

old dear *n.* an old woman.

old-Dutch *n.* mother; also common in the Cockney dialect.

old end *n.* part of a street or neighbourhood where a person had grown up. This term is used exclusively by working-class Brummies who come from poorer backgrounds, as in "I 'ad a mooch down the old end."

old-iron *n.* a penny-farthing pushbike.

Old Sarbot *n.* see **sarbut**.

old Spurrier *n.* "A hard, unbending, crafty lawyer permanently retained by the Mint to prosecute all comers in the district. He had an office near Easy Row and had a busy time of it, gaining for himself a large fortune and an evil reputation" (Tennant, 1983).

olt *vt.* to hold; to grasp, as in the *phrasal verbs* **tek olt** (take hold) and **cop olt** (catch hold) EG "This fire won't tek olt," "Cop olt o' this, will ya?," "I copt olt of orl on 'em and taerned 'em round ther other way from wot they wos astandin" (Squiers, 1917, p.12), and the old rhyme: 'Nicky nacky note, Shoe the lickle colt, 'Ere a nail and theer a nail, An' tek fast olt' (quoted in Rhodes, 1950).

omber *n.* hammer.

omnibus cad *n.* a bus conductor (Palmer, 1979) EG "whether Tinkers or Tailors or Omnibus cads, we can learn them a tune called the Warwickshire lads" (from the street ballad *The Cockney's Trip to Brummagem*, c.1876).

on *prep.* commonly used in place of 'of' EG "Not one on 'em knowed what they was doin', I swear," "All on y' can get stuck in an' 'elp out."

one-eyed jacks *npl.* kippers.

oos-bird *n.* a bastard; an illegitimate child.

oo tosharoon *n.* betting terminology for two shillings.

open-arse *n.* the fruit of the medlar, *Mespilus Germanica* (Northall, 1896).

orse *n.* pronunciation variant of 'horse'; see also **oss**.

orse road *n.* the (horse) road; the street EG "Tell the nippers to keep out o' the 'oss road"; see also **oss road**.

orts *npl.* fragments; morsels; scraps of food or crusts; leavings EG "It is some poor fragment, some slender ort of his remainder" (Shakespeare, *Timon of Athens*, Act IV, Sc. III), "I 'ave me meals when they do, I don't 'ave to eat their outs" (Skeat, 1876).

Oscott *n.* area of Birmingham; meaning the cott (cottage) of a person called Osa, Oscott was first mentioned in 1322 when Thomas de Asteley was given as the "rector libre capelle de Oscote" (the parish priest of the free chapel of Oscott).

oss *n.* pronunciation variant of 'horse' more common in the Black Country.

oss road *n.* variant of 'orse road' (horse road) more common in the Black Country.

otmillo *n.* a boy's game, played thus: "*A* kneels with his face in *B*'s lap, the other players standing in the background. They step forward one-by-one, at a signal from *B*, who says of each in turn, "Otmillo, otmillo, where is this poor man to go?" *A* then assigns each one to a place. When all are dispatched, *A* removes his face from *B*'s lap, and, standing up, exclaims, "Hot!" Hot! Hot!" The others then rush to him, and the laggard is blindfolded instead of *A*" (Northall, 1896).

our kid *n.* used to refer to a brother or other close male relative EG "Our kid would decide whether we stayed a little while longer or returned home, cus I dain't know abaht tellin' the time did I?" (Smith, undated); also common in the Scouse and Mancunian dialects; see also **our wench**.

ourn *pron.* ours; belonging to us; genitive (or *possessive adj.*) of 'us' (Skeat, 1876).

our wench *n.* used to refer to a sister or other close female relative EG "The call from one of our wenches, the old uns, or even on occasions our Mom 'erself, would bring the night's playing to an abrupt halt" (Smith, undated); see also **our kid**.

ousen *npl.* houses; see **housen**.

out-asked *pa p.* "having had the marriage banns published three times" (Skeat, 1876).

outcome *n.* a coming-of-age party or celebration. "Formerly restricted to the twenty-first birthday of an apprentice, which was the expiry date of his indenture (usually after a term of seven years). The 'outcome' was celebrated at the combined expense of the master, the apprentice, and his fellow workmen. At twelve noon, firearms were discharged, and this gave the signal for the distribution of ale. Ordinary dinner hour followed between one and two, and work was resumed from two till five. The outcome supper was held in the evening at a tavern or tea garden, and eating and drinking, singing and dancing were continued until midnight. The apprentice was then taken to a table, crowned with laurel or bays, and encircled by the company, who sang:

> Here's to him that's now set free
> Who was once a prentice bound
> And for his sake, this holiday we make
> So let his health go round, go round,

Go round, brave boys, until it comes to me,
For the longer we sit here and drink
The merrier we shall be.

A 'loving cup' was usually passed round during the ceremony" (Rhodes, 1950). Rhodes (under the pseudonym of John Free Jnr.) noted in the *Birmingham Weekly Post* (Oct. 4 1924) that "when Thomas Crowley died in 1869, Alderman Manton said he had been apprenticed to a packing-case maker, and "by hard work and rigid economy saved £50, but, conforming to the prevalent practice in celebrating outcomes, and being urged by his master to be liberal, he spent the whole in treating his fellow workmen and friends at the Plough and Harrow in the Hagley Road" (Langford, *Modern Birmingham*). The date of this 'outcome' was about 1830." A contributor to the same edition of the *Birmingham Weekly Post* (giving his or her name only as 'H. D.') insisted that outcomes were continuing to be celebrated in the coopering trade at that time.

out-door *n.* off-licence; a shop having a licence to sell alcoholic liquors for consumption off the premises only; still in general use throughout Birmingham.

outride *n.* "the district of a commercial traveller - himself called an 'outride' or 'outrider,' in old times. The terms are almost forgotten" (Northall, 1896).

outrider *n.* a travelling salesperson.

outs *npl.* see **orts**.

oven stopless *n.* see **oven stopliss**.

oven stopliss *n.* an oven lid or cover (Wise, 1861) EG "Sorrow concealed, like an oven stopp'd" (Shakespeare, *Titus Andronicus*, Act II, Sc. IV).

overget *vi.* to recover or recuperate; to overcome, esp. an illness EG "It 'urt us so much when we buried the nipper that we dain't overget it the last four year" (Tomkinson, 1893), "I shan't overget it this long while" (Skeat, 1876).

overhand *n.* a person who organises and oversees piece-work; according to Skipp (1983), factory owners in Victorian Birmingham made piece-rate contracts with workers known as either 'overhands' or 'piece-masters': "The overhand was then responsible for engaging, supervising and paying his own group of workers."

owlud's quid *n.* according to Tomkinson (1893), 'owlud' was a common name for an owl, and a 'quid' was a finger-shaped compacted mass of bones and other indigestible parts of an owl's meal.

owsen *npl.* see **housen**.

owsomdever *adv.* and *conj.* however; nevertheless; at all events (Northall, 1896).

oxford scholar *n.* betting terminology for 5/- in old money; also refers to a time when there were four American dollars to a pound or 20 shillings, hence five shillings was a dollar.

P

pack in *ph v.* to pack (something) in means to stop doing something; to cease an activity EG "Pack irrin yo lot, else I'll gie y' such a wallop!"

pack up *ph v.* like 'pack in', to pack something up also means to cease doing something EG "I've 'ad enough, I'm gonna pack irrup."

pac-wax *n.* the neck tendons of an animal, *ligamentum nuchae* (Northall, 1896).

padded *adj.* dried at the top EG "The ground's gettin' padded now" (Skeat, 1876).

padgell *n.* a trifle; anything of little importance or value; a small amount.

padgelling *adj.* trifling; of small value EG "It's a padgelling way to pay off a debt, but it's all I got."

pailings *npl.* fencing; fences collectively (Geoff Moore).

pain *vt.* to hurt; to cause pain to EG "It was paining 'er so much 'er 'ad to goo to 'orspital."

palatick *adj.* drunk; intoxicated EG "'E was palatick larst night'; from paralytic. In Middle English, paralytic was spelled and pronounced as 'palatyk'; see also **blindo, blotto, bob-howler, canned, kaylied, lagging, market-peart, mopped** and **slaumsey**.

palings *npl.* see **pailings**.

panakin *n.* a very small pan, commonly used to warm a child's food in (Northall, 1896).

panshon *n.* a large glazed earthenware vessel used to store bread.

parish-lantern *n.* the moon (Northall, 1896).

parker *vi.* to pay, esp. in the *phrasal verb* **parker up** (pay up) EG "But oh, lumme, when I 'ad to parker up thaerteen and fower pence fer two fish and chips and two bottles of Waerthington, I daint 'arf git the needle" (Squiers, 1916, p.14).

parky *adj.* cold; chilly; frosty; frequently used in reference to the weather EG "Bit parky, ennit?"; still in common use.

parsley-bed *n.* "baby land; the place where children are created; a euphemism for the uterus" EG "Where do babies come from, mamma?" "Out of the parsley-bed, my dear" (Northall, 1896).

patch *n.* a fool or simpleton EG "A crew of patches" (Shakespeare, *A Midsummer Night's Dream*, Act III, Sc. II).

patched *adj.* foolish (Wise, 1861).

peakie blinder *n.* see **peaky blinder**.

peakies *npl.* see **peaky blinder**.

peaky *n.* see **peaky blinder**.

peaky blinder *n.* a term used to describe members of gangs of young, single males in late nineteenth century Birmingham. Similarly, Manchester had its scuttlers and London its hooligans. Legend has it that gang members stitched razor blades into the peaks of their caps which were then used as offensive weapons, and this is just one account amongst many of how the name originated. It is more likely that the name is derived from the fashion of breaking the peak of the cap so that one part could be brought down low over one eye, hence the peak blinded the one eye. Jones (1998) notes that during the Victorian and Edwardian periods "many references were made by court reporters to men having the appearance of a peaky." He then goes on to state that foul-mouthed peakies often roamed the streets of Birmingham "in drunken gangs, insulting and mugging passers-by." When various gangs fought they did so viciously with steel-tapped boots and heavy belts with sharp buckles, however instances of mugging and attacking general members of the public were rare.

pearl-rot *n.* a pearl-worker; also applied to an ailment common amongst pearl-workers since, as Northall (1896) points out, "pearl-dust has a deleterious effect on workers amongst it."

peart *adj.* lively; healthy (Skeat, 1876).

peck *vt.* and *vi.* to excavate; to dig, esp. coal; to mine, also *n.* a spade or shovel; a digging tool EG "I've got a job I do not like, I neither like the peck or pike, I wish I now was on the strike" (from *Poor Old Wedgebury*, an old street ballad, c.1863), also *n.* an open piece of land, invariably used in connection with Second World War bomb sites, as in "We used to goo and play over the bomb peck"; see also **pleck**.

pearten *vt.* to revive, enliven or cheer (Northall, 1896).

peartly *adv.* brightly; briskly (Northall, 1896).

peff *n.* punishment EG "I gi'im peff" (Northall, 1894).

peffling *adj.* pouring EG "Peffling rain" (Northall, 1896).

pelf *n.* rubbish; refuse (Timmins, 1889); particularly applied to vegetable rubbish (Northall, 1896).

pell *vt.* to bare, reveal or expose (Northall, 1894); usually spoken of the hair EG "Don't pell yer 'air back like that" (Northall, 1896).

pennig *n.* a penny. "I remember as a boy asking exactly what was meant by the flower-girls' cry, "pennig a bunch, vilets; vilets, pennig-a-bunch," and receiving the explanation that it was "penny a good bunch." This very soon slips into pennig-a-bunch when repeated many times in the old sing-song style" (H.B., *Birmingham Weekly Post*, 4 Oct. 1924).

pennywinkle *n.* periwinkle.

perform *vi.* to play up; to misbehave EG "Mom, our dad's 'ad too much t' drink and 'e's performing again!" (K. Carruthers).

perial *adj.* exquisite; excellent; majestic; a contraction, perhaps, of 'imperial' (Skeat, 1876).

Perry Barr *n.* area of Birmingham; Perry Barr takes its name from the Old English word 'pirige', meaning pear tree, and the Celtic word 'barr', signifying a hill top (see also **Great Barr**); at the time of the Domesday Book it was simply known as Perry.

Perry Common *n.* area of Birmingham; part of Perry Barr, the area was taken over by Birmingham in 1928.

phiz *n.* face EG "What is the difference between a photographer and an invalid? One takes your phiz and the other your physic" (Old Sarbot, 1869); a variant of 'fizzog'.

phthysicky *adj.* ill; unwell; sick; see also **tissicky**.

pick-sniff *n.* "an insignificant, paltry, contemptible person" (Northall, 1896).

pick-thank *n.* a pernickety or finical person; one who revels in finding faults (Rhodes, 1950); a toady (Alexander, 1951); a tale-bearer (Wise, 1861) EG "By smiling pick-thanks and base news-mongers" (Shakespeare, *Henry IV (Part 1)*, Act III, Sc. II), also *adj.* "During the rejoicings at Stratford on the conclusion of the Crimean War, I heard a peasant, saying of the public tea-meeting, &c., held in the High Street, 'There will be pickthanking work to-morrow;' that is, tale-bearing, gossiping, not unmixed with grumbling" (Wise, 1861).

piecan *n.* a fool or idiot EG "I felt a proper piecan" (D. Adams).

piece *n.* a slice of bread. Teachers from outside Brum, especially the many who were Welsh, were always puzzled when youngsters stated that they were going home "to 'ave a piece."

piece-master *n.* see **overhand**.

piekelet *n.* see **pikelet**.

pigeon-pair *n.* "offspring consisting of a son and daughter only" (Northall, 1896).

pigeon's milk *n.* something which does not exist; "a nonentity. Greenhorns are often sent to a shop for a pennyworth of pigeon's milk" (Northall, 1896).

piggin *n.* "a small pail-like vessel of wood with an erect handle" (Northall, 1896).

pigsty-doors *n.* trousers which button 'breeches-fashion'; "having the flap instead of fly-fronts" (Northall, 1896).

pikel *n.* a light two-pronged pitchfork used for haymaking (Timmins, 1889).

pikelet *n.* a flattened crumpet; a kind of cake made of flour and water; according to Carpenter (1977), this word was known to J. R. R. Tolkien, who used it often in his correspondence; still in common use.

pikerel *n.* pick.

pilliber *n.* see **pillowbeere**.

pillober *n.* see **pillowbeere**.

pillowbeere *n.* a pillow-case, common c.1600 (Hoddinott and Nikitas).

pillowber *n.* see **pillowbeere**.

pillow breer *n.* see **pillowbeere**.

pillowebeare *n.* see **pillowbeere**.

pillowebeere *n.* see **pillowbeere**.

pillowesbeeres *n.* see **pillowbeere**.

pinfold *n.* a pound for stray animals (Alexander, 1951) EG "If I had thee in Lipsbury pinfold, I would make thee care for me" (Shakespeare, *King Lear*, Act II, Sc. II). Today, the word is recalled in Pinfold Street in the city centre, and one still exists to The Great Stone Inn in Northfield.

pinket *n.* see **pinkit**.

pinkit *n.* a ghost; a spectre or apparition.

piss-a-bed *n.* the dandelion.

piss-ant *vulg.* an unpleasant, contemptible person, also *adj.* pathetic; of little value EG "It's piss-ant stuff."

piss-the-bed *n.* see **piss-a-bed**.

pitch and toss *n.* a gambling game, usually played with half-pence.

pitchback *n.* a boys' game (Northall, 1896).

pitching *n.* the pavement (Northall, 1896).

pither *vi.* to dawdle; to potter about aimlessly.

pithering *adj.* trifling; inconsequential; contemptible EG "Yer pitherin' idiot" (Northall, 1894); now in widespread use.

placket *n.* "the slit in a gown or petticoat which enables the wearer to put the garment on over her head" (Northall, 1896) EG "Let not the creaking of shoes nor the rustling of silks betray thy poor heart to woman: keep thy foot out of brothels, thy hand out of plackets" (Shakespeare, *King Lear*, Act III, Sc. IV).

pleck *n.* a small enclosure of grazing ground; a name given to the 'Old Pleck', a plot of land in Bracebridge Street, Aston to which Birmingham's annual Onion Fair was moved after it was banned in the city itself in 1875. By 1910, the Onion Fair had been moved to the Serpentine Ground close to Villa Park. The word 'peck', as in bomb peck is probably derived from pleck which in turn comes from the Middle English 'plek', meaning a piece of ground.

plim *vi.* according to Tomkinson (1893), this word was used to refer to meat that expands in size during cooking EG "Bacon killed in the prime of the moon plims; that killed in the wane of the moon boils out."

pluck *n.* "the liver, lights, and heart of a sheep" (Northall, 1896).

po *n.* a chamber pot.

podge *vt.* to hit or punch; "to give a blow with the fist" (Northall, 1894), as in the old Warwickshire folk-rhyme:

> Come down the railway
> And see a jolly fight,
> Two dead men
> Podging left and right:
> Two blind men
> To see fair play;
> Two deaf and dumb men
> To shout hooray!

poke *n.* the peak of a cap (Rhodes, 1950).

poothery *adj.* see **puthery**.

pop *vt.* to pawn; to pledge or stake EG "I popped me ring at uncle's"; from which the phrase 'to pop your clogs' appears to have been coined. Thus pop shop is a pawn shop. Pop is also the common word for a fizzy drink such as lemonade and it can also be used jocularly for beer EG "'E's bin on the pop again."

poppy-show *n.* an undue display or fuss EG "It was a right poppy-show" (D. Adams); "an old expression for something that was rather ostentatious" (Tennant, 1983).

posher *n.* a device used to beat clothes in a tub of water in order to rinse them (R. Couling); also common in northern English dialect districts.

pot alley *n.* painted clay marble; frequently shortened to 'pot'; see also **alley**, **alley taw**, **blood alley**, **cat's eye**, **dogger**, **dummox**, **French alley**, **glarny**, **gobbie**, **glass alley**, **gobbie**, **marley** and **steelie**.

pot-ball *n.* "a small dough-dumpling, usually eaten with treacle" (Northall, 1896).

pothery *adj.* see **puthery.**

powk *n.* a stye; an inflamed swelling on the eyelid; according to Warwickshire folklore, powks could be removed by rubbing them nine times with a gold ring (Palmer, 1976); in the dialects of other counties this word is generally used for a pimple anywhere on the body.

prachement *n.* a speech or oration; a corruption, perhaps of 'preachment'.

prate-apace *n.* a gossip or chatterbox (Northall, 1896).

prentice-my-son-John *n.* a boys' game, played thus: "the players fix on a trade, - say that of a butcher. Each player has a chosen joint or portion of a beast for his formula, which he utters as he pitches the back. But before one player makes the back, he arranges in secret with the leader that to name a certain joint or portion shall put the speaker in his place, i.e. 'down.' e.g. one player pitches, crying 'steak' perhaps; another says 'kidney,' and so on, until one unfortunate, who has chosen 'liver,' say, for his formula, finds himself forced to make the back, 'liver' having been the portion prohibited" (Northall, 1896).

prime *n.* a comb used in weaving to loosen the yarn c.1603; mentioned in a Warwickshire household inventory eighty years prior to its first recorded use in the Oxford English Dictionary (Hoddinott and Nikitas).

proper Brummie *n.* a person who is proud to come from Birmingham and speaks the Brummie dialect with pride. In the past such a term would only have been used with regard to white working-class people, but in modern Brum people from many different backgrounds and of any ethnicity can be proper Brummies.

proudflesh *n.* a scab; scar tissue; "a fleshy growth out of wounds and ulcerated surfaces" (Northall, 1896).

proud-tailor *n.* the goldfinch (Timmins, 1889).

puck-fyst *n.* a dried-up toadstool, commonly heard in the expression "Me throat's as dry as a puck-fyst."

pudding bag *n.* a cul-de-sac; a blind alley (Northall, 1896); common until the redevelopment of the 1960s swept away back-to-back Brum.

puddling *adj.* "a person who lives in a house below his means is said to live in 'a poor puddling place'. One who does more business than he has accommodation for, 'does business in a puddling way'. A person who does not pay attention to external comfort or appearance at table 'lives in a puddling way', and anyone who is slow in action 'goes puddling about'" (Northall, 1896).

puff *n.* life; lifetime; lifespan EG "I've never sin such a thing in all my puff" (F. Jones, *The Birmingham Post*, 22 August 1956).

pullback *n.* a hindrance; a disadvantage or drawback (Northall, 1896).

pumps *npl.* soft shoes worn by children for PE at school and for sport; in London these are known as 'plimsolls'.

pun *vt.* to pound (Wise, 1861); from the Anglo-Saxon 'pund'.

pungello *n.* ale; see also **blacking, legs 'n' wings** and **stingo.**

pup *vi.* to excrete or defecate (Northall, 1894).

purgit-hole *n.* Shaw (1930) states that this was the common name for an ash receptacle underneath the grates in coal fires. Tomkinson (1893) states that 'purgatory' was the Worcestershire dialect variant, so the Birmingham word 'purgit' appears to be a corruption of this.

purgy *adj.* peevish; irritable; short-tempered (Northall, 1896).

purgy-hole *n.* see **purgit-hole**.

purler *n.* a bad fall; see also the phrase **to come a purler**.

push *n.* betting terminology for a gang or crowd.

put *n.* an old Warwickshire game; "Put was played with an elongated cube, its four sides marked P, T, H and L, and the two ends, A and D. This die, called the put – hence the name of the game – was thrown up in turn by the players. If the P came up the thrower had to put a marble in the pool. With the T he took one; with the H he could take half the contents of the pool. L meant 'let 'em alone', and the thrower neither took nor lost any marbles. With D the player had to double the number of marbles in the pool, but A meant take all" (Palmer, 1976).

putchen *n.* a trap or snare.

puthery *adj.* spoken of the weather; very warm; close; humid, muggy or stuffy (Marshall, 1796).

pykelet *n.* see **pikelet**.

Pype Hayes *n.* area of Birmingham; the word pype is thought to refer to a stream, and hayes means an enclosure within a chase or manor.

Q

quack *n.* see **duck**.

quartern *n.* a gill.

quat *n.* a stye on the eyelid, or powk (Skeat, 1876); Wise (1861) suggests the word was used more generally to signify "a small pimple, pustule or boil" anywhere on the body, as does Alexander (1951) who adds that it was often used "contemptuously of a person"; Shakespeare uses the word metaphorically in *Othello*: "I have rubbed this young quat almost to the sense" (Act V, Sc. I).

queecer *n.* the wood-pigeon (Timmins, 1889).

queeser *n.* see **queecer**.

Queslett *n.* area of Birmingham; like Oscott, this once was one of the hamlets of the manor of Perry (see **Perry Barr**). It appeared as Quieslade in the sixteenth century and is derived from the Middle English words 'queest', meaning a wood pigeon, and 'slade', denoting a valley. Thus Queslett is the valley of the wood pigeons.

quiddle *vi.* to chew, chomp or munch food slowly in the mouth.

Quieslade *n.* see **Queslett**.

quilting *n.* a beating or thrashing EG "I gi'im a right quiltin', yo should've sin it"; "the metaphor is from the many colours of the patchwork quilt" (Northall, 1896).

quine *vi.* see **qwine**.

quining *n.* see **qwining**.

Quinton *n.* area of Birmingham; with a ridge which is 731 feet above sea level, Quinton is the highest built-up district in modern Birmingham. According to Nash (1781), the name is derived from the Roman sport of quintain. Rosser (1998) points out that a site on Ridgeacre Road West may have been suitable for the sport, and that it was in line with the Roman fort at Metchley in Edgbaston. Another origin for the name was proposed by T. W. Bunting. He felt that it derives from the Latin words Quintana Via, meaning a road which crossed a Roman camp. A third suggestion ascribes the name to the Latin word 'quintana', signifying the market of a camp formed on a 'quintos'. It is difficult to find hard evidence to sustain these assertions. There is no indication of a Roman military road near to Quinton. Indeed, the only Roman road at all which passed through Birmingham was Icknield Street (also known as Ryknield Street), and the absence of a military road to Quinton weakens the case for a Latin origin for the name. Another suggestion is that forwarded by W. E. Hardwick, who states that Quinton may be derived from the Old English words 'cwene', meaning woman, and 'tun', indicating a farmstead. There is also the possibility that 'Quin' arises from the Old English word 'cwen', denoting queen. Yet given that there is no evidence of a queen holding land locally it seems best to explain Quinton as meaning the settlement of a woman. To make matters even more complicated, the district was also known as Ridgeacre. Thus, it was given as Rugacre in a document from 1271. Lastly, it should be pointed out that like Cotteridge, the name of Quinton was usually preceded by 'the'. Accordingly, in 1774 Ambrose Foley of Quyntain in the parish of Halesowen signed a bond in favour of Robert Moore of Birmingham. This is an important document since it predates Nash and lends weight to Margaret Gelling's belief that Quinton is a relatively late name which does refer to "running at the Quintain." However, this sport does not relate to the Romans, rather it was an activity which continued in the countryside until the nineteenth century.

quirk *n.* see **qwirk**.

quitch *n.* couch-grass, *Triticum repens* (Northall, 1896).

qwine *vi.* to line a well with stones.

qwining *n.* the stone lining of a well.

qwirk *n.* a small piece of leather forming part of the finger on a glove.

R

race *n.* a stick EG "A race of ginger" (Shakespeare, *The Winter's Tale*, Act IV, Sc. II), also applied to "the heart, liver, and lights of the pig, lamb, sheep, or calf" (Northall, 1896).

raddle *n.* red ochre; oxide of iron, much used for branding sheep, or for raddling cottage floors and doorsteps, also *n.* rouge, often used contemptuously EG "She was up to 'er eyes in raddle" (Rhodes, 1950). Until the late 1960s and early 1970s, it was common to see older women raddling the front door step and thereby showing their respectability.

ragged-arsed *adj.* used to describe kids who were brought up poor and had no decent clothes.

raggle *vi.* to manage; to get by EG "With a bit of coal, and a loaf of bread, I can raggle along" (Skeat, 1876).

rag-stone *n.* a large grinding stone used for sharpening scythes and other agricultural tools.

rain bat *n.* a beetle; according to superstition, killing one brought rain.

raisty *adj.* putrid; fetid; rank.

ramel *n.* rubbish (Timmins, 1889); more especially applied to rubbish which is occasioned by the employment of bricklayers" (Northall, 1896).

random-shot *n.* "a wild young fellow" (Northall, 1896).

ran-piked *adj.* see **raunpiked**.

rant *vt.* to steal by force; to mug; according to Northall (1894), "boys used this term to signify forcible appropriation of marbles or other toys," and it was also used to indicate "forcible and undue familiarities with females," or 'rape'.

rap *vt.* to exchange; to swap (Northall, 1896).

rattle *vi.* to chatter; to gossip EG "They've bin rattlin' since nine o'clock."

rattletraps *npl.* small objects; small movable items; "sometimes spoken of worthless articles" (Northall, 1896).

raum *vi.* see **rawm**.

raunpiked *adj.* according to Marshall (1796), this was "provincial of *raven-picked*; stag-headed, as an old overgrown oak; having the stumps of boughs standing out of its top."

ravelment *n.* a mess; an entanglement; a general state of confusion or untidiness (Northall, 1896).

ravin *adj.* starving; hungry (Wise, 1861); ravenous (Alexander, 1951) EG "I met the ravin lion when he roared" (Shakespeare, *All's Well That Ends Well*, Act III, Sc. II).

ravlings *npl.* "raw, untwisted threads, drawn, fingered, or worn out of silk or cloth" (Northall, 1896).

rawm *vi.* to strain; to reach awkwardly EG "Don't you rawm over the table like that, you'll do yerself an injury" (Northall, 1896)..

rawpse *vi.* to stretch; to reach higher or further than is comfortable.

Rea *n.* Birmingham river immortalised in verse by Jeffrey (1868):

> No River, Sea, nor Afric's Bey,
> For grandeur equals thee, my Rea.

Alongside Birmingham itself, Rea is one of the oldest place names in Birmingham;

according to Gover, Mawer and Stenton (1936), the name is derived from the Middle English 'atter ee' (at the water). Due to a process known as metanalysis, the 'r' from 'atter' was shifted onto the 'e', becoming 'atte re'. Thereafter the word 'atte' fell out of use, leaving the 're' on its own. The result is that River Rea actually means 'river at the river'. The words 'Rea' and 'ray' are homophonous in Brummagem speech, which means they are pronounced in exactly the same way - as is the case with many words that have an 'ea' in their written form. Thus Weaman Street in the old Gun Quarter of Birmingham's city centre is Wayman Street, tea becomes 'tay', peas are pronounced 'pays' and speak sounds like 'spayk'. Paul Baker is an expert on the music of the renaissance and notes that in the second verse of the ballad *The Great Galleazzo* (1588) the word 'sea' is clearly intended to rhyme with the word 'stay': "Great is the number of ships upon the sea: And their privison wonderfull, But Lord thou art our stay." Ian Glaze, however, notes that the most famous example of the 'ay' sound is in Psalm 23 in the King James Authorised Version of the Bible: "Yea though I walk through the valley of the shadow of death . . ."

rec *n.* public park; a piece of land reserved for public recreation; shortened form of 'recreation ground' EG "I'll see y' over the rec later, alright?"

recklace *n.* see **ricklace**.

reckling *n.* the last-born; the last of a litter (Timmins, 1889).

reddle *n.* see **raddle**.

Rednal *n.* area of Birmingham; in Arthur B. Lock's *The History of King's Norton and Northfield Wards*, he explains that Wreodanhale appeared in 730 in the *Cartularium Saxonicum*. Its meaning is given as the 'halh' (meadow or pasture) of someone called Wreoda. However, 'halh' means either hollow or sheltered place, whilst there is no other evidence that a person called Wreoda actually existed.

reechy *adj.* smoky; black with smoke; unclean (Alexander, 1951) EG "Her richest lockram 'bout her reechy neck" (Shakespeare, *Coriolanus*, Act II, Sc. I), "You'll mek them clothes reechy if you 'ang 'em in the kitchen" (Northall, 1896).

reesty *adj.* see **raisty**.

rennpiked *adj.* see **raunpiked**.

resurrection pie *n.* a pie made with bones which have had most of the meat taken off them; see also **bony pie**.

riband *n.* ribbon (J. Alldritt).

rick *vt.* to wrench, twist or sprain EG "I've ricked me ankle".

rickas *n.* see **ricklace**.

ricklace *n.* local term for the polyanthus flower, apparently a corruption of the Latin 'auricula'. Raven (1978) suggests that the word may be derived from "the expression of secrets or confidences as indicated in the word 'auricular', e.g. word in the ear."

ricla *n.* see **ricklace**.

rid *vt.* to destroy EG "The red plague rid you" (Shakespeare, *The Tempest*, Act I, Sc. II).

riddle *vt.* to sieve.

riddliss *n.* a conundrum or puzzle; a corruption of 'riddle' (Rhodes, 1950).

Ridgeacre *n.* area of Birmingham now known as Quinton; according to Rosser (1998), within living memory older Quintonians pronounced Ridgeacre as Rugacre; there is no doubt that Ridgeacre is made up of the Old English words 'hrycg', signifying a ridge, and 'aecer', meaning a plot of cultivated land; see also **Quinton.**

riffy *adj.* dirty; scruffy; flea-ridden; lousy or nitty; still in common use throughout the Birmingham area. J. R. Acland writes that this word appears in neither the Oxford English Dictionary or any slang dictionary. The nearest words in the OED, 'riff' (meaning a cutaneous eruption) and 'riff-raff' (meaning persons of no importance or social position), give a bit of a clue as to the origins and deeper meaning of the word, but it is a mystery why the word has such a localised usage.

rile *vi.* to romp, roll about or fidget; apparently from the Old French word 'roeler' (to roll), also *n.* a fidget; an active or noisy child EG "'Er's a right rile, 'er is, fer such a littl'un" (Skeat, 1876).

ringy *n.* a game of marbles; when playing, the one shooting at the ring had to "knuckle a line at a fixed distance from it" (F. Lamb, *Birmingham Weekly Post*, Oct. 4 1924).

riz *pa p.* risen; gone up in price EG "The bleedin' butter's riz again!" (Skeat, 1876).

robble *n.* a tangle; a mess, also *vt.* to tangle.

rocks *npl.* children's sweets; see also **cuck-cucks** and **sucks.**

roded *adj.* streaky EG "I'll 'ave a pound o' roded bacon".

rodney *n.* a lazy person; a waster (Rhodes, 1950); Northall (1894) suggests that this word was also used to refer to "a helper on canal paths; the one that opens the locks."

rofe gen *bsl.* 4/- in old money (Harris).

rofe yennups *bsl.* 4d in old money (Harris).

roil *vi.* see **rile.**

roomthy *adj.* roomy; spacious EG "It's roomthy in 'ere, ennit?" (Skeat, 1876).

roozle *n.* a black mood; or "wretchedness of mind" (Northall, 1894), usually in pluralised form EG "'Er's got the roozles again."

ropes *npl.* the entrails of a sheep; from the Anglo-Saxon 'roppas' (bowels; entrails).

Rotton Park *n.* area of Birmingham; the Rotton family was long-established in the Birmingham area – in 1225, a William de Rothon had lands in King's Norton, and in 1601 it was Ambrose Rotton who built Stratford House on Camp Hill, yet there is no evidence linking the family with the district. The earliest mention of Rotton Park is from 1307 when the Warwickshire Assize Roll has an entry for poachers in the "Parcus de Rotton juxta Birmingham" – Rotton Park near Birmingham.

rough-house *n.* an aggressive and uncouth person.

rowings *npl.* refuse from a threshing machine.

Rowley Rag *n.* a local term for the form of hard igneous rock found in the area and used for paving and road making; "in addition to coal, ironstone, limestone and clay, the Midlands yielded a fifth important mineral which proved crucial to industry in the eighteenth and nineteenth centuries . . . the Rowley hills [from where it was quarried] are still scarred by two hundred years spent working the seam" (reported in *Metro*, 3 May 2001, and noted in *Showell's Dictionary*, 1885).

roxy *adj.* over-ripe; very soft; almost rotten (Northall, 1896).

rub-a-dub *n.* local pub; see also **glue pot**.

rubbage *n.* rubbish; waste matter EG "laying rubbage at the Cocke 1s" (Town Book,1671), "levelling rubbidge at Cocke well 2d" (Town Book, 1678).

rubbidge *n.* see **rubbage**.

Rubery *n.* area of south Birmingham; first mentioned as Robery Hills in 1650, the name is derived from the Old English words 'ruh', denoting rough, and 'beorg', indicating a hill or mound; the word hill was added later when folk had forgotten that Rubery already included the word 'beorg'.

ruck *vt.* to crumple or crease EG "Cawn't ye sit deawn? Y're rucking me geawnd" (Rhodes, 1950).

ruckle *vt.* see **ruck**.

ruckus *n.* a fight or brawl EG "'E'd got into a bit of a ruckus at the Queen's."

Rugacre *n.* see **Ridgeacre**.

ruggle *vi.* to struggle, wriggle determinedly or put up a spirited fight.

S

sad *adj.* heavy, esp. said of bread (Skeat, 1876).

saded *adj.* satiated, glutted or full-up, also 'tired', as in the expression 'sick 'n' saded' EG "I'm sick 'n' saded o' my job."

sad-shop *n.* bakery (Palmer, 1979) EG "in Walmer-Lane steel trusses made, in Litchfield-st. a sad-shop" (from an old Brummagem ballad entitled *Birmingham Jack of All Trades*, c.1830).

saft *adj.* stupid; half-witted; unintelligent; a corruption, perhaps, of 'soft' EG "'E's saft in the 'ead, 'e is." Although still in use among older Birmingham speakers, this term is perhaps more common in the Black Country.

said *adj.* obedient; dutiful; servile EG "I do wish you'd be said" (Rhodes, 1950).

saided *adj.* see **saded**.

Saint Monday *n.* Palmer (1976) defines this as "the practice of absenting oneself from work on Mondays," though on what grounds seems unclear: "Workmen in the area into late Victorian times insisted on keeping up Saint Monday: the right to take a holiday on Mondays." A report on the Birmingham metal trades in 1864 complains about this custom: "An enormous amount of time is lost, not only by want of punctuality in coming to work in the morning and beginning again after meals, but still more by the general observance of 'Saint Monday', which is shown in the late attendance or entire absence of large numbers on that day. One employer has on

Monday only about 40 or 50 out of 300 or 400, and the day is recognised by many masters as an hour shorter than others at each end." Customs such as this, Palmer goes on to suggest, were "a conscious or unconscious protest against the clock," but Saint Monday (or 'Fuddling Day', as it was alternatively known) appears to have been as unpopular with wives as it was with factory owners. It reduced the family income and happened to coincide with 'execution day' (wash day), thus causing much marital strife. In the following lyrics from complementary Brummagem street ballads, for example, the husband criticises wash day, and the wife, in turn, criticises Saint Monday:

> The sky with clouds was overcast, the rain began to fall,
> My wife she beat the children and raised a pretty squall.
> She bade me with a frowning look to get out of the way;
> The devil a bit of comfort's there upon a washing day.
> *Chorus*
> For it's thump, thump, scold, scold, thump, thump away,
> The devil a bit of comfort's there upon a washing day.
> St Monday brings more ills about, for when the money's spent,
> The children's clothes go up the spout, which causes discontent;
> And when at night he staggers home, he knows not what to say;
> A fool is more a man than he upon a fuddling day.
> *Chorus*
> For it's drink, drink, smoke, smoke, drink, drink away,
> There is no pleasure in the house upon a fuddling day.

saloop *n.* "a greasy-looking beverage, formerly sold on stalls at early morning, prepared from a powder made of the root of the *Orchis mascula*, or Red-handed Orchis" (Hotten, 1887) EG "in Temple-st. I sold saloop, in Queen-st. a cork-cutter, in Colmore-st. I kept a shop, Sold bacon, cheese and butter" (*Birmingham Jack of All Trades*, c.1830).

Saltley *n.* area of Birmingham; derived from the Old English words 'sealh', which means willows, and 'leah', indicating a clearing, Saltley means the clearing among the willows. The earliest record of Saltley is in a grant from William, son of Nicholas of Saluteley, to William Smith of Erdintone of the moiety (half) of his lands. Dating from the late thirteenth century, it was followed in 1322 by Joan Wrax releasing lands in Salutleye to Henry le Earl.

Saluteley *n.* see **Saltley**.

Salutleye *n.* see **Saltley**.

sarbot *n.* see **sarbut**.

sarbut *n.* a man sent round by the breweries to mingle with customers in public houses and ensure that the right brands were being served; rudely known as a 'bogie' or 'nark'. The same word was also used in the mid-nineteenth century to denote a tell-tale, gossip or busybody. During the late 1860s a poem entitled *Birmingham*, as well as a series of pamphlets (*Brum 1-6* and *Brum: A Parody*) were published under the pseudonym of Old Sarbot, and the expression "Old Sarbot told us" was commonly used as the equivalent of the modern colloquial evasion "a little bird told me" (Rhodes, 1950).

sarment *n.* a sermon (Timmins, 1889).

sarnie *n.* see **sarny**.

sarny *n.* sandwich (R. Phipp).

Satan *n.* a large defused German bomb used as a collecting box for the Spitfire aircraft fund in Birmingham during World War II.

sated *adj.* see **saded**.

saucepand *n.* saucepan (J. Alldritt).

saucepan-lids *n.* children; kids.

sawney *n.* see **sawny**.

sawny *n.* idiot or simpleton; a variant of 'zany'; "apparently the 'sawny' was the merry-andrew who accompanied a quack doctor or travelling dentist" (Rhodes, 1950).

say *vi.* to urinate (Northall, 1894).

scawt *vt.* and *vi.* to kick; to hit with the foot; see also **fissle**.

scour *n.* the shallow part of a river or stream (Northall, 1896).

scouse *vt.* to harry or drive EG "Scouse them dogs out" (Northall, 1896).

scout *vi.* to field at cricket.

scrage *vt.* see **scraze**.

scrat *vi.* to scrabble around for money; to scrape together as much money as possible during hard times EG "'Er's allus scrattin' since old Joe lost 'is job."

scratchings *npl.* pork rind; "the refuse left when the pig's leaf is boiled down to lard" (Skeat, 1876); now in widespread use.

scrawly *adj.* thin and tangled, as corn (Marshall, 1796).

scraze *vt.* to graze, scrape or scratch the outer surface of the skin EG "I've scrazed me knee."

screwton-Newton *n.* a bad mood; the miserables (Northall, 1896) EG "'Er's got the screwton-Newtons again."

scrobble *n.* a tangle.

scrump *n.* an apple (Northall, 1894), also *vi.* to steal apples from private orchards EG "We allus went a-scrumpin' in the summer."

seastorn *n.* a tank for holding water or other liquid. A variant of 'cistern' (Hoddinott and Nikitas).

seen *vt.* saw; *pa t.* of 'see' EG "I sin 'im yesterday" (Upton, Sanderson and Widdowson, 1987).

seg-bottomed *adj.* "rush-bottomed, as in a seg-bottomed chair" (Northall, 1896).

Selly Oak *n.* area of Birmingham; stories are told of how an unfortunate woman called Sarah or Sally was condemned as a witch and killed in this district. An oak stake was driven through her heart and where she was buried an oak tree grew – or else she was hung from an oak tree and buried beneath it. This became known as Sally's Oak and the district name then arose. Certainly there was an oak tree in Selly Oak. It stood at the junction of Bristol Road and Harborne Lane and was planted about 1830 by John Rodway, the owner of Selly Oak House. Cut down in 1909, this great tree did put the 'oak' in Selly Oak, but whoever she was, poor Sally did not give her name to the area. Instead, it is derived from the place name Escelie, the Norman rendering of the Old English 'scelf-leah'. Like Bartley, Weoley and Northfield village, Escelie was one of the original Old English settlements in the parish of Northfield and it means the clearing on the 'scelf' – the dead flat land – and there are several such areas in Selly Oak. This interpretation is much stronger than that which derives Selly from 'selwe leah', meaning hall in the clearing, or another which explains that Selly means salt and is thus the salt way.

Selly Park *n.* area of Birmingham; in the nineteenth century, Selly Park Farm was actually in Weoley, at the junction of Weoley Park Road and Gibbins Road. However, the modern district lies to the east and is cut through by the Pershore Road. To the west it merges imperceptibly into Bournbrook, to the south it is cut off from Stirchley by the Bourn, to the east it is marked off by the River Rea, and to the north its limit with Edgbaston is the Bourn Brook; see also **Selly Oak**.

set *vt.* to let; to grant to a tenant EG "ye barne and croft which Mr Jennens is tenant to, shall be set to ye Usher of the Free School under a rent proportionable to others after the expiration of the present lease" (Order of the Governors, *King Edward's School Records* Vol. II, 10 April 1765).

setlass *n.* a thrawl for barrels; "a platform, or ledge of bricks or tiles, around a cellar, on which to place barrels" (Northall, 1896).

settlas *n.* see **setlass**.

settle *n.* a long wooden seat with arms and a high flat, solid back; from the Anglo-Saxon 'setl'; still in common use.

set-to *n.* a fight or brawl EG "'E 'ad a bit of a set-to with the gaffer."

shacklety *adj.* shaky; rickety; unstable.

shaggy *n.* a ghost, spectre or apparition EG "Watch out or shaggy'll get yer" (D. Adams).

sharabang *n.* a vehicle; from the French char-a-banc.

Shard End *n.* area of Birmingham; the earliest mention of Shard End comes in a document from 1334 when it is written as 'le Sherd'. Joe McKenna feels that Shard End is taken from the Old English word 'sceard' and may mean a gap or pass in the Forest of Arden. This seems more likely than the suggestion that Shard is derived from the Middle English 'sherd' which denoted an isolated part of a manor. In this case, Shard End was a remote part at one of the ends of the manor of Castle Bromwich.

share *n.* a short wooden sheath stuck in the waistband to rest one of the needles in whilst knitting (Skeat, 1876).

shaver *n.* "a sharp youth" (Northall, 1894).

shelacking *n.* see **sherricking**.

Sheldon *n.* area of Birmingham; the Domesday Book has no mention of Sheldon, although it does include an entry for Machitona. This became Mackadown and means the settlement ('tun') of a person called Macca. It is obvious that this manor later became that of Sheldon. The entry of the Domesday Book states that Machitona was held from Turchill by Alnod. In 1221 the lord of Makinton was

Ansel de Scheldon. The inclusion of the French 'de' in his name suggests that Ansel took his name from part of the manor where there was a 'scelf' or shelf hill. If this is the case, Sheldon shares the same derivation as Selly. The 'don' part of the name may be from the Old English word 'dun' signifying hill.

shell *vt.* to procure earnings or tips; a term used by Birmingham coachmen in the nineteenth century. According to a report in *Metro* (10 April 2001), coachmen "were often extrovert characters who were much admired by the public and used all kinds of tricks to amuse passengers. One man could throw his whip to twist around the stem of a man's pipe and remove it from his mouth. Descending Hagley Hill [on the Hagley Road coaching route between Birmingham and Kidderminster], the drivers prided themselves on being able to lasso a duck from the marshy ground around them and land it on the lap of a very surprised box-seat passenger." However, not all passengers were enamoured of these antics, and coach drivers often had to resort to other means to extract tips. The majority of a coachman's income was earned from tips, and the practice of extracting them from reluctant passengers - known as 'kicking' or 'shelling' - involved the coachman approaching passengers with his hand outstretched, saying: "I am leaving you now, Sir."

shellalaking *n.* see **sherricking**.

sherlaking *n.* see **sherricking**.

sherricking *n.* a firm reprimand, warning or admonishment EG "I gave 'im a darn good sherrickin'." Since 'to coat' someone also means 'to give someone a ticking-off' (EG "I gave 'im a good coatin'"), it appears that sherricking, shelacking, sherlaking and shellalaking are all variants of the word 'shellac', a spirit varnish (D. Evans, and D. Whyle).

shimmy *n.* a shirt or blouse (Skeat, 1876); a corruption., perhaps, of 'chemise'.

shine *vt.* to steal, esp. apples (Northall, 1894).

shindy *n.* a row; an argument or quarrel (Northall, 1896).

shiny-bat *n.* the common garden-beetle (Northall, 1896).

shisn *pron.* see **hern**.

shive *n.* a slice EG "It is easy to steal a shive of a cut loaf" (Shakespeare, *Titus Andronicus*, Act II, Sc. I).

shog off *interj.* go away EG "Will you shog off? I would have you solus" (Shakespeare, *Henry V*, Act II, Sc. I), and "Shall we shog? The king will be gone from Southampton" (Shakespeare, *Henry V*, Act II, Sc. I); appears to be derived from the Welsh word 'ysgogi' (to jolt).

short-arse *n.* a short person; still in common use.

shovel-board *n.* a part of the table marked out for the game of shove ha'penny; "a portion of the table in some of the Warwickshire public-houses is still marked out as the shovel-board, upon which a coin is jerked with the open hand to a given mark, the winner being the person who jerks it nearest. A tradition exists in Stratford that Shakespeare used to play shovel-board at the Falcon" (Wise, 1861).

shrammed *adj.* cold; frozen EG "Stick the fire on, I'm shrammed."

sick 'n' saded *adj.* see **saded**.

sideboards *npl.* side-whiskers; sideburns EG "'E en't 'alf got a whoppin' pair o' sideboards on 'im, en't 'e?" (Upton, Sanderson and Widdowson, 1987).

sidespurns *npl.* the spreading roots of trees; an old agricultural provincialism (Marshall, 1796).

siden *adj.* crooked, bent or bowed.

sigh *vi.* to waste; to dissipate or diminish, as in the *phrasal verb* **sigh away** (fade away) EG "'Is powk's a sighin' away now."

sile *vt.* to quench or slake EG "D'yo think I'm a silin' me thaerst with tha?" (Squiers, 1916, p.3).

sink *n.* a cesspool; a pit for collecting sewage (Kenington, 1878).

skanky *adj.* a modern word used by youngsters to denote something horrible EG "It was really skanky. I didn't like the place at all."

skewiff *adj.* crooked; awry; not straight; now in widespread use.

skew-whiff *adj.* see **skewiff**

skewwiff *adj.* see **skewiff**.

skim-dick *n.* a type of cheese made from skimmed milk (Northall, 1896).

skimmington *n.* according to Tomkinson (1893), this was a "rough play got up for the annoyance of unpopular individuals." It usually consisted of some kind of a procession, in which likenesses of the offending persons were carried through the village or town accompanied by "the beating of tin kettles and other discordant noises," and it appears that skimmingtons were typically concluded with the ritualised burning of the effigies.

skinner *n.* betting terminology for a good result for a bookie.

skinny *adj.* mean; tight EG "'Er's dead skinny, 'er is."

skip-pan *n.* a dustpan.

skraze *vt.* see **scraze**.

skrinch *n.* see **skrinsh**.

skrinsh *n.* a very small amount; "the smallest possible portion of anything" (Northall, 1894).

slack *n.* fine coal rubble. Poorer Brummies were often sent to buy slack and not coal.

slacken-twist *n.* a dawdler; an idler (Northall, 1896).

slade *n.* "a tract of land which bears evidence of an ancient landslip (slide), hence the vale at its base" (Northall, 1896).

slan *n.* the sloe, *Prunus spinosa*; from the Anglo-Saxon 'slan' (sloes).

slang *n.* a tent used for performances by mummers (actors in a folk play) EG "Let's 'ave two pennorth at the slang," also *n.* a watchchain (Rhodes, 1950), and *adj.* long and thin, as in 'a slang field' or 'a slang room' (Northall, 1896).

slaumsey *adj.* maudlin, esp. when in a half-drunk state; see also **blindo, blotto, bob-howler, canned, kaylied, lagging, market-peart, mopped** and **palatick**.

sleck *n.* slack or small coal.

slommick *vi.* to slouch; to shuffle or walk in a slovenly manner (M. Baylis), also *n.* a dishevelled, unkempt or generally untidy person (Skeat, 1876).

slommicky *adj.* slovenly; dishevelled (Northall, 1896, and Rhodes, 1950).

slommock *vi.* see **slommick**.

slommocky *adj.* see **slommicky**.

slommuck *vi.* see **slommick**.

slommucky *adj.* see **slommicky**.

slop *n.* a policeman (Rhodes, 1950), also *n.* "a short white frock gathered into a band at the waist, worn instead of a coat" (Skeat, 1876).

sloughe *n.* see **sluff**.

slow-swift *n.* a dawdler or idler; one who is slow at work.

sluff *n.* the pool at the end of the midden that ran through the buildings; see also **suff**.

slug *vt.* to throw, esp. stones; "Slugging was a form of fighting practised in the [eighteen] nineties by gangs of peaky blinders, until stamped out by the cat o' nine tails. Also used for snowball fighting. Variant of 'slug', an irregular missile of lead used for loading blunderbusses" (Rhodes, 1950).

slummick *vi.* see **slommick**.

slummicky *adj.* see **slommicky**.

slummock *vi.* see **slommick**.

slummocky *adj.* see **slommicky**.

slut farthings *npl.* small, hard lumps of dough left in loaves of bread after baking; "an indication that the kneading had not been done properly" (Palmer, 1976); see also **lazy backs**.

Small Heath *n.* area of Birmingham; mentioned in 1461 as Small Hethe and in the 1511-12 Rental of Bordesley Manor as 'le Small Hethe on Coventry Wye', the word small means narrow and thus Small Heath was the Little Heath.

Smerrick *n.* pronunciation variant of Smethwick.

smoke-shop *n.* a tavern; a public house (Northall, 1896).

smother *n.* a topcoat or overcoat.

snap *n.* food EG "We'm gonna 'ave us some snap" (R. Phipp).

snape *vi.* see **sneep**.

snatch *n.* smell EG "The smoke from that chimbley in Montague Street's got a snatch as sticks in yer boko," also *n.* taste EG "This beer's bad; it's got a nasty snatch."

snead *n.* see **sned**.

sneap *vt.* to hurt; to cause pain.

sned *n.* the bent stick to which a scythe is attached or hung; "the handle of a scythe" (Northall, 1896); from the Anglo-Saxon 'snaed'.

sneep *vi.* to snub, disregard or shun.

snever *interj.* a contracted form of the popular Brummagem phrase 'so soon as ever'.

sog *n.* gooseberry (Northall, 1894); see also **goose-gog**.

sop *n.* a meal made from stale bread over which was poured the drainings of the tea pot. It was well known in the hard times of the 1920s and 1930s. The word is derived from the Old English 'sopp', meaning a piece of bread dipped in liquid; see also **dipper**.

sord *n.* see **sward**.

sough *n.* see **suff**.

soughe *n.* see **suff**.

sound *adj.* fine; okay; used in reply to the greeting "Alright?" by Irish Brummies in the 1970s and has now become a common reponse EG "Alright?" "Yeah, sound."

spade-bone *n.* the shoulder-blade; perhaps, as Marshall (1796) suggests, "the shoulder-bone of a horse or ox, was the *spade* of our ancestors."

spadge *n.* a slang term for a sparrow (Jim Hunt).

Sparkbrook *n.* area of Birmingham; in Old English 'spearca' meant brushwood and Sparkbrook may mean the brook where brushwood grows.

sparrow grass *n.* asparagus.

sparsy *n.* sixpence.

spavined *adj.* diseased; derived, according to Raven (1977), from the term applied to the diseased hockjoint of a horse EG "They'd have licked all the spikes on a spavined hedgehog" (from the mid-nineteenth century Midlands street ballad *The Darlaston Dog-Fight*).

specs *npl.* see **specks**.

specks *npl.* badly bruised apples and sometimes other fruit which were sold cheaply by greengrocers EG "Looking back I can see me queuing for the Tupp'nny crush on a Sat'day arternoon arter a look at ole mon Blackwell's, an' scroungin' some specks (fruit turning bad) ta stuff while we wus watchin' Buck Jones, Johnnie Mack Brown, or the Whisperin' Shadder" (Smith, undated).

Spiggit 'n' Fossit *n.* a wooden tap on a barrel; "the 'fossit' is the part inserted into the cask; the 'spiggit' is the plug" (Tomkinson, 1893).

spike *n.* workhouse EG "'Oo put the old man in the spike?"

spinney *n.* a clump, small plantation or grove (Marshall, 1796).

split-arse *n.* a derogatory term for a woman.

split-in-the-ring *n.* a boys' game, played thus: "a mark is made within a ring. Each player casts his spinning-top at this mark, attempting to manage the cast so that the top may strike fairly, and then spin without the ring; for, should the top remain within, it becomes the mark for the other players, and they attempt to split it with their own tops" (Northall, 1896).

splits *n.* a game of marbles; according to Northall (1896), "One player holds one of his own marbles, plus a marble of his opponent, over the back of his own head, and then drops both - his object being to separate the marbles as far as possible; for the opponent then shoots with his own marble at that of the first player, and wins it, if it be struck."

splod *adj.* flat-footed.

splother *vi.* to slaver; to dribble or let fall in small drops; usually applied to saliva trickling from a child's mouth "You got an 'ankerchief, our wench? The littlun's splotherin' again."

splotherer *n.* a person who sprays saliva when talking; see also **splother**.

spockle *vi.* to drizzle; to cover with droplets of water; Ann James write that spockle was often used by her grandmother when she was frying eggs and the fat had jumped EG "The fat's spockled me arm!"

spod *n.* a nerd; a person who has few friends and takes life a little too seriously.

spondulux *n.* money (Geoff Moore).

spoofer *n.* a person who makes things up; a teller of tall tales; mostly used lightheartedly with regard to children EG "You're a right spoofer, you are."

spool *n.* reel, esp. of thread (Upton, Sanderson and Widdowson, 1987); though 'bobbin' is the dominant variant in the north, and 'reel' is dominant in the south of England, 'spool is still quite commonly used throughout the Midlands.

spout *vt.* to pawn; to give as security for repayment of borrowed money (Palmer, 1979) EG "she is gone to her uncle's to spout a shawl for a shilling" (from the old Birmingham street ballad *Tally-man!*, c.1845-61).

sprack *adj.* quick; lively; alert (Northall, 1896).

sprat *n.* a threepenny piece.

sprightle up *ph v.* to cheer up; to liven up; "to be brisk, lively" (Northall, 1894).

springer *n.* betting terminology for a little-known horse put in a race to win.

spug *n.* see **spuggy**.

spuggy *n.* a sparrow (J. Alldritt).

spurn *n.* the main root of a tree (Marshall, 1796).

squab *n.* a sofa; a settee, also *n.* a small pigeon.

squash *n.* an unripe pea-pod (Wise, 1861).

squench *n.* thirst.

squilt *n.* a pimple; a pustule; a small reddened swelling on the skin.

squit *n.* nonsense (Northall, 1894); now more commonly used to refer to diarrhoea.

squitch *n.* garden weeds for burning; applied mainly to the weeds couch-grass and fiorin, which were known as 'quick grass' (due to the rapidity of their growth) in Elizabethan husbandry, but frequently used to describe any type of garden weed.

squob *n.* an old-fashioned sofa.

squoze *vt.* past tense of squeeze EG "'E squoze it."

stag-alone-y *n.* see **staglioney**.

staglioney *n.* a running game; according to Rhodes (1950), "a leader was chosen, and the other players scattered as he chased them. When caught, a player joined hands with the leader and the two chased the others, each one who was caught linking up in turn until the line encircled the last uncaught player. 'One, two, three, staglioney!' was the cry of the leader who began the game." Northall (1896) gives a slightly different and much more detailed account: "one boy is chosen stag, and runs after the other players, holding his clasped hands, palms together, in front of him, trying to *tick* any one he can. The first boy he touches joins hands with him, and they run together, and try to *tick* other players, and so form an ever-lengthening chain, the boys at each end of the chain ticking others with their disengaged hands, till all are caught - the first one caught becoming 'stag'. The other players may break the chain if they can, and ride the disengaged members back to the den. The stag's rhyme of warning when starting from den is *Stag-alone-y, my long pony, kick the bucket over.*"

stagger-bob *n.* a very young calf (Northall, 1896).

stail *n.* a long broom handle (Rhodes, 1950); a handle of any kind, as in "fork-stale and plow-stale" (Marshall, 1796); 'stail' is the more probable spelling, since the word appears to be a contracted form of either 'broom's tail', 'fork's tail', or 'plough's tail', etc.

stale *n.* see **stail**.

standy *adj.* unruly; disobedient.

stank up *ph v.* to dam; to restrict the flow of water EG "She had stanked up [dammed] the water, which was just beginning to trickle over her" (Palmer, 1976).

starchy *n.* a haughty or toffee-nosed person EG "'E's a right starchy, 'im".

starky *adj.* dry.

statty *n.* "statute fair of the kind held, for example, on Kings Norton Green" (Tennant, 1983).

statute-caps *npl.* woollen caps, "compelled to be worn by an Act in 1571, for the encouragement of the woollen trade" (Wise, 1861) EG "Well, better wits have worn plain statute-caps" (Shakespeare, *Love's Labour's Lost*, Act V, Sc. II).

Stechford *n.* area of Birmingham; in either 1300 or 1301, William of Berwode granted lands in Wodibromwis to Alice daughter of Adam Smith of Stichesford. Twenty-six years before, Stycheforde was described as a hamlet, whilst in 1345 it was spelt as Stycheforde. According to Victor Skipp, the name might mean the sticky ford, that is the ford with sticky soil. The district remained Stichford until the mid-nineteenth century, when the railway station was mistakenly named Stechford.

steelie *n.* ball-bearing used as a marble; see also **alley, alley taw, blood alley, cat's eye, dogger, dummox, French alley, glarny, glass alley, gobbie, marley** and **pot alley**.

steely *n.* see **steelie**.

steen *n.* an earthenware pot; derived, perhaps, from the Anglo-Saxon, since it appears to share the same root as the German word for stone ('Stein').

step-'n'-fetch-it *n.* a pole lathe: "a cord was fastened at the free end of the pole, round the wood and continued to the treadle; when pressed down this spun the wood round and when released was pulled back by the spring of the pole" (H. Hall, *Birmingham Weekly Post*, 4 Oct. 1924); according to Northall (1896) the same term was also applied in the old Warwickshire dialect to a person with an irregular gait; see also **hoppety-kick**.

stepper *n.* a treadmill EG "Now 'e's grindin' wind 'n' corn an' runnin' up the stepper at Warwick Gaol" (Exile, *Birmingham Weekly Post*, 1930).

Stercan lei *n.* see **Stirchley**.

Stichesforde *n.* see **Stechford**.

Stichford *n.* see **Stechford**.

stick *n.* a measure of beer, smaller than half a pint, which cost two pence in old money;

T. L. King writes that "if you had had half a pint and wanted it topping up you had a stick put in it," also *vt.* to bear; to withstand or endure EG "I can't bleedin' stick 'im, I can't."

stick-and-a-rag *n.* an umbrella.

stickler *n.* a jobsworth or pedant; a person who adheres stubbornly and unco-operatively to petty rules; someone who shows too much interest in minor details EG "'E's a stickler fer detail, 'e is," "Watch 'er – 'er's a stickler fer the rules, I'm tellin' yer"; still in common use.

stiff *n.* a complimentary ticket given by the management for displaying placards and bills EG "Shan't see yer termorra, Bill. Me and Liz got a stiff for the play."

stingo *n.* strong ale EG "May he always have plenty of stingo and pence, and Wilkinson's [a Midlands iron master, inventor and innovator] fame blaze a thousand years hence" (from *John Wilkinson*, an old street ballad popular in the late nineteenth century), "While old Thomas was drinking Sarah's health in Stingo, 'Carrol singers were heard at the door'" (Palmer, 1976); see also **blacking, legs 'n' wings** and **pungello**.

stinker *n.* a cold; flu EG "I aint 'arf copt a stinker an'all" (Squiers, 1916, p.1).

Stirchley *n.* area of Birmingham; according to Arthur B. Lock, Stirchley was first mentioned in the *Cartularium Saxonicum* of 730 as Stercan lei. In Old English 'styrk' meant a young bullock or heiffer and the name thus signifies the clearing or pasture for such animals. However, there are problems with this interpretation for the 730 reference actually relates to a 688 mention of a place in Wiltshire. Joe McKenna states that the original name was Streetly and that it meant the settlement, 'leah', by the Roman road – in this case the Icknield Street (Ryknield Street). Apparently at some stage in the eighteenth century, a map maker's 'ee' was mis-read and replaced with a 'u'. This led to Strutley and hence the Sturchley Street which was shown on Sherriff's Map of 1796. The shift to Strutley can be explained in this way. Certainly, Stretley Street is mentioned in an indenture of 1658 and local people continued to call the place Strutley into at least the late 1800s.

stitchwhile *n.* a moment; an instant; a jiffy EG "I'll be back in a stitchwhile" (Northall, 1894).

stock-axe *n.* a tool resembling a pick-axe, but having flat ends for cutting, one end being in a line and the other at right angles with the helve or handle.

stock-eekle *n.* the Wood-pecker; also common in the Worcestershire dialect.

Stockland Green *n.* area of Birmingham; some people feel that Stockland means where livestock were kept, but it is more likely that it is derived from the Old English word 'stoc', meaning an outlying farmstead. The 'green' would emphasise that it was a cultivated area in the midst of woodland or heathland. This interpretation would fit in with the position of Stockland Green which lies on the edge of the old manor of Erdington and close to the borders of the manor of Witton.

stopless *n.* see **oven stopliss**.

stopliss *n.* see **oven stopliss**.

strap-ail *n.* strap-oil; stirrup-oil, which, according to Tomkinson (1893), was "a mythical commodity, supposed to be retailed by a shoemaker, saddler, or leather dealer; its purchase usually being entrusted to some mischievous lad (probably on the first of April), who (if caught) receives, instead of oil, a few strokes from the tradesman's strap"; see also **pigeon's milk**.

straumpse *vi.* to loll about; to lounge or sprawl ' EG "Stop straumpsin' about in that chair 'n' get some fleekin' work done, will ya" (Tennant, 1983).

stretcher *n.* a tall tale; an unbelievable story.

strike *interj.* a contraction of 'God strike me down!' EG "Strike, that's as much as ther Villa" (Squiers, 1916, p.14), also *n.* "a bushel; the common term" (Marshall, 1796).

strommock *vi.* to dawdle; to walk in a slovenly or ungainly manner (Northall, 1894).

Strutley *n.* see **Stirchley**.

stumour *n.* wrong or misleading information.

Sturchley *n.* see **Stirchley**.

Stycheforde *n.* see **Stechford**.

sucks *npl.* children's sweets EG "Do you want some suck?"; see also **cuck-cucks** and **rocks**.

suff *n.* a sewer; a covered drain of any size EG "306 foote of plancks for the soughes" (*King Edward's Accounts*, March 1669), "Stay away from the suff or you'll get the fever!" In Scene I of Act V of Shakespeare's tragedy *Troilus and Cressida*, Achilles the great Greek hero is talking to a fellow army commander, Patroclus, when they are joined by Thersites, "a deformed and scurrilous" man marked out by his bad temper and biting invective. Foolishly, Patroclus enters into a slanging match with Thersites, who crushes his opponent with the most scathing crescendo of curses: "Now the rotten diseases of the suff, the guts-griping ruptures, catarrhs, loads o'gravel in the back, lethargies, cold palsies, raw-eyes, dirt-rotten livers, wheezing lungs, bladders full of imposthume, sciaticas, limekilns I' th' palm, incurable bone ache and the rivelled fee-simple of the tetter, take and take again such preposterous discoveries!" Tennant (1983) suggests that the word "may have been derived from 'surface' – i.e. the main drain taking away all the surface water"; see also **sough** and **soughe**.

sugar-babby bricks *npl.* cobbles (Tennant, 1983).

summat *pron.* something; an undefined thing EG "She got summat out of 'er bag," "Wasamarra with yo' bloody lot, 'ave ya' lost ya' tongues or summat?" (Smith, undated); still in common use.

Summer Lane *n.* area of central Birmingham; dating back to at least 1289, when Ranulph son of Walter of Barre released to Roger of the Somerlone a messuage in Wodibromwys and Erdintone, the name is derived from the fact that it was the main route to Perry and Walsall and could only be used in the summer.

summut *pron.* see **summat**.

suss out *ph v.* to find out; to discover EG "Ar, they soon sussed 'im out"; now in widespread use.

Sutton Coldfield *n.* area of north Birmingham; there is no doubt that Sutton means the south farmstead or village, but there is controversy as to which place Sutton was south of. In his *Antiquities of Warwickshire*, William Dugdale proposed that Sutton was south of Lichfield, but since then another interpretation has suggested that Sutton was so called because it is south of Cannock Chase. The addition of Coldfield is mentioned first in 1269 and is derived from the Old English words 'col' meaning charcoal and 'feld' signifying open land. Thus Sutton Coldfield is the south village where there was open land in which charcoal was produced. In the later Middle Ages, the charcoal burners operated to the west of the Warwickshire town on the heathland which stretched into Staffordshire.

swaddy *n.* a soldier; a corruption, perhaps, of 'squaddy'.

swank *n.* panache; swagger; used in the Midlands before being more widely adopted (Rhodes, 1950).

sward *n.* bacon rind (Northall, 1896).

sweet *adj.* great; excellent; superb EG " 'Ow's it gooin?" "Sweet, ar."

sweet-wort *n.* the liquor in which malt has been infused prior to the addition of hops (Tomkinson, 1893); also common in the Worcestershire dialect.

swell-mob *n.* "that class of pickpockets who, to escape detection, dress and behave like respectable people" (Partridge, 1972) EG "When the Swell-Mob comes down, we must look out for squalls, or they'll bolt with the Organ out of the Town-hall" (from an old street ballad entitled *The Cockney's Trip to Brummagem*, c.1876).

swell-mobsman *n.* criminal cant for cut-purses who dressed respectably; this term may not be Brummie in origin, but there is plenty of evidence to suggest that it was used widely in the area during the nineteenth century; see also **swell-mob**.

swilker *vt.* to spill or splash.

swill *vt.* to rinse; to wash lightly (Upton, Sanderson and Widdowson, 1987); variants such as 'rinsh', 'rense', 'sind' and 'stream' are common in other English dialects, but 'swill' still appears to be the dominant variant in the West Midlands.

swipes *n.* weak or inferior beer (Raven, 1977) EG "There's eightpence tobacco, and seven farthings swipes" (from the old Brummagem street ballad *How Five & Twenty Shillings Were Expended in a Week*).

swob *n.* a sailor.

swoddy *n.* see **swaddy**.

swopson *n.* a heavily-built woman; used in a humorous sense (Rhodes, 1950).

swyme *vi.* to feel giddy, dizzy or light-headed.

syke *n.* bacon; esp. common in the Stratford-upon-Avon dialect (Northall, 1894).

T

ta *interj.* thanks; the usual way to express gratitude in Brum.

tabber *vi.* to drum; to make a drumming noise; to tap a rhythm with the fingers.

tabor-and-pipe *n.* a musical instrument, or pair of musical instruments, consisting of a tabor, or tambourine, and a small pipe. The tabor was suspended from the left arm and beaten, or tabbered, with a small stick held in the right hand; the pipe was held to the mouth and played with the left hand simultaneously.

tachin-end *n.* a waxed thread made by a shoemaker with a bristle at each end instead of a needle and used primarily for sewing leather; pronunciation variant of 'attaching end'.

tack up *ph v.* to improve; to abate; to let up, esp. as in the weather.

taerter *n.* see **tater**.

tageous *adj.* tedious; troublesome; disobedient or naughty; according to Skeat (1876), "this points back to the old pronunciation of tedious as [taidius]."

tallit *n.* a hayloft.

tally-man *n.* although probably not Brummie in origin and common in many other dialects, tally-man was a well-known term amongst Brummies in the early twentieth century; "it refers to a door-to-door salesman who collects the price of his goods in instalments – with interest" (Palmer, 1979), as in the old Brummagem street ballad *Tally-man!* (c.1845-61):

> Pray Mrs. Ginger are you at home?
> Bawls out the Tally-man,
> No, Mr. Swindle, I'm not, she cries,
> And you must understand
> That call when you will my husband swears
> You shall not have a mag,
> Since you've turned rogue, you took me in,
> For your things are not worth a gag.

Tame *n.* a Birmingham river; from the Romano-British 'Tamesis' – the origin of which is uncertain but may indicate a dark river.

tan *vt.* to hit EG "I'll give yer such a tanning if you don't packirrup!"

tank *vt.* to hit, beat or thrash; see also **lamp**, **larrup** and **thrape**.

tanker *n.* a man employed specifically for the threshing of corn with a flail during harvest-tide.

tanna mana *n.* slang term for the 'pits' (cheap seats) in a picture house EG "There was another exit door just on the left inside the passage, but that was for the exclusive use of the patrons in the Stalls, the 'ninepennies', as was the front foyer the exclusive exit for the gallery patrons, the 'gods bobs'. We could not use either of these exits to force our illegal entry, but had to be satisfied with the pits, or the 'tanna mana'" (Smith, undated).

tant *vi.* to tempt or persuade EG "I must admit I was tanted, but I dain't do it."

ta-ra *interj.* goodbye; farewell; another popular form of address at parting in Brummagem is: "Ta-ra a bit."

tat *vi.* to collect second-hand goods, as a tatty-man (rag-and-bone-man) does EG "'E allus teks the 'oss 'n' cart out tattin' of a wick-day," also *n.* an item or items bought from a second-hand shop or car boot sale EG "'E brought back tons of tat from that car boot sale larst Sunday."

tater *n.* potato EG "Pd for plants and taters for Green wife to sett her garden with" (Poor Law extracts from overseers accounts at Great Barr, Staffordshire, 1759) and "A bot o' sheep's jimmy with baked taerters and taernips" (Squiers, 1916, p.6).

tatter *n.* see **tatty-man**.

tatty *adj.* old and shabby; of little value; no longer in pristine condition.

tatty-man *n.* a rag-and-bone-man; a person who collects and deals in second-hand goods.

tay-kettle-broth *n.* see **tea-kettle-broth**.

tea-kettle-broth *n.* bread and hot water with added butter, herbs, onions and salt.

teem *vt.* to pour (usually a cup of tea) EG "Teem us a cuppa".

tenchlee *n.* a green or stock-field, possibly Anglo-Saxon in origin. The earliest settlement in the Acock's Green area of Birmingham was at a small hamlet called Tenchlee, close to Whislow Meadow c.1275, though its name disappeared from the map in the later Middle Ages.

terrify *vt.* to damage or destroy EG "Them birds've bin terrifying me cabbages" (Skeat, 1876).

tettenal *n.* a small pear.

tewer *n.* a narrow passage EG "I want 'er as lives up the tewer" (Skeat, 1876).

T.H. *bsl.* 8d in old money (Harris).

that there, those there *dem. pron.* and *dem. adj.* pointing out people or things EG "all that there Tenemente and those theare Byldings and Gardeyns nowe in the tenure or occupation of the seid Thomas" (*The Records of King Edward's School*, 1565).

theirn *pron.* theirs; belonging to them; genitive (or *possessive adj.*) of 'they' (Skeat, 1876).

them *dem. pron.* and *dem. adj.* those, as in: "Which things?" "Them things over there!"

thessole *n.* see **es-hole**.

thief-in-the-candle *n.* a part of the wick protruding from the main portion, and causing the candle to burn unevenly; also common in the Worcestershire dialect.

thin-bottle *n.* a bottle of sterilised milk; in Birmingham sterilised milk comes in thin bottles and pasteurised in fat bottles.

this'n *dem. pron.* and *dem. adj.* literally 'this one' EG "Which one yo' arter?" "This'n."

Thomas *vi.* see **a-Thomasing**.

thone *adj.* damp and cold; "not thoroughly dry" (Marshall, 1796).

thrape *vt.* to hit, beat or thrash; see also **lamp**, **larrup** and **tank**.

threepenny hop *n.* a social dance (K. Carruthers).

three-straws *n.* a game of pitchback, which, according to Northall (1896), is played thus: "Three rows of earth, sand, &c., are placed in parallel lines about a foot and a half apart. Each player is careful not to step or descend upon these 'straws' when pitching over the boy who makes the back, lest he himself should be forced to take the other's place. The one that makes the back has several positions, which he takes up by turn, when the last player pitches and cries 'Foot it': (1) Both feet outside the first straw; (2) A foot on each side of the first straw; (3) Both feet inside; (4) Both feet between the first two parallel lines; (5) Both feet before the second straw, &c.

When the three straws are passed, and the one 'down' is told to 'foot it', he does so by placing one foot lengthwise against the other resting sideways, and then bringing the side-long foot, still sideways, in advance, and, lastly, setting the now rear foot beside, but in front of its fellow; and again makes the back. This goes on until the distance is so great that one leaper, less agile than his fellows, fails to reach the 'back', or steps over or on the last straw to do so, when he is 'down'. If the last player forgets to cry 'Foot it' at any time in the game, he himself goes 'down'. I imagine that the rows are called 'straws' because they are *strewn* or *strawn*. When the one 'down' has a foot on each side of the middle straw - a position which is called 'the fly' - each leaper must clear his back and the three straws. Should one tread on the first or last straw, or start from the space between straws *one* and *two*, or alight between straws *two* and *three* (this not always), he is 'down'. But, when the one that makes the back has advanced his position, each leaper is allowed to start from the space between the first and second straws. When the maker of the back has both feet over the third straw, it is allowable to leap from the space between straws *one* and *two*, or *two* and *three*. Sometimes the one 'down' does not continue to foot it further, but returns, step-by-step, to his original position before the first straw, should no leaper blunder meanwhile, when a new game is begun. The method adopted to determine which player shall make the back is to procure the same number of various lengths of straw, or blades of grass, as there are players. These are held by one player, usually with the visible ends even, and each player, in turn, selects any length he may fancy. The one that has the shortest length must make the back. If a previous game has been played, and one player has made the length throughout, he is exempt from the drawing."

thrial *n.* a group of three; used only in the game of cribbage, when three cards of the same denomination are played consecutively.

thrice-cock *n.* the old Warwickshire dialect word for a missel-thrush (Palmer, 1976).

throstle *n.* the thrush (Rhodes, 1950).

throwed *pa t.* and *pa p.* threw; thrown EG "'Er throwed summat at us," "'E's throwed it away." If a verb is regular, the past tense and past participle have an *–ed* ending EG "I clean*ed* the windows," "I have clean*ed* the windows." When the past tense and past participle do not end in *–ed*, the verb is irregular EG "I *spoke* to her yesterday," "I have *spoken* to her." In standard English, the transitive verb 'throw' is irregular EG "I *threw* it away," "I have *thrown* it away," but in the Brummagem dialect (as is the case with many other verbs) 'throw' is given a regular *–ed* ending; see also **drawed, knowed** and **learned**.

thrup'ny hop *n.* see **threepenny hop**.

thrussle *n.* see **throstle**.

thunderball *n.* the poppy; according to Northall (1894), 'thunderball' was a variant favoured in the dialects of surrounding areas: "It is believed by children that to pluck it will draw down the 'bolts of heaven' on them. Venus and Jove - or possibly Venus and Vulcan - seem to be in conjunction here."

tibbyhog *n.* local variant of 'bob-howler' (A. Sealey).

tiddlywink *n.* "A small public house licensed for the sale of beer, cider and tobacco" (Northall, 1896).

tig *n.* a game of chase when the youngster who is on has to catch and touch (tig) the others. "Tig, you're on!" is the usual cry when somebody has been caught.

tik *n.* credit EG "Give us tik, will yer?"

tip-cat *n.* an old Warwickshire children's game, which, according to Halliwell (1855) was played thus: "The *cat*, which is made of some very firm wood, pointed at both ends, resembles a small shuttle, but having the angles from the centre more acute, so that a smart and well-directed blow with a bat-formed stick shall cause it to rise from the ground, when the player endeavours by a second stroke to drive it as far as possible. This diversion has considerable resemblance to 'trap-ball', save that the cat in this game answers the double purpose of trap and ball." Northall (1896) adds: "when the striker has driven the *cat* to a distance, he gives the other player a chance to become batsman by allowing him a certain number of leaps from the cat towards the ring. Should the leaper succeed in reaching the ring by these leaps, he becomes batsman and the former holder must cast the *cat* . . . A ring is scored in the ground, and one player casts the *cat* towards it from a certain mark. Should the *cat* fall in the ring, and remain there, the batsman is 'out', i.e. must resign the bat. If the *cat* falls on the line of the ring, one tip and drive (called 'one pen'uth', pennyworth) only are allowed: if it falls entirely without the circumference 'three pen'uth' - three tips and three drives - are regular. The usual formula of the batsman - after the *cat* is cast - is 'Rise cat, turn cat, all the way along, and all outs wherever it goes', which allows of his placing the *cat* in any favourable position for the tip, or taking it from any hollow or inconvenient place into which it may fall. Should the one who casts the *cat* cry '*No* rise cat', &c., this advantage is forbidden. The game, in some form, is of world-wide fame, I believe: and is said to be pictured amongst the mural decorations of the ancient Egyptians." Tip cat was played widely in the back streets of Brum until the 1950s. It is also played in the Indian sub-continent. In the Pakistani Punjab it is known as 'gulee danda' and in Bangla Desh as 'tagore'.

tisiky *adj.* see **tissicky**.

Tissa *n.* see **Tyseley**.

Tisseleye *n.* see **Tyseley**.

tissicky *adj.* ill; unwell; sick EG "All the upset's made me feel a bit tissicky" (Hampson, 1936, p.6); see also **phthysicky**.

tittle-tattle *n.* idle gossip; chatter of little consequence or importance; rumour. Walker (undated) states that the etymology of this term is highly unusual since it joins the Norman 'tittle', meaning 'a small particle', with the Middle English 'tatalen', meaning 'to gossip'.

titty-babby *n.* a cry-baby.

tittymog *n.* a child frequently at the breast; according to Northall (1894), 'mog' or 'moggy' was, "in several counties, a term applied to a calf," and an alternative term for suckling was **lugtit**.

tizzicky *adj.* see **tissicky**.

tizzie *n.* sixpence.

token *n.* an omen or portent; a death-sign EG "I'm certain summut has come to my son, for I saw his token last night; it was a white dove flew out of the bed-curtains, and was gone in a minute" (Skeat, 1876).

Tom-and-Jerry *n.* a tavern; a public house (Northall, 1896).

tommy *n.* a snack or light meal; "provisions given to workmen in manufacturing districts, instead of money" (Northall, 1896).

tommy note *n.* see **tommy shop**.

tommy shop *n.* "the Truck Act of 1831 was an attempt to curtail the system by which workers were paid partly or wholly in tokens or credit notes [or 'tommy notes'], which could only be spent at company shops. These were known as *tommy shops*, and the goods they sold, often at inflated prices [and of inferior quality], as *tommy*. The last word is still occasionally heard, even today, with the meaning simply of *food*" (Palmer, 1979) EG "It is concerning Tommy shops, and the high field ruffian he pays you with a tommy note, you must have that or nothing" (from an old Brummagem street ballad entitled *The Tommy Note*, c.1817-27).

torpedo *n.* a small sugar-coated liquorice sweet shaped like a torpedo (Jim Hunt).

torpedo loaf *n.* a baguette; a long narrow loaf of white bread with a thick crust EG "I can see that van now, dark blue, with gold lettering on both sides and the rear, with a red back up, advertising BRADFORD'S BREAD & CAKES. In addition on the rear doors only was their Trade Mark, a red circle with gold dots on it representing the pimples on the bottom of their cottage loaves, small and torpedo loaves" (Smith, undated).

torril *n.* a person who looks weak, worn-out or exhausted (Northall, 1896).

tosheroon *n.* five shillings ('half a tosheroon' was equal to half a crown).

touch *vt.* to borrow; to obtain the use of EG "'E says, "I 'ope yo'll be happy," and touched me fer seven and a tanner" (Squiers, 1916, p.10).

traipse *vi.* see **trapse**.

tranklements *npl.* miscellaneous accessories or accoutrements (Northall, 1896); paraphernalia; oddments; trinkets (Rhodes, 1950).

trap *vt.* to leave, taken from the way greyhounds leave the traps in dog racing.

trapse *vi.* to ramble, stroll or wander slouchingly EG "He'd come trapesing from the garden" (Hampson, 1936, p.6), also *vi.* to walk EG "We 'ad to trapse it all the way back in the rain."

treepot *n.* a flower pot (B. Prettyman); Sheridan also calls flower pots 'bough pots' in *The School for Scandal*.

trencher *n.* a wooden platter (sometimes painted) for fruit c.1605 (Hoddinott and Nikitas).

trinamanoose *n.* any item that children are forbidden by their parents to touch (Northall, 1894).

trinklements *npl.* see **tranklements**.

troach *n.* "a kind of cough sweet common in early days. *Collins Dictionary* gives us 'troche' – another name for lozenge, which in turn is derived from 'trohiskos' (Greek) – a little wheel" (Tennant, 1983).

trollymog *vi.* to walk about heavily and aimlessly; Northall (1894) states that this was a particularly common term in Lichfield.

trots *n.* diarrhoea; also known as 'back door trots' (Tennant, 1983).

trussen *vt.* to place trust in; to have supreme confidence in something or someone EG "I wun't trussen him far as I could chock 'im."

tubthumper *n.* a cooper.

tum *n.* contracted form of 'stomach' EG "I've got a bit of a dicky tum."

tumberill barge *n.* see **barge**.

tuner *n.* a loom maintanance worker (Raven, 1977) EG "Tuner should tackle me loom, 'e'd rather sit on his bum" (from *Poverty Knock*, an old Brummagem street ballad popular during the nineteenth century).

tunkey *adj.* short and thick of build.

tunnelback *n.* a type of house EG "They've cleared whole streets of tunnelbacks, destroyed a neighbourhood, and shifted half the families right out to Chelmsley Wood" (from the ballad *Summer Lane*, sung by Mr Laurence 'Pummy' Rogers of Sheldon, Birmingham; collected by Roy Palmer, 20 July 1975). Back-to-backs predominated in Summer Lane, but tunnelbacks emerged from the 1870s as councils began to pass bye-laws regarding housing and which effectively banned back-to-backs. Builders still attempted to get as many houses as possible into a small space, so they developed long terraces which had narrow frontages with a front room, middle room and back kitchen (and a bedroom above each). The back kitchen and bedroom 'tunnelled back' into the yard of the house, hence the name. This type of dwelling can still be seen in Bournbrook, Alum Rock, Small Heath, Sparkhill and Stirchley.

tup *n.* a ram (Skeat, 1876).

tup'ny crush *n.* the queue for the cheapest seats at the Saturday afternoon showing in a cinema (Tennant, 1983) EG "Looking back I can see me queuing for the Tupp'nny crush on a Sat'day arternoon arter a look at ole mon Blackwell's, an' scroungin' some specks (fruit turning bad) ta stuff while we wus watchin' Buck Jones, Johnnie Mack Brown, or the Whisperin' Shadder" (Smith, undated).

tuppence all over *n.* a very close, cropped haircut.

turn-again-gentlemen *n.* the tiger-lily, *Lilium martagon* (Northall, 1896).

tussock *n.* a tuft of coarse grass; a sod (Skeat, 1876).

twang *n.* accent; the sound of someone's speech EG "'Er 'ad a bit of a West Country twang."

twiggen *adj.* wickered; made of or covered with basketwork, in use c.1615 (Hoddinott and Nikitas); with a wicker covering (Alexander, 1951) EG "But I'll beat the knave into a twiggen bottle" (Shakespeare, *Othello*, Act II, Sc. III).

twiggne *adj.* see **twiggen**.

twinter *n.* a two-year old animal c.1605 (Hoddinott and Nikitas).

twist *vi.* to cheat; to be deceitful EG "I copped 'im twistin' at cvards last night."

twister *n.* a cheat, a deceitful person.

twit *n.* a tell-tale, as in the children's rhyme: "Tell-tale twit, your tongue shall split, and all the little birdies will have a little bit."

twizzle *vt.* to intertwine or interweave; to twist or turn (Northall, 1896).

two 'n' a kick *n.* two shillings and sixpence (K. Jenks).

two-three *adj.* a few; some; several; an indefinite number or quantity EG "'E's got two-three more in 'is pockets" (S. Kay); see also **couple-a-three**.

Tyseley *n.* area of Birmingham; it is first recorded as Tisseleye in the Subsidy Roll of 1327 and would appear to mean the clearing made by a person called Tissa, but according to Margaret Gelling, the name might signify "the sacred grove of Tiw." As recalled in 'Tuesday', Tiw was the Old English god of war. If he is brought to mind in Tyseley, then it would push back the origins of the district to the early stages of the Anglo-Saxon settlement in Birmingham – perhaps to the seventh century. The naming of the place after a pagan deity could only have occurred at a time when the worship of the old gods was still carried on by a minority of the Old English (see also **Weoley**). However, if Tyseley does not originate from a sacred grove, then it would have emerged when Tissa made a clearing some time before the Norman Conquest of 1066.

U

um *n.* home EG "I'm gooin' um Monday wick," "When yo gerra mota car ole mon, you can come 'ere an' put it in that shed at the top of the gardin, until yo gu um again" (Smith, undated); also heard in the Worcestershire and Black Country dialects, though the variant 'wum' is slightly more common in these areas.

umber *n.* rubbish c.1630 (Hoddinott and Nikitas).

umming and arring *vi.* hesitating or dallying; taking a long time to decide EG "'Er's ummin' 'n' arrin' a bit, en't 'er?"; see also **iffing and offing** and **ivvering and ovvering**.

uncle *n.* see **uncle's**.

uncle's *n.* a pawnbroker.

unked *adj.* terrible; ghastly EG "'Is leg's an unked sight" (Skeat, 1876).

unthatched *adj.* hatless, also used to denote baldness (Old Sarbot, 1869).

urchin *n.* a hedgehog; "in *Venus and Adonis* Shakespeare calls the boar "urchin snouted," that is, with a nose like a hedgehog. The common notes on the passage say, "urchin, that is, sea-porcupine." But the word is the common term in Warwickshire and the midland districts for a hedgehog, which is so called in old works on natural history" (Wise, 1861) EG "Ten thousand swelling toads, as many urchins" (Shakespeare, *Titus Andronicus*, Act II, Sc. III).

urge *vt.* to provoke; to exacerbate or annoy EG "'Er don't 'alf urge us, some days" (Skeat, 1876).

us *possessive adj.* our; belonging to us EG "We 'ave us own tongue" (Upton, Sanderson and Widdowson, 1987); no longer in widespread use, but 'us' is still frequently used in place of 'me', as in "Gie it us will yer!"

uting *n.* see **yewtinge fatt.**

utingfatt *n.* see **yewtinge fatt.**

V

varges *n.* see **vergis.**

varsal *adj.* universal (Timmins, 1889); "so corrupted and yet it is used by our great poet, and the most frequent application of the word as a provincialism is precisely with the same adjunct - the *varsal world*" (Northall, 1896) EG "She looks as pale as any clout in the versal world" (Shakespeare, *Romeo and Juliet*, Act II, Sc. IV).

verdinyre *n.* see **vergis.**

vergis *n.* the acidic juice of crabapples or unripe fruit, used in cooking and for dosing animals c.1613 (Hoddinott and Nikitas); often used critically EG "That tastes as sour as vergis."

versal *adj.* see **varsal.**

W

wad *n.* a slice of cake EG "Fancy a cup o' tea an' a wad?" (R. Couling).

wag *vt.* to play truant EG "I wagged the afternoon off," "I was copped waggin' it"; still in common use among schoolchildren.

wagman *n.* truant officer.

walkathon *n.* a term first coined by the Birmingham radio station BRMB in order to publicise a long-distance walk across the city in aid of charity.

Walkerishethe *n.* see **Walker's Heath.**

Walker's Heath *n.* area of Birmingham; this district of King's Norton was first recorded as Walkerishethe in 1314 - twenty-six years later, a Richard le Walkere of King's Norton was noted in the Feet of Fines and it seems likely that his family gave its name to the heathland thereabouts.

walk-the-moon *n.* children's game: "One player is blindfolded, and stands astride. The other players cast their caps between his legs, from the front, and one cries 'Walk the moon!' He walks at pleasure, until he treads on a cap, when the others buffet its owner, who afterwards becomes 'Walker'" (Northall, 1896).

wallop *n.* beer EG "It was a cracking pint of wallop," also *n.* a heavy blow or sudden loud noise; see also the phrase **wallop, Mrs Cox.**

wallspring *n.* an old Warwickshire agricultural provincialism for "a cold, wet, springy, or spewy part of land" (Marshall, 1796).

Walmley *n.* area of the 'Royal Borough' of Sutton Coldfield, Birmingham; its name signifies a warm clearing and is best known for its association with the manufacturing Websters of Penn Hall.

wammel *n.* mongrel; an animal, esp. a dog, of a mixed breed; derived from the Old English 'hwaemelec' (Walker, undated); also common in the Black Country dialect.

wanteye *n.* a rope or band used to secure the load on a pack-horse's back c.1613 (Hoddinott and Nikitas).

wap *vt.* to hit EG "I'll gie yo such a wap if yer doan pack irrup!" Wap is from the Middle English word meaning to strike and is used in the poem *Patience*: "Bot at a wap hit here wax and away at another."

Ward End *n.* area of Birmingham; a family called Ward were recorded as living locally from the end of the thirteenth century, and this is more than likely how the name came into being; Ward End Hall was mentioned first in 1425, and it is obvious that the family owned land locally for a William Ward is noted as having an estate in the records of King Edward's School, whilst in 1590-1, a John Warde of Brymicham left lands and houses in Birmingham, Aston, Lytle Bromwich, Great Bromwich and Bordesley to his cousin.

Warstock *n.* area of Birmingham; according to Showell's *Dictionary of Birmingham*, Warstone Lane in Hockley took its name from the Hoarstone which was "supposed to have been an ancient boundary mark." Similarly, Warstock was recorded first in 1331 as le Horestock. 'Har' is thought by many to mean a boundary and it is believed that by about 1500, the 'h' had become a 'w' in the local dialect. However, the Old English word 'har' did not mean boundary, rather it signified hoary, grey or white with age. Thus the first part of Warstock is difficult to deduce, although stock means an outlying settlement – which Warstock was in relation both to Yardley and King's Norton.

Washwood Heath *n.* area of Birmingham; part of the manor of Saltley, Washwood Heath lies on the high ground above the valley of the River Rea. The eastern boundary of that manor was the Wash Brook, thus providing part of the name of Washwood Heath. According to A. D. Mills, in Old English a 'waesc' was a stream used for washing sheep or clothes. However, Margaret Gelling feels that 'waesc' may have the sense of 'land covered with water', as in The Wash. The earliest reference to the district is from 1454 when it was written as Wasshewode. This suggests that there was a wood above the Wash, whilst the reason for the addition of heath is apparent from J. Tomlinson's *A Map of Saltley Manor*, published in 1760. It shows that the greater part of Washwood Heath was uncultivated and thus heath or waste land. The only fields were to be found lying alongside the Rea and in the basin formed by the flowing of that river into the Tame.

wassail *vi.* to sing Christmas carols in the traditional Warwickshire manner; according to Palmer (1976), wassailing continued in Warwickshire, "particularly in the deep south of the county," till the early twentieth century. Savage (1923) comments: "The people . . . would wend their way by the light from a candle placed inside an improvised lantern, usually a swede, carved in the shape of a man's face, to the farm houses, and after knocking on the door would enter in, singing the following wassail carol":

> Wisselton, wasselton, who lives here?
> We've come to taste yer Christmas beer.
> Up thu kitchen and down thu hall,
> A peck of apples ull serve us all.
> Holly and ivy and mistletoe;
> Give us some apples and let us goo;
> Up with yer staocking, on of yer shoe,
> If yer ant got any apples, mony ull do.
> My carol's done, and I must be gone,
> No longer can I stay here.
> God bless you all, both great and small,
> And send yer a happy new year.

wassail bowl *n.* a bowl used by carol singers: "The drink in the bowl – and it has been suggested that the 'gossip's bowl' in *A Midsummer Night's Dream* was a wassail [or 'wassal'] bowl – was made of ale, nutmeg, ginger, toast, and roasted crabs or apples. It was sometimes known as 'lamb's wool'" (Palmer, 1976) EG "Carrol singers were heared at the Door. On its being opened, two tall Women entered, bearing between them a large Wassal Bowl, finely dress'd on the outside with Holly, Misseltoe, Ribbons, Laurustinus, and what other flowers could be had at that season" (from the reminiscences of Sarah Chandler, c.1759, published in Palmer, 1976); see also **wassail**.

Wasshewode *n.* see **Washwood Heath**.

wassin *n.* throat (J. Alldritt); from the Old English 'wasend' meaning 'gullet' (Walker, undated); also common in the Black Country dialect.

wassock *n.* see **wazzock**.

watcha *interj.* hallo; a common Brummie greeting; see also **wha'ppen**.

water bewitched *n.* weak tea (Rhodes, 1950).

wavelly *adj.* thin and flexible EG "The blade on this knife's a tad wavelly" (T. Jones).

wazzock *n.* an idiot or fool; often used affectionately EG "Yer great wazzock!"

weddergetter *n.* a ram let out for breeding (Marshall, 1796).

Wedgbury *n.* see **Wedgeberry**.

Wedgeberry *n.* Wednesbury EG "Colliers from Hampton and Bilston, likewise, and Wedgbury nailers are struck with surprise" (*A New Song on the Opening of the Birmingham and Liverpool Railway*, c.1837), also applied to Wednesbury-ware generally EG "Wedgeberry brass," and often used disparagingly EG "Wedgeberry trash"; first used c.1609 (Hoddinott and Nikitas).

weds-and-forfeits *n.* "this designation of a youthful amusement, better known under the name of *forfeits* only, is still in use, although the principal word is fast giving way" (Halliwell, 1855).

Weeley *n.* see **Weoley**.

weigh-jolt *n.* a see-saw (Northall, 1896).

Weleie *n.* see **Weoley**.

Weleye *n.* see **Weoley**.

wellygogs *npl.* wellington boots.

wench *n.* "a young maid; still used in its primitive sense as a term of endearment throughout the midland districts" (Wise, 1861) EG "Why there's a wench, come on and kiss me Kate" (Shakespeare, *The Taming of the Shrew*, Act V, Sc. II). In the Middle English poem *Cleanness*, probably written by the same author as *Sir Gawain and the Green Knight*, 'wench' is used for 'girl' and it appears to be derived from the Old English 'wencel', meaning 'child'. Unlike other parts of the country where the use of wench can be seen as derogatory and as implying a serving girl or a lusty woman from medieval times, in Brum and the Black Country it is a term of affection and respect. In particular, 'our wench' refers to an older sister - the one who acted as a little mother, minding and caring for her younger brothers and sisters, but having precious little time for herself.

Weoleg *n.* see **Weoley**.

Weoley *n.* area of Birmingham; this name is pronounced 'weeley', as was indicated in 1644 by a receipt signed by Susanna Marrist of Weelie Park in the parish of Northfield for a legacy under the will of Robert Glover. Better known as Weoley Castle, the place has an intriguing origin. Spelled as Weleye in 1264 and thereafter with variations such as Wheolig, Weoleg, Weleie, and Weeley, some accounts ascribe its derivation to the Old English words 'hweol', meaning a circle or wheel, and 'ig' or 'ey', signifying an island. Thus it would mean a round island. As proposed by Arthur B. Lock, the moated manor house of Weoley (the Castle) is in the valley of Stonehouse Brook, is surrounded by hills, and was on an island in the midst of a lake. This interpretation is plausible, but more likely is the suggestion that perhaps Weoley recalls a 'weoh' or 'wih', a heathen shrine in a glade or 'leah'. As Margaret Gelling has maintained, to the west of Birmingham places like Wednesbury and Wednesfield (called after the pagan god Woden), probably received their names because they were strongholds of paganism after the majority of the local Anglo-Saxons had become Christians. This could have been the case with Weoley. Certainly, the place was one of the first Old English settlements in Northfield Parish – along with Selly, Bartley and Northfield village. Like them it was sited on boulder clay with a stream nearby and it lay between the Bourn Brook and the Stonehouse Brook. The Domesday Book of 1086 does not mention Weoley, although many people believe it is recorded under Escelie (see **Selly Oak**).

werk *n.* work; Brummies usually pronounce the word as 'werk'. It is from from the Old English we(o)rc. Werk is spelled like this in the Middle English poem *Sir Orfeo*, written in the South Midlands dialect in the early 1300s and in the mystical treatise, *The Cloud of Unkowing*, written in the North-East Midlands dialect in the late 1300s.

werret *vi.* to fret or worry; to tease (Hampson, 1936, p.5).

werreting *n.* a worry or worriment EG "Stop yer werritin'" (S. Kay).

werrit *vi.* see **werret**.

werriting *n.* see **werreting**.

wetchered *adj.* wet through; soaked to the bone EG "Don't stand out in the rain without a coat, you'll be wetchered in five minutes" (Northall, 1896); a corruption, perhaps, of 'wetshod'.

whack *n.* house; home EG "Let's goo round our whack"; according to Mrs Hawkesford, the word was probably derived from the habit landlords used to have of saying 'That's yer whack' after they had given you the key to a two-up-two-down.

whaling *n.* a beating or thrashing EG "It's bloody strange fer yo' ta gu rushin' orf ta school like this, what's a marra, yo bin playin' up agin? Cus if yo' 'ave I shall soon bloody find out, an' then yow'll gerra bloody good whalin'" (Smith, undated).

wha'ppen *interj.* hallo; a contracted form of the greeting 'what's happening?', originating from the West Indian Brummie community and popularised in the 1980s by the chart-topping Birmingham band The Beat who used it as a title for one of their albums; see also **watcha**.

whelt *adj.* wheeled.

Wheolig *n.* see **Weoley**.

wherret *vi.* see **werret**.

wherreting *n.* see **werreting**.

which *n.* a chest, coffer or container; a hutch, common c. 1621 (Hoddinott and Nikitas).

whiffle *vt.* and *vi.* to shake (Northall, 1894); see also **whoffle**, and the phrase **Walsall whoffler**.

whinnock *vi.* "to whimper; to cry fretfully or querulously, as a young child does; to whine" (Northall, 1896).

whitche *n.* see **which**.

whit leather *n.* tough white leather made from horse hide; commonly used in the saying 'tough as whit leather'.

whittaw *n.* a saddler, or collarmaker (Marshall, 1796).

whit-tawer *n.* see **whittaw**.

whoffle *vt.* and *vi.* see **whiffle**, and the phrase **Walsall whoffler**.

whole-foot-one *n.* a game of pitchback: "One player makes a back. The other players pitch over, the last crying 'Foot it'. The one 'down' then places his right foot at right angles to his left, and brings the left in advance of the right, sideways, and, lastly the right close and parallel to the left. So the game goes on until one player cannot leap the distance, when he is forced to make the back. But he does not commence at the first place again, but takes the last position of the one 'down' before him; and now the players may hop to reach the back. When another player fails, he goes 'down' and a stride is added to the hop, and, finally, a hop, stride, and jump are allowed. The player that fails now begins at taw again, and the game goes on *ad lib*" (Northall, 1896).

whopstraw *n.* a country clown (Northall, 1896).

Wichton *n.* see **Witton**.

wick *n.* pronunciation variant of 'week' EG "Bloody 'ell she could lay into ya, when she belted yower arse yo felt it forra wick arter" (Smith, undated).

wicketts *n.* a person who is fonder of meat than of vegetables.

Wicton *n.* see **Witton.winding-sheet** *n.* "an imperfection in a burning candle caused by some small obstacle, such as a hair, in the tallow, which causes this to curl or wind into a rough resemblance to drapery. It is supposed to foretoken a death in the family" (Northall, 1896).

windy *adj.* frightening EG "It worn't arf windy."

wingell *vi.* to murmur or whimper incessantly (Northall, 1894); a corruption, perhaps, of 'whinge'.

winnock *vi.* see **whinnock**.

Winson Green *n.* an area of Birmingham noted first in 1327 when it was written as Wynesden; in the Warwickshire volume of the English Place Name Society it is suggested that this indicated the hill, 'don', of a man called Wine. Joe McKenna feels that a better explanation is the derivation from the Old English word 'winn', meaning a meadow. Thus Winson Green would be meadow hill green. Certainly the land drops quite sharply to the north of Winson Green Road. This topographical feature supports both interpretations as far as the 'don' element of Winson Green is concerned. It remains debatable as to which case is the stronger for the origin of 'Win'. Locally Bordesley was pronounced with a barely discernible 'd' so that it became Bor'sley (see **Balsall Heath**). Similarly, it is most likely that Wynesden was spoken as Wynes'n. This shift is indicated by two documents separated only by 30 years. In 1592, John Barebon of Wynsdon Greene leased land from Ambrose Phillips; whilst in 1622, Sir Walter Erle, knight, and Anne his wife, conveyed to Edward Bests of 'Wynson greene' in the parish of Birmingham, smith, premises and lands at Winson Green and Smethwick.

Winterval *n.* literally 'Winter Festival'; a highly controversial term first coined by Birmingham City Council in the late 1990s to refer to a program of festive events over Christmas and the New Year; not, as many religious leaders and politicians were quick to believe, a substitute for Christmas, but merely a title for the whole program of winter festivities, of which Christmas is the central point. The following lines from a Christmas message by Mark Santer, the Anglican Bishop of Birmingham, was typical of the kind of response from religious groups generally: "What madness is in store for us this Christmas? I confess I laughed out loud when our city council came out with 'Winterval' as a way of not talking about Christmas. No doubt it was a well-meaning attempt not to offend, not to exclude, not to say anything at all. Now it seems, the secular world, which expresses respect for all, is actually embarrassed by faith. Or perhaps it is Christianity which is censored." William Hague, the Conservative MP, was equally censorious: "It's time we halted the march of political correctness. Can you believe that Birmingham's Labour

Council decided to rename Christmas 'the Winterval'? . . . I want all these people who despair of this politically correct idiocy to know that we are going to govern for them." A council spokesperson at the time, however, said Christmas was at the heart of Winterval, and pointed out that publicity material included Christmas greetings and traditional images, including angels and carol singers.

Witton *n.* area of Birmingham near Aston; there are a number of Wittons throughout England and normally they originate from the Old English words 'wudu' meaning a wood and 'tun' denoting a farmstead. Thus Witton would be the farmstead in or by the wood. However, A. D. Mills, a place-name expert, believes that Witton in Birmingham comes from the Old English 'wic' signifying a dairy farmer. He bases this suggestion on the recording of Wichton in 1186 and Wicton in 1235. This interpretation is supported by Margaret Gelling and is much stronger than the suggestion that Witton means the farmstead of Witta.

woffle *vi.* to date, court or woo EG "Gooin' wofflin'?".

woffle-eyed *adj.* cross-eyed.

woffle-legged *adj.* lame.

woolly-bear *n.* a caterpillar (Northall, 1894).

wopples *n.* an eye infection causing the eyelashes to become stuck together (A. Parkes).

worn't *vi.* wasn't; was not; negated past tense form of the first and third person singular of the verb 'to be' EG "It worn't me as did it."

worrit *vi.* see **werret**.

worriting *n.* see **werreting**.

Wreodanhale *n.* see **Rednal**.

wrile *vi.* see **rile**.

writ *pa t.* wrote EG "I writ it down last night, before I went to bed."

wruggle *vi.* see **ruggle**.

wurrit *vi.* see **werret**.

wurriting *n.* see **werreting**.

Wynes'n Green *n.* see **Winson Green**.

wynowynge cloath *n.* a sheet used in separating grain from chaff, common c.1618 (Hoddinott and Nikitas).

Wynsdon Greene *n.* see **Winson Green**.

Wynson greene *n.* see **Winson Green**.

X

X's gen *bsl.* 6/- in old money.

X's 'n' X's *bsl.* 6/6d in old money (Harris).

X's yennup *bsl.* 6d in old money (Harris).

Y

yampy *adj.* mad; crazy; insane EG "'Er's as yampy as a March 'are, 'er is."

yam-yam *n.* a derogatory term for a person from the Black Country.

yap *vi.* to talk idly; to gossip or chatter EG "We 'ad a good 'ole yap."

yapple *vi.* to gobble greedily.

yarb *n.* herb (Skeat, 1876).

yard *n.* courtyard; from the late 1700s to the later 1800s, thousands of back-to-back houses were built in Birmingham. Many of them were erected in terraces behind the houses which fronted on to the street. They were up an entry and in a courtyard or 'yard', as was the term used by working-class Brummies. The yard was a communal space in which children played and washing was hung out and where the communal facilities were located. Amongst these were the brewus, miskins and lavatories.

Yardley *n.* district of Birmingham lying to the east of the city centre; the earliest mention of Yardley is in a document from 972 when it was given as Gyrdleah. In Old English this meant the wood or clearing ('leah') where rods or spars ('gyrd') are made. Another possibility put forward by Victor Skipp is that 'gyrd' meant a yard, and in the Anglo-Saxon period this could also indicate a quarter of an acre and thus a small plot of land. In this case, Gyrdleah would be the small clearing. Whatever its exact meaning, the area around Yardley village would have been cut out of thick woodland – as were many other settlements both in the parish and elsewhere in greater Birmingham. In the Domesday Book of 1086, Yardley was given as Gerlei and because it was a member of Beoley it was not recorded separately.

yarnest *n.* a portion of wages paid in advance to bind the bargain upon hiring a servant (Marshall, 1796).

Yarnton *n.* see **Erdington.**

yawnups *n.* a stupid oaf EG "Yer great yawnups!" (Skeat, 1876).

yennup *bsl.* one penny.

Yenton *n.* old name for the Erdington area of north Birmingham, as in the anonymous old rhyme (Palmer, 1976):

Sutton for mutton, and Tamworth for beeves;
Yenton for a pretty girl, and Brummagem for thieves.

Yerdington *n.* see **Erdington.**

yewtinge fatt *n.* a vat used for soaking the grain in brewing, common c.1600 (Hoddinott and Nikitas).

yeyling howse *n.* a place in which wort is left to ferment in brewing c.1614 (Hoddinott and Nikitas).

yo *pron.* you; contrary to the mispronunciation of the Brummie accent in many television programmes, the second person pronoun 'you' is articulated not as 'yow' but as 'yo'; as in "Where yo' bin?" 'Yow' is the variant more commonly heard in the Black Country dialect.

yourn *pron.* yours; belonging to you; genitive (or *possessive adj.*) of 'you' (Skeat, 1876); literally 'your one'.

yowe *n.* pronunciation variant of 'ewe' EG "'Er's dressed up like an old yowe lamb fashion" (Northall, 1896).

yowk *vi.* to yelp in reaction to a sudden pain, as when struck; see also **zowk**.

yslaked *adj.* muted; silenced (Alexander, 1951) EG "Now sleep hath yslaked hath the rout" (Shakespeare, *Pericles*, Act III, Sc. I).

ytingfatt *n.* see **yewtinge fatt**.

Z

zilch *n.* zero; nothing.

zonked *adj.* tired; worn out; as in "I'm zonked out."

zowk *vi.* to cry out; to yelp in reaction to a sudden pain, as when struck EG "'E dain't 'alf zowk when 'is old mon was a-beltin' 'im one, I can tell yer"; see also **yowk**.

Brummagem phrases

A blind man on a galloping horse would be glad to see it. "Said to one who cavils at the smallness of a thing, or makes a fuss over some trifling defect" (Northall, 1894, and S. Kay).

A Christmas gambol oft can cheer the poor man's heart through half the year. (Palmer, 1976).

A creaking gate lasts longest. (Win Tainty).

A fool above the shoulders. Stupid; simple; half-witted EG "If yer expectin' us to do a wick's work fer twothree fardins, yer must think we'm fools above the shoulders" (Northall, 1896).

A fool's a monkey's master. "Said to one who calls another a fool" (Northall, 1896).

A gardener has a big thumbnail. Often said when somebody is attempting to convince others of their innocence or ignorance of some minor infringement, e.g. a gardener manages to carry off a great deal of his master's property without being conscious of it (Northall, 1894).

A gift on the thumb is sure to come; a gift on the finger is sure to linger. Old Warwickshire proverb (Timmins, 1889).

A good deal to chew but little to swallow. "Once said of shop-bread by old country people" (Northall, 1894), but now used indiscriminately to criticise anything which is of little substance.

A good old farmer's clock. An accurate and dependable timepiece (Northall, 1894).

A good one to send for sorrow. "Spoken of an idler" (Northall, 1894).

A good year for nuts is a good year for babies. (Palmer, 1976).

A head like a bladder of lard. Said of someone with a bald and shiny head (Northall, 1894).

Airship in a cloud. Sausage and mash (K. Carruthers).

A lane! A lane! A cry warning the spectators at a bull-ring to open an avenue for the dog to pass through on its way to the bull at the stake (Rhodes, 1950).

A lick and a promise and better next time. "Alluding to a hasty wash given to a child, dish, etc." (Northall, 1894).

All on one side like a bird with one wing. Lopsided; off balance (Northall, 1894).

All over aches and pains like Trotting Bessie. According to Northall (1894), this phrase was common in the Harborne area of Birmingham (formerly Staffordshire) in the late nineteenth century. It is unknown who or what Trotting Bessie was.

All over the shop. Irregular; erratic and unpredictable; messy EG "'E's a crap driver – 'is steering's all over the shop" (Dean O'Loughlin); also everywhere; in every place EG "'E's left 'is cowin' books all over the shop again."

All that caper. All those goings-on EG "Our old mon'd never of approved of all that caper."

All tittery to tottery. "From laughing to staggering" (Northall, 1894); said of a person having a fit of the giggles.

All you can reap and run for. According to Northall (1894), this was a phrase "much used to express the total sum of money that can be accumulated in an emergency" EG "Twothree fardins is about the best I can reap 'n' run fer."

A long thing and a thank you. Commonly said of anything lengthy and meandering with no particular value.

A lowing cow soon forgets her calf. (Northall, 1894).

A mess for a mad dog. "Said of a meal compounded of various ingredients" (Northall, 1894).

A miller is never dry. A common retort, usually from a person who has been accused of drinking too heavily (i.e. a miller never waits to be thirsty before drinking).

And the suet. Often added to the end of another person's utterance if their expectations appear to fall something short of the mark. Albert Charles writes that he was recently talking to a neighbour, a proper Brummie, about the price of houses. During the chat Albert mentioned that he would expect a certain amount for his house, should he put it on the market, and the neighbour replied '. . . and the suet', meaning 'and the rest'. Albert hadn't heard the phrase since he was a kid when it was apparently very common indeed.

A nice name to go to bed with. Often used ironically to express disapproval of a child's absurd or unusual name EG "Jus' fancy, to christen the poor kid Pharaoh: that's a nice name to goo to bed with, ennit?" (Northall, 1896).

A nod's as good as a wink to a blind horse. (Northall, 1894).

Any road up. Anyway; anyhow.

A pig in a poke. Something not worth its value EG "'E's bought a right pig in a poke."

A poor hap'orth of cheese. A sickly child (Northall, 1894).

A public house would want but two customers, him and a man to fetch away the grains. "Said of a noted drinker" (Northall, 1894); see also **he's a good man round a barrel but no cooper.**

As bent as a nine bob note. Crooked; counterfeit; illegal; often said of someone who is untrustworthy.

As big a fool as Kitty Bitt. (Palmer, 1976).

As big as a bonk 'oss. As big as a bank horse (i.e. a large horse that worked on a pit bank) EG "'E's as big as a bonk 'oss, 'im" (S. Kay).

As big as a parish oven. Said of someone who has a big mouth or loose tongue EG "'Er's got a mouth on 'er as big as a parish oven, 'er 'as" (J. Burgess).

As big as bull beef. Pompous; self-important; conceited (Palmer, 1976).

As black as a grate. Dirty; filthy; unclean EG "Yer donnies're black as a bleedin' grate!"

As busy as a cat in a tripe shop. Absorbed; overworked; engrossed EG "'Er's busy as a cat in a tripe shop right now" (Northall, 1894).

As dark as a black pig in a bean rick. (Palmer, 1976).

As deep as Garry. "Hazlitt (1882) has "As deep as Garrick," and remarks that he found this current in Cornwall, where Garrick [a celebrated Shakespearean actor] could scarcely have been very familiar" (Northall, 1896).

As dim as a Tok H Lamp. Stupid; slow on the uptake; a reference to the small flame on the Tok H badge (J. Houldey).

As dirty as Dudley Street. Filthy; unclean EG "'Is 'ouse is as dirty as Dudley Street" (Old Sarbot, 1869).

As drunk as a bob 'owler. Intoxicated; inebriated (Mary Bodfish); see also **bob-howler**.

As dummle as a donkey. Stupid; dim-witted (Northall, 1896).

As false as God's true. Deceitful; mendacious; fallacious (Northall, 1896).

As fat as a match with the brimstone off. (Northall, 1894).

As fat as a tunkey pig. Obese; overweight; a 'tunkey pig' was a piglet that had been fattened-up for Christmas (S. Kay).

As fierce as a four-year-old horse. Spirited; mettlesome (Northall, 1896).

As fond of a raw place as a bluebottle. "Said of one always ready for a quarrel, or anxious to touch on grievances" (Northall, 1894).

As full as a blow'd mouse. Stuffed; crammed; full up (Northall, 1896).

As full of megrims as a dancing bear. Grumpy; in a bad temper EG "'Er was as full o' megrims as a dancin' bear when 'er 'eard" (Northall, 1894).

As gain as a glass eye. Useless; ineffectual; serving no useful function (i.e. as useful as a glass eye to actually see with) EG "'E's as gain as a glass eye at footie" (S. Kay).

As handy as a pig with a musket. Clumsy; incompetent; awkward EG "'Er's about as 'andy as a pig with a musket, 'er is" (Northall, 1894).

As hard as the devil's nagnails. (Northall, 1894).

A silver new nothing to hang on your arm. A stock answer to children who ask their parents if they have bought anything for them from the shops; according to Northall (1894), "A tantadlin tart" was also once a common reply.

As jolly as a sandboy. (Northall, 1894).

As joyful as the back of a gravestone. (Northall, 1894).

As lean as a lath. (Northall, 1894); 'as thin as a lath' is the modern day equivalent.

A slice from a cut cake is never missed. Usually said to gloss over a breach of some moral law (Rhodes, 1950).

As melancholy as a gib-cat. (Shakespeare, *Henry IV (Part 1)*, Act I, Sc. II).

As merry as Momus. (Northall, 1894).

As modest as an old whore at a christening. (Northall, 1894).

As much sense as a suckling duck. Nonsensical; incomprehensible; unintelligible EG "This is mekin' about as much sense as a sucklin' duck to me" (Northall, 1896).

As noisy as Bedlam. Loud; disorderly EG "It's as noisy as Bedlam in 'ere" (Old Sarbot, 1869); also common in other dialects.

As old as my tongue and a little bit older than my teeth. An evasive reply to the question, "How old are you?" (D. Dodd).

As old as Adam / As old as Methuselah. "The former refers to time: the latter to longevity" (Northall, 1894); also common in other dialects, as well as languages such as Italian.

As pleased as a jay with a bean.

As prime as His Worship. Delicious; tasty EG "This feed's as prime as 'is Worship" (Old Sarbot, 1869).

As proud as a dog with two tails.

As red as a turkeycock's jowls.

As red as Roger's nose who was christened in pump water.

As red as the rising sun at Bromford. According to Northall (1894), this phrase was well known in Warwickshire, and alludes "to Bromford, 1 mile S.E. from Erdington, par. Aston juxta-Birmingham, where there was a mill on the Tame prior to the Norman conquest." Though a forge mill still existed on the old site in the late nineteenth century, the phrase is thought to refer to the sign of some old public house in the area.

As right as a ribbon. Seemly; proper; becoming (Northall, 1896).

As rough as a bear's backside. (Palmer, 1976).

As rough as chopped gos. Literally 'as rough as chopped gorse'; uncouth; common (Northall, 1896); Palmer (1976) has 'as rough as goss chopped off the common' with the same meaning.

As round shouldered as a grindstone.

As sandy as a Tamworth pig. According to Northall (1894), this was usually "spoken of a red-haired woman," and implied that she looked "likely to prove concupiscent and prolific."

As savage as a tup.

As sharp as Joel Hedge, who cut the bough from under him. (Palmer, 1976).

As short as a Marchington wake-cake. Usually said of a person's temper (Northall, 1894).

As smart as a master sweep.

As solid as old times. (Northall, 1894).

As sound as an ackern. Good; solid; trustworthy.

A still bee gathers no honey. (Northall, 1894).

As straight as a dog's hind leg. Not to be trusted (K. Carruthers).

As straight as a pound of candles. Usually said of a person's hair if unusually straight (Northall, 1894).

As sure as fate or death. Without doubt; certainly; definitely; according to Northall (1894), similar phrases were, "As sure as I'm alive," "As sure as you're born," and "As sure as you're there."

As the monkey said as he put his hand in the commode, "There's more to this than meets the eye." (Ian Hawthorne).

As thick as gutter mud.

As thick as inkleweavers. Common local proverb up until the late nineteenth century (Northall, 1896).

As thick as two short planks. Stupid (K. Carruthers).

As thin as a fardin rushlight. Fat; rotund; obese (Northall, 1894).

As thin as ha'penny ale. EG Small beer at 2d per quart.

A swarm of bees in May is worth a load of hay; a swarm of bees in June is worth a silver spoon; a swarm of bees in July is not worth a butterfly. (Timmins, 1889).

At first blush. At first sight; without consideration EG "At the first blush I thought the feller was sane enough" (Northall, 1896).

A trip up the cut in a coalboat. This refers to children's Sunday School and other outings whereby the youngsters were taken out on a narrowboat on the canal.

A warm May makes a fat churchyard. (Palmer, 1976).

A whistling woman and a crowing hen will frighten the devil out of his den. (Timmins, 1889); more common is: "A whistling woman and a crowing hen are good to neither God nor men."

Barnaby bright, Barnaby light, longest day, shortest night. St Barbnabas' Day falls on the 11th June, but, as Palmer (1976) points out, this old Warwickshire folk-rhyme "more properly applies to the 21st June since the change of calendar in 1752."

Be as quick as you can, and, if you fall down, don't stop to get up. "A jocular incentive to one going on an errand" (Northall, 1894).

Best bib and tucker. Sunday best; "metaphorical for holiday clothes" (Northall, 1896).

Better a belly bost than a good thing lost. (Palmer, 1976).

Better a man that's ne'er been born than pare his corns on a Sunday morn. (Palmer, 1976).

Better an ugly patch than a handsome hole. Often said in reply to youngsters who moan about the patches on their clothes.

Better a quick penny than a dallying shilling.

Better long little than soon nothing.

Better than a bob in the eye with a broomstick. Better than nothing (Palmer, 1976).

Black your behind and go naked. Advice given to a person who complains about having nothing suitable to wear (Northall, 1894).

Blind man's holiday. Twilight; a dim light or partial darkness, "when it is too dark to see to work" (Northall, 1896).

Blow my buttons! An old Warwickshire expletive listed in Northall (1896).

Book of hard names. An account book (Northall, 1896).

Born but not buried. Commonly used in reference to wrongdoers who appeared to have got away scot-free EG "Theym born but not buried" (anonymous contributor, Kings Heath).

Borrow to save. This phrase refers to someone who is always borrowing money to spend because they can't save their own money.

Bread and pull it. According to Northall (1894), this was a common retort when somebody was asked what they had had for dinner, esp. when they hadn't actually had anything at all; another common reply was 'gravel hash', "which really means a walk on the roads. Another reply is 'chums and chair knobs'." See also the phrase **to box Harry and chew rag**.

By degrees, as lawyers go to heaven. (Northall, 1894).

Catchings, havings; slips go again. A street phrase, usually spoken by someone who finds themselves cornered and about to be arrested (Northall, 1894).

Cat, you bitch, your tail's afire. The idea of a cat bearing fire in its tail is commonly found in many folk-tales and verses, though there appears to be no satisfactory explanation for why this should be so.

Chance the ducks. In the old Warwickshire dialect, to do something and 'chance the ducks' meant to do it, come what may and regardless of the consequences.

Chapping it. Having a good time out with the lads; see also **wenching it**. Also used with regard to girls who are going out looking for chaps.

Cheer up – yer a lung time dead. (Win Tainty).

Choke up, chicken, more a-hatching. Said to a child who chokes on food, other common variants being, "Cough up, chicken," and "Choke up child, the churchyard's nigh" (Northall, 1894).

Come day. Go day. God send pay day. An old Brummagem folk-rhyme; according to Palmer (1976), 'Sunday' was often used in place of 'pay day'.

Come to my arms, my little bundle of charms. "Said, jocularly, to a woman" (Northall, 1896).

Compliments pass when beggars meet.

Cough it up, it might be a gold watch. John Essex writes that this was often said to someone with a noisy or irritating cough.

Cry! You'll piss the less. Usually addressed to children who cry 'unreasonably' (Northall, 1894); Win Tainty writes that variants such as the following were also fairly common: "Goo on, cry – the more yer cry yo'll widdle the less,

Curses, like chickens, come home to roost. (Northall, 1894).

Cut and come again. Expressing 'take a share and come again freely for more' (Northall, 1896).

Cut off his head but mind you don't kill him. "A mock injunction to one about to beat a child for some wrongdoing (Northall, 1894).

Cut them on Monday, cut them for health; cut them on Tuesday, cut them for wealth; cut them on Wednesday, cut them for news; cut them on Thursday for a new pair of shoes; cut them on Friday, cut them for sorrow; cut them on Saturday, see your sweetheart tomorrow; cut them on Sunday, cut them for evil; for all the week long will be with you the devil. According to Warwickshire folklore, cutting fingernails or toenails had a meaning, depending on the day of the week (Palmer, 1976).

Daft ha'p'orth. An idiot or fool EG "You daft ha'p'orth!" or "You soppy ha'p'orth!" (S. Kay). Normally used affectionately towards someone who has done something nice and the recipient goes, "You shouldn't a-done it y' daft a'porth."

Damn my sinks! An old Warwickshire expletive listed in Northall (1896).

Deeds are Johns, and words Nans. "A local version of the proverb - Deeds are males, but words females" (Northall, 1894).

Deritend wake Sunday, the first day of winter. "Deritend, in the parish of Aston juxta-Birmingham, is divided from the south-east side of the town by the river Rea. The chapel there is dedicated to St. John the Baptist, the calendared date of whose beheading is Aug. 29" (Northall, 1894).

Dilly-dally brings night as soon as hurry-skurry. A phrase expressing a similar sentiment to Mohandas K. Ghandi's declaration that "there is more to life than increasing its speed."

Dirty stop out! Said jocularly when a young person has stopped out later than is usual.

Docker me! An old Warwickshire oath listed in Northall (1896).

Dog bite me! An old Warwickshire oath listed in Northall (1896); according to Mary Bodfish, her grandfather (Joe Bodfish, 1872-1946) often used a very similar expression when annoyed beyond endurance: "Dog bite me be hanged!"

Dog bite old rope! "An expression of surprise or amazement" (Tennant, 1983).

Doing bird. Serving a prison sentence; a three month sentence was known as 'a carpet', six months as 'half a stretch', and one year as 'a wool'un' (K. Carruthers).

Don't be always don'ting. Said to a person who seems pessimistic about everything (Northall, 1894).

Don't Care was hanged. According to Northall (1894), usually said to a reckless or impatient person who exclaims that they don't care.

Don't do it a that'n, do it a this'n. Don't do it that way, do it this way (Rhodes, 1950).

Don't drink water with yer dinner – yer meat'll turn to leather. (Win Tainty).

Don't drown the miller's eye. Be careful not to add too much water to the flour when mixing dough. Northall (1894) suggests that the 'miller's eye' was probably "that part of the [corn-grinding] machinery which is in the aperture in the upper revolving stone, beneath the hopper, through which the corn passes."

Don't put old heads on young shoulders. Don't give children adult responsibilities (anonymous contributor, Kings Norton).

Don't sigh, but send, I'd run a mile for a penny. "Said to one who sighs without apparent cause" (Northall, 1894).

Drenched to the kith and kin. Wet; soaked through; soaked to the bone EG "'Er's drenched to 'er kith 'n' kin" (Jeffrey, 1868).

Dressed to the nines. Smart or fashionable EG "'Er's dressed to the nines tonight" (R. Couling).

179

Dressed up like an old yowe lamb fashion. "Spoken of an elderly woman dressed in girlish attire" (Northall, 1896).

Drunk as a boiled owl. (Northall, 1894).

Even-leaved ash, or four-leaved clover, you'll meet your true love before the day is over. (Timmins, 1889).

Every dog has his day, and a cat has two afternoons. (Northall, 1894).

Every hands while. Every now and again; intermittently; whenever necessary, possible or convenient EG "Mind and see to the chickens ev'ry 'ands while" (Northall, 1896).

Every little helps, as the old woman said as she made water in the sea. (Northall, 1894).

Every time you speak you lose a mouthful. Said to children who are talkative at the dinner table (K. Carruthers).

Fall o' the leaf. Autumn (Skeat, 1876).

Fern-seed I sow, fern-seed I hoe, in hopes my true love will come after me and mow. It was once believed that fern-seed had mystical powers, and, if gathered with certain rites on Midsummer Day, could render a person, (esp. young women) invisible; according to Wise (1861), this rhyme was usually repeated as fern-seed was scattered in a garden at midnight on Midsummer's Eve, and Palmer (1976) writes that if the girl doing so wanted to know who her future husband would be, "She would then see the young man's image."

Fire and water; good servants, but bad masters. (Northall, 1896).

Fives to play sixes up seven street. Mind your own business (Steve Dean).

For two pins. Reason, or lack of reason, for doing something EG "Fer two pins I'll lamp yer one" (D. Adams).

Fourpenny one. A hard blow or punch EG "I gi' 'im a fourpenny one on the boko" (E. Yorke).

Fun and fancy; gee up, Nancy. "A phrase intimating that a thing is said or done in jest" (Northall, 1894).

Get a jerk on! Hurry up! (Mary Bodfish).

Get on and you go to Moseley; get honour and you go to Edgbaston; get honest and you leave Brummagem. A typically light-hearted and self-deprecating Brummagem proverb, quoted in Keith Hancock's autobiography *Country and Calling* (1954). "When people make jingles of this kind about themselves," Hancock remarks, "they usually do so in a spirit of affectionate tolerance, and it always seemed to me that differences of material and social circumstances counted for less with Birmingham people than their feeling that they were all citizens of the same city, and no mean city at that."

Get your head under that tap you've got enough dirt to plant carroway seeds. (K. Carruthers.

Give it some bell oil! Give it some elbow grease; "get stuck in or give it all you've got when doing something physical" (Paul Williams).

Go and piss down your leg and play with the steam. Said to express annoyance; Joan Burgess writes that "any of us (ten in all) who annoyed our father in some way would usually be dismissed in this manner."

Go and throw shit at your photo. Similar to "Go away!," or "Clear off!" (Joan Burgess).

God bless the Duke of Argyll! "Whenever [my grandmother] had an itchy back, she would stand against the arch of the doorway rubbing it and say this as she did so" (A. Trapp). According to *Brewer's Dictionary of Phrase and Fable* (ed. Kirkpatrick, E., 1993), the ninth Duke of Argyll erected a row of scratching posts around his property so that his cattle could rub against them, and this is how the phrase appears to have originated (G. Sly). Louise Lorne Road, which joins Alcester Road with Trafalgar Road in Moseley, was named in honour of Princess Louise, the fourth daughter of Queen Victoria and wife of the second Duke of Argyll.

Good shot o' bad rubbidge. Good riddance; frequently said of a person or thing cheerfully discarded (Northall, 1896).

Go to Hanover! Get lost; go away (John Essex); see also **go to Smerrick!**

Go to Smerrick! Telling someone to go to Smerrick (Smethwick) was akin to today's "Clear off!" or "Get lost!" According to Northall (1894), this was a local version of "Go to Jericho!"

Guy flip! An expression of surprise; Mike Cotton writes that this was similar in sentiment to the current expressions 'Crikey!' and 'Flippin' 'eck!"

Half past kissing time, time to kiss again. A humorous reply to someone who asks the time (Northall, 1894).

Handy bandy, sugar-candy, cut my throat and double hang me. Job! Job! Job! At ten o'clock at night. "In the North Midlands, when a boy wishes to assure a companion of the truth of some act or promise, he utters these words, intimating that he would be prepared for, or deserving of these terrible punishments, should he prove false. He prods his throat with his forefinger at each mention of the word 'job'" (Northall, 1896).

Happy is the bride the sun shines on; blessed is the corpse the rain rains on. (Timmins, 1889).

Have a wash before yer goo ta bed, or you might wake up and find yerself dead. (Win Tainty).

Hawthorn bloom and elder flowers will fill a house with evil powers. (Palmer, 1976).

Heads a penny! Often said when a child has bumped his or her head; Northall (1894) suggests that this was probably an abbreviated form of some longer phrase, the origin of which is unknown.

He always had a crooked elbow. Often said of an alcoholic, or a person who has been fond of drinking ever since they were young; "'crooked elbow' refers to the bent position of the arm in lifting a mug or glass to the mouth" (Northall, 1894); see also the phrases **he holds his head back too much** and **he's a good man round a barrel, but no cooper.**

He couldn't stop a pig in an entry. He's bow-legged (Tennant, 1983).

He'd forget his head if it was loose. Said of an absent-minded person.

He'd give him the top brick of the chimney. Said of a parent who spoils his child (Northall, 1894).

He doesn't know A from a bull's foot. He is stupid; he's slow on the uptake (Christine Kendell).

He doesn't know A from a bunch of carrots. He is stupid; he's slow on the uptake (Christine Kendell).

He doesn't know where is behind hangs. Often said of an arrogant, vain, or "insufferably proud" person (Northall, 1894).

He'd rob Jesus of his shoe-strings. (Northall, 1896).

He'd skin a flint for a ha'penny, and spoil a sixpenny knife doing it. Said of a mean and miserly person; according to Northall (1894), 'he would flay a flint' is "a proverb of remote times - Abdalmalek, one of the Khalifs of the race of Ommiades, was surnamed, by way of sarcasm, Raschal Hegiarah, that is *the skinner of a flint*."

He'd skin a turd for a farthing. He'd do anything to earn some money.

He'd take snuff through a rag. See **he'd skin a flint for a ha'penny, and spoil a sixpenny knife doing it**.

Heeper, peeper, chimbley sweeper, had a wife and couldn't keep her; had another, didn't love her, heeper, peeper, out goes she. An old Warwickshire dialect children's rhyme. "In a close community," writes Palmer (1976), "everyone knew how well or otherwise married couples got on together," and merciless rhymes such as this were fairly common in the Birmingham area.

He'll never make old bones. Spoken of a frail or sickly child (Northall, 1894).

He makes the bullets and you shoot them. Said to a person who does the dirty work for someone else.

He ought to have been a fireman – he's that good at dowting them. Said of a heavy drinker (K. Carruthers); see also **he's a good man round a barrel, but no cooper**.

Here goes ding-dong for a dumpling. Similar in sentiment to the current phrase: "Here goes nothing." Northall (1894) suggests that this phrase is probably derived from "the old sport of bobbing with the mouth for balm dumplings immersed in hot water."

Her's the cat's mother. "Said to someone who uses the possessive *her* of the third person instead of the nominative *she*" (Northall, 1894); "Who's 'er, the cat's mother?" was a common retort in the twentieth century from mothers referred to as 'her' or 'she' rather than the more courteous 'mom'.

He's a good man round a barrel, but no cooper. He's an alcoholic; a drunkard (Northall, 1894).

He's a right Brahma. According to C. Goodall, this phrase referred to a person who was a bit of a nuisance, someone who was a hindrance or annoyance to others. In some parts of Birmingham, however, 'Bramah' appears to have been used as an expression of admiration or praise; see also **brahma**.

He's fit for nothing but to pick up straws. He's useless; dim-witted (Northall, 1894).

He's that lucky he'd fall off the top of Rackhams into a new suit.

He's that slow he couldn't catch a cold.

He's too slow to take cold dinners. He's dopey; slow on the uptake (Mary Grosvenor).

He wants to know the back of Meg's arse. He wants to know everything (about someone or something); said of someone who is very nosey.

He was born under a threepenny planet. Said of someone who is "avaricious or a curmudgeon" (Northall, 1894).

He wouldn't give a blind man a light. Said of someone who is mean (K. Carruthers).

He wouldn't give away the droppings from his nose on a frosty morning. He's mean and miserly (Northall, 1894).

He wouldn't give you the parings of his nails. He's mean; stingy; miserly (Northall, 1894).

His dad'll never be dead as long as he's alive also **her mom'll never be dead as long as she's alive.** Usually said of sons or daughters who closely resemble their parents in appearance, personality or manner (Northall, 1894).

How many beans make five? A common question, in both the old Warwickshire and Worcestershire dialects, when attempting to test a person's sharpness or vigilance; a reply (or 'retort courteous') was not always given, but for those in the know the correct answer (or 'quip modest') was, "A bean and a half, a bean and a half, half a bean, and a bean and a half." According to Northall (1894), "to say of a person that 'They know how many beans make five' is to speak very highly of their shrewdness."

How're you frogging? How are you?; a common greeting in the neighbourhood of Sutton Coldfield in the late nineteenth and early twentieth centuries, though - as Northall (1894) points out - "not unfamiliar in other parts of Warwickshire."

How's the enemy? What's the time? (Palmer, 1976).

How's-yer-father. An argument or disagreement EG "I've just 'ad a right old 'ow's-yer-father with the missis" (R. Couling).

Hungry Harborne, poor and proud. An area of Birmingham once notorious for its grinding poverty. According to Northall (1894), "ancient documents preserve several parish place-names which suggest poverty; Kenward, *Harborne and its Surroundings*, 1885, pp. 44-45, mentions Wilderness Farm, Bareland's Coppice, Mock Beggar Farm, &c."

I can't see for looking.

I could eat a cock-eyed kid with measles. (Jo and Pete Chance).

I could eat a scabby horse. (Ian Trow).

I couldn't give a kipper's dick. I'm not bothered; I couldn't care less.

I cry Nicklas! See **nicklas** (Northall, 1896).

I'd as soon hear a rake and basket. Usually said of "discordant singing" or any unpalatable noise (Northall, 1894).

I en't got a latch-lifter. I haven't got enough money to go to the pub (E. Yorke).

If horse muck was pudding nobody would starve. (K. Carruthers).

If in your house a man shoulders a spade, for you or your kinsfolk a grave is half made. (Timmins, 1889).

If so be as how. "If so be as how I've done my work in time, I'll come across" (Northall, 1896).

If the sage-tree thrives and grows, the master's not master, and that he knows. (Timmins, 1889); as Palmer (1976) points out, "popular feeling despised the household where the man was not the master," and these mysogynous sentiments are clearly expressed in this old Warwickshire folk-rhyme.

If you buy a broom in May, you're sure to sweep a corpse away. (Palmer, 1976).

If you'd live to be old, strip before you sweat and dress before you're cold. (Palmer, 1976).

If you don't mind what you're about, you'll get over Moulden's Bridge. According to Palmer (1976), this old Warwickshire saying means that if you don't care about anything, you'll turn out bad: "It recalls the name of the bridge over which prisoners passed to Warwick gaol and assizes."

If your bees fall sick and die, one of your house will soon in churchyard lie. (Timmins, 1889); as Palmer writes in *The Folklore of Warwickshire* (1976), "the well-being of the bees and of the household seem to have been closely linked" in days gone by.

I'll be soysed! An old Warwickshire expletive listed in Northall (1896).

I'll it yo' that 'ard, our kid, yo'll meet yerself comin' back. (K. Carruthers).

I'll not make fish of one and fowl of another. I do not have favourites; I refuse to favour one over another (Northall, 1896).

I'll pull your ears as long as a donkey's. A warning to wayward children (Old Sarbot, 1869).

I'll see your nose above your chin. A threat, usually addressed to children (Northall, 1894).

I'm eating my white bread now instead of at the end of my days. (Northall, 1894).

In a jilt of rags. Usually said of a ragamuffin, or somebody of generally unkempt appearance (Northall, 1894).

In dock, out nettle. "A saying or charm. It is believed that a person severely stung with a nettle will obtain relief from rubbing the part with dock-leaves, repeating this phrase three times" (Northall, 1896).

I never done nothing; I never wanted nothing; I don't want no more; They 'en't got none left; There 'en't no-one 'ere; She can't find no book and others are all examples of what is known to the layman as *the double negative*, and to linguists as *multiple negation* or *negative concord*. It frequently occurs in the speech of Brummies, as it does in the speech of people from other working-class dialect areas, but it is universally regarded as 'sub-standard' and 'wrong'. Of course, dialect relates not only to words but also to grammar. In this case, the double negative is a grammatical form used primarily for emphasis or stress, but which has been lost in standard English. As Montgomery (1998) points out, the double negative is not a modern phenomenon: "at earlier periods multiple negation can be found in all dialects, including the English of Chaucer and of Shakespeare, so neither in numerical nor historical terms would the standard seem 'more correct' than the non-standard." Standard English permits only one negation per sentence, and so dialects that allow double or even triple negation are viewed as subordinate. As Trudgill (1983) asserts, however, there is nothing intrinsically inferior about negative concord: "grammatical forms which are most typical of working-class dialects have low status, because of their association with groups who have low prestige in our society. This low status leads to the belief that these forms are 'bad' and they are therefore judged to be 'wrong'. Evaluations of this type are therefore clearly social judgements about the status of the speakers who use particular forms, rather than objective linguistic judgements about the correctness of the forms themselves."

In quick sticks. Rapidly; quickly; promptly.

In the old pickle. Pregnant (Northall, 1894); according to a report in *Metro* (11 May 2001), Charles Lloyd of the Lloyds banking family had fifteen children in eighteen years by his wife Mary and referred to her condition as "being in the old pickle" when she was with child; see also **making feet for baby's stockings.**

It's all a bag of moonshine. It's an illusion; nonsense; rubbish (Northall, 1896); often said in reference to gossip, rumour, or shallow talk.

It's all for the back and belly. Usually implying that food and clothing are "the main objects of all endeavour" (Northall, 1894).

It's all my eye and Betty Thomas. It's not true; it's all a pack of lies (M. Ravenhill).

It's a poor hen that can't scrat for one chick. (Northall, 1894).

It's just struck a copper baldheaded. A common reply when asked the time (I. Hawthorne).

It's looking a bit black over the back of Bill's mother's. It looks overcast; it looks like it's going to rain (B. Osborn, R. Phipp and T. Knibbs). Although used commonly in Brum, this is a term used generally across the country.

It tastes of what never was in it. Usually said when food has been overcooked or burnt (Northall, 1894).

Jack-a-making-pancakes. "The reflected sunlight thrown upon the ceiling from the surface of water" (Tomkinson, 1893).

Jack's alive at our house. "Said on an occasion of noisy merriment. There is a well-known game at forfeits, in which a lighted spill is passed from hand to hand, the players saying meanwhile –
> Jack's alive, and likely to live,
> If he dies in your hand
> You've a forfeit to give

187

- that may have originated this phrase: for, as the spill burns lower and lower, there is much haste to place it in the hands of the next player, and this is carried on amidst much cheering and laughter" (Northall, 1894).

Jimmy Johnson squeeze me. This saying, which was common c.1830-40, appears in a song called *The Brummagem Lad*:

> I came up to London to see the Queen,
> And all the grand sights I was willin',
> But, when I came to look over my cash,
> I found I'd took two bad shillin',
> But a Brummagem Lad is not to be had;
> If he is, Jimmy Johnson squeeze me."

It is unknown whether the song was founded on the phrase or vice-versa (Northall, 1896).

Just like horse muck from China. Far-fetched; used in reference to a tall story (K. Carruthers).

Just the thing, like old Berry's wife. (Palmer, 1976).

Keep your lamps trimmed. Keep your eyes open (K. Carruthers).

Kippers and curtains. Well-off; posh; people described as 'all kippers 'n' curtains' feign importance in some way, and pretend to be superior to others. Often applied to those living in the Harborne, Edgbaston and Sutton Coldfield areas of Birmingham (E. Yorke). It tends to be used towards those who put up appearances and show off the externals but haven't really got much.

Kissed, cursed, vexed, or shake hands with a fool. Often said by someone whose nose itches - "hoping for the first lot, but prepared for either" (Northall, 1894).

Kissing goes by favour. Old Warwickshire proverb (Rhodes, 1950); see also **favour**.

Knee-high to a grasshopper. Young; a child EG "I knew you when you was no more than knee-high to a grasshopper" (R. Couling).

Like a bag of muck tied up ugly. Also **like a bundle of shit tied up ugly**; used to suggest that someone looks bulging, shapeless and (generally) unsightly EG "'Er looks like a big bag o' muck tied up ugly" (Northall, 1894, and Joan Burgess).

Like a blue-arsed fly. Said of someone who is in a hurry EG "'Er's bin dashin' around like a blue-arsed fly all arternoon."

Like a bulldog licking piss off a thistle. An ugly or unattractive person is commonly said to have a face like 'a bulldog lickin' piss off a thistle' (C. Weekes).

Like a cat on a hot bake-stone. "A person is said to go like a cat on a hot bake-stone (or backstone) when treading cautiously, and with apparent fear and uneasiness" (Northall, 1896).

Like a chip in porridge. Of no effect; making no discernible difference EG "Like a chip in porridge, neither good nor harm" (Northall, 1896).

Like a dog in a doublet. Spindly; gangling; weedy EG "'E's a mere dog in a doublet" (Northall, 1894).

Like a frog in a fit. Drunk; tipsy; inebriated EG "'E's like a frog in a fit" (Northall, 1894).

Like a glede under the door. Commonly used to imply that something or someone does not sound very appealing EG "'Er's got a voice on 'er like a glede under the door" and "Theym mekin' a noise like a gleed under a door" (P. Collins and S. Kay).

Like a marley in a tin can, all rattle. All talk and no action; said of someone who is abnormally fond of gossiping and little else (K. Carruthers).

Like an old hen scratching before day. Working unsociable hours (Northall, 1894).

Like a pawnshop. Said of someone who is gullible and believes anything, no matter how far-fetched it is (K. Carruthers) EG "'Er's like a pawnshop 'er is, 'er'll tek anythin' in."

Like a pea on a drumhead. See **to pop about like a parched pea on a shovel**.

Like a pigeon pair. Said of two people very much alike in their ways (K. Carruthers).

Like a toad out of a tree - thump! (Northall, 1896).

Like a tomtit on a round of beef. Diminutive; small; insignificant; "a little person is said to look so when situated on some coign of vantage" (Northall, 1894).

Like Bassen's miller, always behind. (Palmer, 1976).

Like death on a mopstick. Infirm; unhealthy; ill (Northall, 1896).

Like dogs in dough. Unable to proceed or make headway (Northall, 1894); making no discernible progress.

Like Hunt's dog. Undecided; unsure (Palmer, 1976).

Like snow in a harvest. Unwelcome; unwanted; unexpected (Northall, 1894); a person who looks a little down in the dumps is also said to look 'as pleasant as a snow in harvest'.

Like the back end of a bus. Ugly; unattractive EG "'Er's got a phiz like the back end of a bus, en't 'er?"

Like the wreck of the Hesperus. Untidy; dishevelled, esp. in reference to a person's general appearance (anonymous contributor, Kings Norton). The Hesperus was a schooner wrecked near Gloucester, Massachusetts in 1839 and was made famous in a ballad by H. W. Longthorne - a ballad that was learned widely by schoolchildren.

Live and learn, die and forget it all. (Northall, 1896).

Long-look'd-for, come at last. (Northall, 1896).

Long tom and a'penny in the bottle. Said of two people walking together, one of whom is noticeably taller than the other (I. Hawthorne).

Love of lads and fire of chats is soon in and soon out. A Derbyshire proverb also used in the Birmingham area during the nineteenth century (Northall, 1896).

Making feet for baby's stockings. Pregnant; with child (Northall, 1894).

Man proposes, God disposes. Often said when plans had gone awry (J. Burgess).

March, the month to open the windows and let the fleas fly out. (Northall, 1896).

March will search, and April try, but May will tell you if you live or die. (Timmins, 1889).

Married in white, you have chosen all right; married in green, ashamed to be seen; married in grey, you will go far away; married in red, you will wish yourself dead; married in blue, love ever true; married in yellow, you're ashamed of your fellow; married in black, you will wish yourself back; married in pink, of you he'll aye think. (Palmer, 1976).

Marry the miskin for the muck and get pisened with the stink on it. An old Warwickshire proverb warning that if you marry for money you'll live to regret it (Northall, 1896).

Michaelmas chickens and parsons' daughters never come to any good. (Northall, 1894).

Money and fair words. Common response to the question: "'Ow much was it?", esp. with children (K. Carruthers).

Much of a muchness. Almost identical; very much the same EG "These cakes are a bit much of a muchness"; still in common use.

My belly thinks my throat's cut. A common expression used when feeling hungry.

My cake's all dough. According to Northall (1896), this is "expressive of mischance or disappointment" EG "My cake is dough: but I'll in among the rest" (Shakespeare, *The Taming of the Shrew*, Act V, Sc. I), and the old Warwickshire folk-rhyme *O, Dear, O!*:

> O, dear, O!
> My cake's all dough [i.e. sad, heavy]
> And how to make it better
> I do not know.

My eye! An interjection implying a good deal of disbelief (Old Sarbot, 1869). Now in widespread use.

My Ga! An old Warwickshire oath listed in Northall (1896).

Neither my eye nor my elbow. Neither one thing nor the other; neither here nor there (Northall, 1894); interestingly, Palmer (1976) has 'neither my arse nor my elbow' with an identical definition.

Neither sick nor sorry. Said of someone who has caused annoyance or trouble of some kind but shows little remorse (Northall, 1894).

Never in the rain of pig's pudding. Used to refer to something that will never happen.

Nick at need. At a pinch (Northall, 1896) EG "I'm nothin' to 'im at ordinary times, but 'e's glad enough of us nick-at-need."

No carrion will kill a crow. (Northall, 1894).

No cocks eyes out. Blood sports were a popular entertainment in the Midlands up until the late nineteenth century, and cockfights were held on a regular basis in Birmingham: there were pits behind the Salutation Hill in Snow Hill (c.1798), Duddeston Hall (c.1747), the Old Crown Inn in Deritend, and sites were also opened at Smallbrook Street in 1809, and Coleshill Street in 1817. "Although it was made illegal in 1849," writes Palmer (1976), "cock-fighting took a long time to disappear and it left its mark on the language. 'No cocks eyes out' was a Warwickshire expression, meaning 'no great harm has been done, therefore you can get on with what you have been doing'. 'That cock won't fight' means 'that won't be any good'. 'To quarrel like fighting cocks' is self evident," and there is still a Fighting Cocks public house in Moseley.

Not worth a tinker's curse. Worthless; valueless (Northall, 1894).

Off, like a jug handle. (Northall, 1896).

Old Exile's put his check in. Commonly used as a euphemism for death.

Old Sarbut told us so. A local version of the phrase "A little bird told me"(Northall, 1894); see also **sarbut** for a full definition of this word.

One of these days yo'll meet yerself comin' back. Said to someone who is always rushing around.

One over the eight. Drunk.

One white foot, buy a horse; two white feet, try a horse; three white feet, look well about him; four white feet, go away without him. (Timmins, 1889). Before the first seeds of the industrial revolution were sown in the English Midlands, people were solely reliant on the land, and horses were vital to the agricultural economy. As Palmer (1976) writes, "they were much prized, and purchased with great care," and this old Warwickshire folk-rhyme appears to be offering advice on which is the best type of horse to buy.

On the arm. Courting.

On the bounce. Achieving something consecutively EG "Villa's new striker scored three goals on the bounce yesterday."

On the lash. A newer Irish Brummie term for a heavy drinking session; to go out on the lash means to go out with the intention of getting drunk.

On the mace. See **on the strap**.

On the pop. Going out drinking heavily.

On the razzle. Going out for a drink and a good time.

On the rob. Going out looking for something to steal.

On the strap.. To have something 'on the strap' meant to have goods on the slate (on credit) at the huckster's (corner shop) which sold just about everything EG "Our entry faced the grocery shop Amy Keedwell where we got our food on the strap, out in the book and pay on Friday" (E. Williams, quoted in *Brummagem* Issue No.2); see also **on the mace.**

On the tap and tar. Cadging; borrowing with no intention of paying back.

On the treacle stick. Out of work and claiming benefit; before that the phrase referred to claiming outdoor relief from 'The Parish' - usually in the form of tokens for coal and bread.

Out of the road of the coaches. Safe; secure; out of harm's way (Northall, 1894).

Over the left shoulder. Antagonistic; adverse; "contrary to custom" (Northall, 1894); to do someone 'a kindness over the left shoulder' is to do them an injury; a similar phrase is also common in some French dialects.

Paws off, Pompey. Don't touch (Northall, 1894).

Pick up your nalls and cut. Pack up your stuff and leave.

Pride must be pinched. "A reproof to one who complains of tight boots, garments, &c." (Northall, 1894).

Pull the other one, it's got bells on it. Said, whilst holding out an arm, to people fond of a tall tale or two, or in reaction to anything which seems unbelievable; now in widespread use.

Put a pitch plaster in your mouth. Shut up; be quiet (Northall, 1894).

Put in with the bread and pulled out with the cakes. An old Warwickshire folk-phrase spoken of a slow, half-witted or simple person (Northall, 1896).

Put the wood in the hole. Shut the door (E. Yorke).

Put your face straight or I'll put it straight for you. Said to a youngster who is sulking; see also **to play your face.**

Put your hand out and feel if you're in bed. "Said to one who expresses a mistaken impression" (Northall, 1896) EG "Yer dreamin', mate - put yer 'and out 'n' feel if yer in bed."

Rain before seven, fine before eleven. (Timmins, 1889).

Ring finger, blue-bell, tell a lie and go to hell. Said to emphasize a promise, often with fingers crossed (Timmins, 1889).

Round the houses. Trousers (K. Carruthers).

Run round the table and get fed up! According to Win Tainty, this phrase was a stock response to children who constantly moaned about being hungry.

Sam who? According to Northall (1894), this was a common Warwickshire street phrase in the late nineteenth century, similar in sentiment to "So what?": "a sort of contemptuous 'put off.' *Exs.* 'I'll punch your head;' 'I'll tell your gaffer!' *Ans.* 'Sam who?'"

San fairy Ann. I dont care; it doesn't matter; from the French, "Ça ne fait rien" (D. Adams).

Shake your feathers! Hurry up!

Shake your shift and give the crows a feed. An insult implying that the person to whom it is addressed is flea-ridden (Northall, 1894).

She'll make the lads sigh at their suppers. "Said of a pretty or attractive girl" (Northall, 1894).

Shift your feet from up the ess-hole. Move your feet away from the fire; stop lounging around (S. Kay).

Shitting luck is good luck. Often said by someone who treads in excrement, or, as Northall (1894) puts it, is "befouled by mischance." As Wright (1872, p.146) suggests, this phrase probably originates from the ancient term for manure ('gold dust'), which in turn probably originates from the agricultural value of dung, or perhaps from its natural colour: "The Anglo-Saxon vocabularies have preserved another name *gold hordhus*, a gold treasure house, or gold treasury, which is still more curious from its connexion with the name *gold finder* or *gold farmer*, given as late as the seventeenth century to the cleaners of privies."

Short and sweet, like a donkey's gallop. See also **short and sweet, like a roast maggot** (Northall, 1894).

Short and sweet, like a roast maggot. (Northall, 1894, and Mary Bodfish).

Shut your mouth and give your arse a chance. Be quiet, you're talking gibberish (S. Chapman).

Silence in the pigmarket, and let the old sow have a grunt. (Northall, 1894).

Sit further back and you'll get a longer ride. (K. Carruthers).

Six of one and half a dozen of the other. "Said of opposite parties in a quarrel, misdemeanour, scheme, &c., when the right or wrong of the matter in question cannot be fixed on either side with certainty" (Northall, 1894); said when two people are arguing over whose fault it is and both are to blame (K. Carruthers).

Slow and steady wins the race. (Northall, 1894).

Sneeze-a-bob, blow the chair bottom out! Said to a person who sneezes (Northall, 1894).

Sneeze on Monday, sneeze for danger; sneeze on Tuesday, kiss a stranger; sneeze on Wednesday, have a letter; sneeze on Thursday, something better; sneeze on Friday, sneeze for sorrow; sneeze on Saturday, see true love tomorrow. (Timmins, 1889).

Sold again and got the money. "A dealer's phrase, when a bargain is closed, and the money is paid. It is used figuratively, too, when a person is 'sold' or choused" (Northall, 1896).

Some day, or never at the farthest. An evasive answer to a person (esp. if a child) who keeps asking for something (Northall, 1894).

Some day when Nelson gets back. Said in reply to the question, "When are we going to the seaside, mom?" (K. Carruthers).

Soon crooks the tree that good gambrel would be. Old Midlands proverb (Northall, 1896); see also **gambrel**.

Sound love is not soon forgotten. (Northall, 1894).

Spare 'em. A theoretical place where ill-mannered or generally disliked people are reputed to come from; "the limbo of uncouth folk" (Northall, 1894) EG "'E comes from Spare 'em."

Spotted and spangled like Joe Danks's Devil. An old Warwickshire dialect phrase; according to Northall (1894), Joe Danks was "an itinerant showman, who exhibited a wretched creature whose attractions comprised skin eruptions and a spangled suit."

Steady past your Granny's. Be careful (E. Hawker).

Stick your two thumbs up your arse and sit on your elbows. Also **sit on your thumb till more room do come** (Northall, 1894); often said "when all the seating was taken up and someone had complained of having nowhere to sit" (Joan Burgess).

Straight off the reel. Straight away; immediately; without hindrance (Northall, 1894).

Strip of piss. Skinny; gangly; scrawny EG "'E's a thin strip o' piss."

Swelp me Bob. Contracted form of "So help me God" (David Grainger). A. Sealey also writes that **Well, self me Bob** was another variant of this phrase.

Ta-ra a bit. Goodbye; ta-ta; see you soon (C. Butters).

That cock won't fight. "That won't be any good" (Palmer, 1976); often said of any weak or unsatisfactory plan or line of argument (Northall, 1894); similar in sentiment to the phrase **that won't hold water**; see also the phrase **no cocks eyes out**.

That'll tickle your gig. That'll make you laugh; according to Northall (1894), "there appears to be some play on *gig*, a wanton, and *gig*, slang = pudendum. The phrase is now used of anything likely to cause mirth, or even brisk movement of the body."

That's about my barror. That's all I can do; I can't manage any more; "by 'barror' is intended, possibly, *barrow-load*" (Northall, 1894). Also used when referring sarcastically to someone who has done something not worthy EG "That's just about 'is barrer." In both cases, 'barror' and 'barrer' are pronunciation variants of 'barrow'.

That's a cock. Usually said after spitting, esp. when the saliva contains mucus.

That's a rhyme, if you'll take it in time. Often said by someone who unintentionally makes their words rhyme; similar in sentiment to the contemporary phrase 'I'm a poet and I don't know it'.

That's it if you can dance it. Similar to the current phrase 'if the cap fits, wear it'.

That's killed my pig. It's all over; I'm finished; "I am dealt the finishing stroke" (Northall, 1896).

That's settled my hash. See **that's killed my pig** (Northall, 1896).

That's the chap that gnawed the cheese. Usually said in an accusatory tone to point out a person guilty of some offence (Northall, 1894).

That's the last the cobbler threw at his wife. That's the end of the argument; that's the last I want to hear of it; often said to end an argument; "the play is on 'last'. Actually, the *last word* is meant" (Northall, 1894).

That's the stuff for trousers. Said in reference to anything good or pleasing; "this phrase once had a definite meaning, no doubt, but is now used of any good thing" (Northall, 1894).

That sticks in my craw. I don't believe it; I won't swallow that.

That's what you are! "A street phrase, and deadly insult" (Northall, 1894); apparently, this was usually said after someone had blown their nose in full view of the addressee. A common retort to this insult was 'there's two friends parted'.

That's yer whack! That's your lot EG "'E's 'ad 'is whack"; said of someone who has had their quota or fair share.

That was our bed and we lay on it. Said by someone who accepts their lot; used to express a feeling of resignation or submissiveness either in the past or the present.

That won't pay the old woman her ninepence. "Said of aught not equivalent to given value, in money or kind" (Northall, 1894).

The best of the boiling. The best and most worthy member of a family.

The bigger the man, the better the mark. The bigger a man is, the more there is to aim, or strike at in a fight (Northall, 1894).

The colour of the devil's nutting bag. Dingy; dowdy; "bad-coloured" (Northall, 1894, and Palmer, 1976).

The devil hung in chains. An old Warwickshire dialect phrase for a cooking turkey dressed with sausages.

The ghost of Old Flam. In the old Warwickshire dialect, any mysterious noise was said to be caused by this spectre (Northall, 1894); the origin of the name 'Flam', however, remains a mystery.

Them as ask don't get, them as don't ask don't want. (Joan Burgess).

The oak before the ash, a summer of splash; the ash before the oak, a summer of smoke. (Timmins, 1889).

The old woman's picking her geese. It's snowing.

There and back to see where it is. Common Brummie response to a child's question, "Where you bin, Mom?" (K. Carruthers). Another variant of this phrase is "There and back to see how far it is."

There en't no babby washed. Nothing has happened; nothing has been achieved; no progress has been made (D. Adams).

There's more old ale in you than fourpenny. Said to a quick and sharp-witted person; according to Northall (1894), in the late nineteenth century fourpenny was "beer at 4*d*. per quart."

There's no cock's eyes out. Usually said in reference to a non-event, or when something expected had failed to materialise; also said "when a matter goes off tamely . . . it recalls the days of cock-fighting" (Northall, 1894); also common in the Black Country dialect.

There's no profit got from feeding pigs but their muck and their company. (Northall, 1894).

There's nothing done without trouble, except letting the fire out. (Northall, 1894).

There's nothing gained by being witty; fame gathers but wind to blather up a name. Old Warwickshire saying (Northall, 1896).

The sandman's come into your eyes. You look sleepy; tired; usually addressed to children (Northall, 1894).

The whole hog-shead. The whole hog; the full monty (Jeffrey, 1868).

This en't gettin' the babby a new bonnet. Nothing is happening; nothing is being achieved; no progress is being made (S. Kay).

This en't gonna feed the babby. Nothing is happening; nothing is being achieved; no progress is being made (S. Kay).

Three jumps at the pantry door and a buttered brick. An exasperated reply to the constant nagging of children, esp. to the question "What's for tea, mom?" (D. Dodds).

Three sheets to the wind. Drunk; inebriated; intoxicated EG "'E got 'ome three sheets t'the wind last night"; also common in the Black Country dialect (Walker, undated).

Throw your orts where you throw your love. "This is admonitory, not a piece of advice: some add 'and in bigger pieces!'" (Northall, 1894).

Tick-tack, never change back, touch cold iron. The binding sentence upon the completion of a sale, deal or exchange by children, at the same time touching a piece of iron with the finger (Rhodes, 1950).

To be brother and Bob. To act like Siamese twins; to be inseparable (Northall, 1894).

To be down on your duff. To be out of luck; to be down in the dumps (Northall, 1894).

To be full of good keep. To be happy; cheerful.

To be given a whaling. To receive a good hiding; to be thrashing as punishment for some transgression EG "I just 'eard old Jonesy givin' 'is nipper a good whalin' over that bost winda."

To be given a wigging. To receive a telling off EG "'Er gave 'im a right good wiggin' when 'e gorrin."

To be in on the mace. To enter on the credit side of an account.

To be in on the nail. To pay out in full.

To be in the club. To be pregnant.

To be in the family way. To be pregnant.

To be in your oiltot. To be very pleased EG "'E's in 'is oiltot over summat." Tennant (1983) suggests that this phrase probably originated from "the old habit of a worker drinking a tot of olive oil on payday to line his stomach before going out drinking, supposedly to stave off getting too drunk."

To be measured for a new suit of clothes. To receive a beating or thrashing EG "'E was measured fer a new suit of clothes last wick by them roughs up Livery Street."

To be off the hooks. Mary Bodfish writes that this had an altogether different meaning to the similar sounding phrase 'to be let off the hook' (to be allowed to go free), and meant "to be unwell, but not seriously ill."

To be on a hiding to nothing. To put in a lot of work for little reward; to work hard for no material gain EG "Yer on an 'idin' to nothin', you are" (R. Couling).

To be on a line with someone. To be angry about something; according to an anonymous contributor from Kings Norton, a common response to this was often, "Well, slide down the prop then."

To be on the bite. To be on the borrow, looking for something to cadge EG "Ayeup, 'e's on the bleedin' bite again" (R. Couling).

To be on the box. To be off work, sick (E. Yorke).

To be on the knocker. To sell items from door to door (K. Carruthers).

To be on the rantan. To be angered, maddened or enraged EG "'E's on the rantan again" (Raven, 1978).

To be put to your trumps. To be embarrassed (Northall, 1894).

To be sick of the simples. To be silly or stupid; according to Northall (1894), in the Warwickshire dialect of the late nineteenth century it was common to say to "the performer of a foolish action, 'I'll have you cut for the simples'."

To be struck all of a heap. To be surprised, astonished or flabbergasted (Northall, 1894).

To be the very spawn of a person. To resemble someone else very closely; to be alike (Northall, 1894).

To be up in the boughs. To be in a rage; to be in a bad temper (Northall, 1894).

To be up the stick. To be pregnant.

To be whitewashed. "To pass through the bankruptcy courts" (Northall, 1894).

To blow sugar and hurricanes. Usually applied to the weather when it has turned nasty, implying that there's a fierce wind; to blow a gale EG "It's blowin' sugar 'n' 'urricanes out there" (Jeffrey, 1868).

To blow the bubble. To reveal something; to make something known; to give away a secret EG "That's it. 'Er's gone an' blowed the bubble."

To blow your bags out. "To eat a heart meal" (Northall, 1896).

To box Harry and chew rag. To go on a diet; to eat very little (Northall, 1894).

To bring the beans to the boil. To get married; to put up the banns of marriage EG "Theym bringin' the beans to the boil."

To burn daylight. To light a candle or switch on a light before it is dark EG "Come, we burn daylight, ho" (Shakespeare, *Romeo and Juliet*, Act I, Sc. IV).

To call someone out of name. "To call anyone by what is not their proper name" (Skeat, 1876).

To carry the grind stone. To look after a spouse during a period of illness; commonly used in the 1800s to refer to a man who is looking after his wife during her pregnancy; also common in the Worcestershire dialect.

To cast a spavin. To throw a fit or overreact; Paul Williams writes that a spavin is a part of a horse near the hoof, and suggests that the phrase may be an embellishment of 'to cast a shoe'.

To catch it. To receive a scolding, thrashing or other punishment, as in the following Midlands folk-rhyme quoted in Northall (1896):
A. You'll catch it when yo get 'um.
B. What for?
A. Breaking the bottle and spilling the rum,
and kissing your sweetheart all the way 'um.

To catch the chat. To receive an admonishment or reprimand of some kind; to be told off (Northall, 1894).

To change the name and not the letter is to change for worse and not for better. An admonishment for future brides (Palmer, 1976).

To clear your feathers. To clear all existing debts; to "rub off old scores" (Northall, 1894).

To cock a deaf one. To feign ignorance EG "'E's cockin' a deaf'un."

To come a purler. To fall heavily EG "'E came a right purler over them steps."

To come from Gornal. To be vulgar and coarse EG "'Er must come from Gornal"; to say this suggested that someone came from a place "renowned for the oddness and rudeness of its inhabitants" (Northall, 1894). The people from Gornal were unfairly seen as uncouth. In reality they were hard-working and neighbourly folk.

To come the madam. To assume airs and graces; to put on a superior manner EG "You can stop comin' the madam with me, my lady!"

To come your ways. To come here: usually addressed to children in an encouraging tone (Northall, 1896) EG "Look to't, I charge you; come your ways" (Shakespeare, *Hamlet*, Act I, Sc. III), "'Come your ways, come your ways" (Shakespeare, *Troilus and Cressida*, Act III, Sc. II), and "Ay, go your ways, go your ways" (Shakespeare, *As You Like It*, Act IV, Sc. I).

To cop out. To be caught in the act of committing some minor misdemeanour, or to be told off for doing so EG "'Er dain't arf cop out when the old mon fount out."

To cop the fork. To be displeased with something; to take umbrage EG "'Er's copped the fork about summat" (Tennant, 1983, D. Morris, and Mary Bodfish).

To crack a Solomon. To skive off work; according to Paul Williams, this term was usually applied to someone who was "having a day off work when they weren't ill – usually the day before a big pigeon race."

To credit. To believe; to give credence to (Geoff Moore) EG "You wouldn't credit it, would ya?"

To creep up someone's sleeve. To attempt to obtain a favour by coaxing or wheedling (Northall, 1896).

To crock up. To stock up or store (Northall, 1894).

To cry roast meat. To boast or brag about something; Northall (1894) gives two more specific definitions: "(1) to make known one's good luck. (2) to boast of women's favours."

To cry the mare. "Harvest time in the villages of the West Midlands in the early 18th century was celebrated with a custom called crying the mare. The field reapers tied together the tops of the last heads of corn or 'mares' and then stood some distance away to throw their sickles. The winner was the first person to cut the knot" (reported in *Metro*, 6 March 2001).

To cut it fat. To boast, brag or show off (Palmer, 1979) EG "They sport the blunt and cut it fat with the pretty girls of Brummagem" (from an old ballad entitled *Pretty Girls of Brummagem*, c.1833-5).

To cut your stick. To leave; to depart or withdraw from (Palmer, 1979) EG "Oh, if you are Mr. Cheatem, the Tally-man, you'd better cut your stick" (from the old Brummagem street ballad *Tally-man!*, c.1845-61).

To dispute with Bellarmin. To hit the bottle; to become an alcoholic or drunkard; "The Bellarmin - a dutch mug or jug - is a varied form of our Toby Tosspot, Greybeard, &c.: but the face upon it was popularly likened to the visage of Cardinal Bellarmin, the bitter opponent of the reform party in the Netherlands, in the latter part of the sixteenth and early seventeenth centuries" (Northall, 1894). According to Halliwell (1855), 'bellarmin' was also a "burlesque word used among drinkers to express a stout bottle of strong drink."

To do a moonlight. To do 'a moonlight flit' meant to move out of lodgings under cover of night, usually to escape the attention of bum bailisses.

To do a runner. To make a sharp exit; to escape EG "There was just too many on 'em. We 'ad ter do a runner."

To do something off your own bat. To do something on your own initiative; to do something without waiting to be asked.

To draw in your horns. To lose ground in an argument or fight (Northall, 1894).

To draw the long bow. To lie or exaggerate (Northall, 1894).

To draw the yoke together. To collaborate with another person; to work in tandem (Northall, 1894).

To drop a rick. To make a mistake – not, as in other dialects, 'to drop a brick'; it is unknown why the letter 'b' is dropped in Brummagem English.

To drop your jib. To become displeased or surly EG "What have you dropped your jib for?"

To eat like a pig chobbling coal. To eat noisily, with your mouth open EG "Y'sound like a pig chobblin' coal with them cuk-cuks."

To fall into the huckster's hands. To be cheated or duped (Northall, 1894).

To fetch copper. To strike fire from stone with iron; according to Northall (1894), children in both Staffordshire and Warwickshire used to "run swiftly along the paved side-walks striking sparks therefrom with their nailed shoes, and use the phrase."

To fix the bottom on someone. To become a parasite (Northall, 1894).

To fly the kite. To enjoy yourself; a common phrase in many English dialects, but its meaning in the old Warwickshire dialect appears to be unique.

To get hammered. To get drunk; to become intoxicated.

To get the forehorse by the head. To clear all debts; "to see one's way clear" (Northall, 1894).

To get the sack and a bag to put it in. To lose your job (K. Carruthers).

To give a Bewdley salute. To tap on the ground with a walking stick when passing an acquaintance (Northall, 1894).

To give someone Bell Tinker. To beat, "as tinkers clout a pot" (Northall, 1894).

To give someone the pip. To annoy, bother, hinder or disturb someone (D. Adams).

To go a-hopping. To pick hops (Palmer, 1979) EG "My father is gone a hopping, and he wanted to get a donkey on the tally" (from the street ballad *Tallyman!*, c.1845-61).

To go all round the Wrekin. To go the long way round; to go on an unnecessarily long journey or errand; still in common use.

To go a-Thomasing. "To go round on St. Thomas' Day, begging for Christmas gifts" (Skeat, 1876).

To go away bag and baggage. To leave, taking all moveable possessions; Northall (1896) states that this is probably a military phrase.

To go away breech in hand. To leave defeated, beaten, or crest-fallen (Northall, 1894).

To go birding. To go out looking for girlfriends.

To go home with the parish lantern. To travel home by moonlight (Northall, 1894).

To go off hopper-arsed. To get the wrong end of the stick.

To go off like one o'clock. To leave "with as little delay as a workman gets off to dinner when the clock strikes one" (Northall, 1894).

To go out of your own country and all others, into Walsall. According to Northall (1894), "Walsall was formerly regarded as a rough, 'ill-conditioned' place, inhabited by boors. There is a tale that a pedestrian had need to ask passers-by the way to this place. He said to the first man he met, 'Is this the way to Walsall?' The reply was 'Ah!' The second man he questioned replied 'I suppose so.' The third answered 'Go to H___!' Thank you,' said the pedestrian, 'I am evidently nearing your town.'"

To go the raps. To do something quickly; energetically; violently; similar to the phrases 'to go ten-to-the-dozen' or 'to go like the clappers'.

To go to the foot of the stairs. To be dumbfounded or surprised; similar to "I'll be damned!" or "I'll be blowed!" EG "Well, I'll goo to the foot of the stairs" (S. Kay).

To go up the spout. To be pawned (Palmer, 1979) EG "On Saturday he his clothes gets out, on Sunday proudly struts about, but on Monday his togs go up the spout" (from an old Brummagem ballad entitled *Pretty Girls of Brummagem*, c.1833-5).

To hack and hew. To stumble or hesitate in speaking or reading aloud (Northall, 1896).

To have a bob on yourself. According to Mary Bodfish, people who have got a bob on themselves think very highly of themselves; always used reprovingly – particularly when a person's high self-regard seems completely unjustified.

To have a bull and cow. To argue; to have a dispute or fall out over something EG "I 'ad a right bull 'n' cow with the old-Dutch last wick."

To have a cob on. To be mardy; to look miserable and moody "'E's got a right cob on 'im over summat" (R. Couling, and Robert Lowe).

To have a dog in your belly. To be bad-tempered (Northall, 1894).

To have a face as long as Livery Street. To look sad, miserable or melancholic (R. Couling, J. Barklam, and Yvonne Rideout) EG "Wasamara with yo' snivellin' an' grizzlin', an' look at yer bloody ferce, it's as lung as Livery Street, w'at ya' bin up to, yo' ain't bin fightin' again'ave ya?" (Smith, undated); also used to refer to a long and rambling story or tale (R. Powderhill). Livery Street was once one of the longest streets in Brum.

To have a face like a bag of frogs. To be ugly or unattractive EG "'E's got a phiz like a bag of frogs."

To have a face like a fourpence. To look miserable.

To have a face like a wet Saturday night. To look sad or miserable.

To have a face that would stop a clock. To be ugly or unattractive (Northall, 1894).

To have a quid in your gob. To have a 'put-on' or affected accent EG "'E's got a quid in 'is gob" (Tennant, 1983).

To have a slate or two missing. To be barmy, mad or insane.

To have eyes like piss-holes in the snow. To look unattractive or unappealing.

To have it rough. To have a tough time of it; to suffer EG "We dain't arf 'ave it rough when we was nippers."

To have no cotter. To cease communication with others; often said when somebody had decided to stop talking or being friendly with others; 'to have no cotter with someone' means to break off relations with a person because they have done something wrong or unacceptable EG "I won't have no cotter with 'em no more" (Joan Burgess), "Doan 'ave no cotter with 'em"; see also **to take no cotter.**

To have no oil in your lamp. To have no common sense EG "'En't yer got no oil in yer lamp?"

To have someone on the carpet. To reprove or reprimand (Northall 1896).

To have the brass skimmer rubbed over your face. To be impudent or audacious EG "'Er's 'ad the brassen skimmer rubbed over 'er face, 'er 'as" (Northall, 1896).

To have the face ache. To be angry, cross or grumpy EG "'Er's got the face ache over summat or other" (H. Taylor).

To have your arse in your hand. Mary Bodfish writes that this phrase, which is still very popular, means "to be obdurately sullen and bad-tempered," and it is often said of children who appear to have their tails between their legs after a telling-off.

To have your jacket trimmed. To be beaten up EG "'E's 'ad 'is jacket trimmed by some o' them roughs."

To hop the twig. To speed by; to travel quickly (D. Morris).

To jet like a crow in the gutter. To strut; to swagger (Palmer, 1976).

To keep someone to their cake and milk. To keep someone under strict supervision; to watch over someone; "to keep someone within bounds, or to any firm rule" (Northall, 1896).

To kick the bucket. To die; "Truth, 'tis said, lies in a well, Pursuit is all in vain, We kick the bucket going down, And ne'er come back again" (Old Sarbot, 1869). Now in widespread use.

To kick up Bob's a-dying. "To make noisy merriment" (Northall 1894).

To knock it on the head. To put an end to something EG "Knock that noise on the bleedin' 'ead, will yer? I can't get to kip."

To learn the thieves' alphabet. To be engaged in illegal or nefarious activities (Old Sarbot, 1869).

To leather someone's pig. To beat someone, either in a fight or an argument (Northall, 1894).

To look as if you have murdered a turnip and washed your face in its blood. To look ill, sickly or generally unwell (Northall, 1894); an old Warwickshire dialect phrase.

To look like a boiled turnip. See **to look as if you have murdered a turnip and washed your face in its blood**.

To look like a dog that has burned its tail. To look ashamed; "discomposed" (Northall, 1894).

To look two ways for Sunday. To be thoughtless, careless or improvident (Northall, 1894).

To make a maygame of someone. To mock, ridicule or scorn (Northall, 1894).

To make brick walls. To eat hastily or greedily and without chewing (Northall, 1894).

To make someone dance without a fiddle. To give someone a telling off; to scold (Northall, 1894).

To make the neddy. To strike gold; to amass a fortune or large profit (Northall, 1894).

To meddle and make. To interfere EG "So I sez to 'im, I sez, you've no call to come to me for the keys, I sez, I en't gonna meddle 'n' make, and the keys en't in our 'ouse, I sez" (Skeat, 1876), "For my part, I'll not meddle nor make no further" (Shakespeare, *Troilus and Cressida*, Act I, Sc. I), "Quoth the young cock, I'll neither meddle nor make" (Old proverb).

To mend your draught. To have another drink (esp. beer).

Tomorrow goes by of itself. (Northall, 1894).

Too fat to turn or spin. (Northall, 1896).

Too much for one, and not enough for two, like the Walsall man's goose. From *The Hungry Man from Walsall*: the title of a popular comic song. The origin of this proverb, according to Poole (1880, p.25), is that "a Walsall man, when asked if he and his wife were going to have a goose for their Christmas dinner, replied 'No;' for said he, "the goose was a silly bird - too much for one to eat, and not enough for two.'"

Too thick to thrive. "Said of livestock too abundant in a place" (Northall, 1894); it seems probable that this phrase might also have been said of people, but there does not appear to be any extant record of this.

To pay footing. To pay a fine or forfeit on first doing anything (Northall, 1896); see also **foot-ale**.

To pay forehand rent. "To pay down the rent prior to the occupancy" (Marshall, 1796).

To pick up your crumbs. To regain health after an illness.

To play Hell and Tommy with someone. To mess somebody about; to play around, confound or confuse; to harass or vex (Northall, 1894); see also **to play the bear**.

To play Old Boots. See **to play the bear**.

To play Old Gooseberry. See **to play the bear**.

To play Old Harry. See **to play the bear**.

To play the bear. To inflict heavy damage (Palmer, 1976); similar in meaning to the phrase **to play Hell and Tommy with someone**, but also applied to inanimate objects, such as crops EG "The frost 'as played the bear with the tater tops" (Northall, 1896), "The pigs have been in the garden and played the bear with it" (Wright, 1898-1905); according to Northall (1894), the Gloucester dialect has the variant **to play the very Buggan with someone** ("Buggan = Old Bogey, Satan, or any evil spirit").

To play the wag. To play truant; to stay away from school (Geoff Moore) EG "I suppose it would be fair to say that 'playing the wag' (being truant from school) was an occasional accepted thing, amongst us kids anyway in my schooldays" (Smith, undated).

To play your face. To sulk.

To pop about like a parched pea on a shovel. To be fidgety, jittery or jumpy (Northall, 1894); see also **like a pea on a drumhead**.

To pour water on a drowned mouse. To continue hitting or arguing with someone who has already been beaten; "to cast out spite on one past vengeance" (Northall, 1894).

To pull a fast one. To deceive or cheat EG "Are you tryin' ter pull a fast'un?"

To put the bite on. To borrow, beg or cadge (esp. money).

To put the mockers on. To spoil or ruin something EG "That dain't 'alf put the mockers on it, I can tell ya!"

To quarrel like fighting cocks. (Palmer, 1976); see **no cocks eyes out**.

To queer the pitch. To ruin something; to spoil a good thing EG "'E's queered the pitch"; also common in the Worcestershire and Black Country dialects (Walker, undated).

To quis the fat. To gossip or chatter (Palmer, 1979) EG "Each place of fashion they are at, drink their champagne and quis the fat" (from an old Brummagem ballad entitled *Pretty Girls of Brummagem*, c.1833-5).

To riddle the gledes. To sift through the embers of a coal fire.

To ride a free horse to death. To abuse someone's hospitality, patience or kindness (Northall, 1894).

To rattle like a bibble in a can. To chatter or gossip incessantly EG "They bin rattlin' like a bibble in a can all day, them two"; see also **to rattle like a pea in a collander**.

To rattle like a pea in a collander. To chatter or gossip incessantly.

To rough it. Not, as is the contemporary definition of the phrase, to sleep rough or outdoors, but to have a hard time of it EG "We dain't arf 'ave to rough it when we was young, I can tell yer."

To run like the clappers. To run really fast EG "We 'ad to run like the clappers to gerraway."

To sell someone a pen'orth. To tell a fanciful tale, with intent to deceive (Northall, 1896).

To send someone to Coventry. To ignore or stop communicating with someone; Shakespeare uses this phrase in a slightly different form but identical sense when Falstaff says to Bardolph: "Get thee to Coventry," and it is still in common use throughout Birmingham.

To set the dice on someone. To cheat, con or swindle (Northall, 1894).

To shut your knife. To die EG "'E shut 'is knife last wick."

To sing like a Bromwich throstle. To make a din as frightful as a donkey braying (Ursula, 1988). According to Northall (1894), "a Bromwich throstle' is a donkey," and West Bromwich is, of course, the place meant.

To sing like a muckbird. "To emit a continuous mournful sound in a minor key" (Northall, 1896).

To spite your belly for the sake of your back. To go without food in order to buy expensive clothes (Northall, 1894).

To sport the blunt. To flash money around; to be extravagant (Palmer, 1979) EG "They sport the blunt and cut it fat with the pretty girls of Brummagem" (from an old ballad entitled *Pretty Girls of Brummagem*, c.1833-5).

To stand to your pan-pudding. To be firm; to stand your ground or hold your position (Northall, 1894).

To stare like a throttled Isaac. (Northall, 1894).

To stick up your stick. To die (Northall, 1894).

To stick your spoon in the wall. To die EG "'E stuck 'is spoon in the wall last March."

To stuff your hodge. To eat your fill; to eat as much as you possibly can (Northall, 1894); still in common use.

To sup sorrow by the spoonful. According to Northall (1896) this was commonly heard in phrases relating to matrimonial intentions EG "Ah! If she marries that fellow, she'll sup sorrow by the spoonful."

To take a dekko. To have a look EG "Eeyar, tek a dekko at this"(E. Yorke).

To take no cotter. To take no notice EG "Doan tek no cotter of 'em, our kid."

To take tea in the kitchen. To drink tea from the saucer (Northall, 1894).

To take the pug. To be offended by something.

To take up the cudgels for someone. To fight someone else's battle (Northall, 1894).

To talk on the strap. To boast, brag or show off; used to refer to someone who is telling a tall story EG "I 'eard 'er talkin' on the strap again" (Joan Burgess).

To talk the legs off an iron pot. To chatter or gossip incessantly; similar in meaning to the contemporary phrase 'to talk the hind legs off a donkey'; often said of a person who is skilled in rhetoric, or has 'the gift of the gab' EG "'Er could talk the legs off an iron pot, 'er could."

To take the rise. To take the piss out of someone; to mock or belittle; still in common use.

To tan someone's hide. To administer a beating or thrashing; "to chastise" (Northall, 1894).

To think a lie, like Cox's pig. This saying, according to Palmer (1976), "refers to an unfortunate animal who thought his breakfast was arriving when in fact the butcher was coming to kill him."

To throw the belt off. "Used when someone was talking about work too much. Probably referred to the overhead shaft drives in factories. To stop a machine the operator pulled a lever to throw the belt off the drive pulley on to an idler pulley" (Tennant, 1983).

To tumble to pieces. To give birth (Northall, 1894).

To turn up the eyes like a duck at thunder. To be scared or frightened of something;

to take fright; "an inferior, or corrupted version is 'like a dying duck in a thunderstorm'" (Northall, 1894).

To walk an Alderman's pace. To walk sedately and with gravity (Northall, 1894).

To walk like a cat in pattens. To potter about aimlessly; to loiter or dawdle (Northall, 1894).

To watch someone's waters. To keep someone under surveillance; to keep an eye on someone; to keep someone under close observation (Northall, 1894).

To wear the yellow. To be jealous; according to Northall (1894), this phrase also meant "to be free, one's own master, or a bachelor" EG "Give me my yellow hose again" (old song).

To win the whistle. To lose; to win nothing at all (Northall, 1896).

To wipe someone's eye. To see what someone else fails to see (Northall, 1894).

To work a flanker. To attempt to gain something by dishonesty or deceit.

To work by the grit. To carry out piece-work; "to undertake work in the gross, to contract for it" (Skeat, 1876).

Trimmed up like a ham bone. Smartly dressed; (K. Carruthers).

Two heads are better than one, even if the one's a sheep's. "An extended version of the well-known and ancient proverb. 'A sheep's' head, in folk figure, means a daft or unreasoning head" (Northall, 1894).

Two short of a dozen. Lacking in common sense or intelligence; not all there (K. Carruthers).

Two swedes to a ton of mutton. "A formula used by one who does not wish to gamble for high stakes. 'I'll bet you a button' belongs to the same class of saying" (Northall, 1894).

Two-year breeders never ha'done. An old Warwickshire dialect phrase, "said of married people whose first children are born one child two years after the other" (Northall, 1894).

Up a daisy! also **ups a daisy!** and **whoops a daisy!** "Addressed to a child when taking it up into the arms; or in lifting it from the ground after a fall" (Northall, 1894); still in common use in the West Midlands.

Upright and down straight. Equitable; fair and square; honest (Northall, 1894); similar in meaning to **aysam-jaysam.**

Up the suff. Lost; missing (Tennant, 1983).

Up the wooden hill to Bedfordshire. Upstairs, to bed; EG "Our Mom allis liked us up the wooden hill to Bedfordshire by seven o'clock ev'ry night, but the three big uns were allowed up until ten" (Smith, undated); frequently shortened to "Up the wooden 'ill" (go to bed), esp. when talking to children (R. Powderhill).

Use your loaf! Use your head; think about it.

Wallop, Mrs Cox. According to Mary Bodfish, her father Jim, who was born in Ladywood in 1911, often uttered this phrase "on hearing a sudden loud noise." Now the title of a musical by Laurie Hornsby that played to packed houses at the Crescent Theatre in 2000 and at the Birmingham Repertory Theatre in June 2001.

Walsall whoffler. Said of a person who is either bandy-legged, or seems unsteady on their feet; from 'whoffle' (to shake). According to Northall (1894), "the inhabitants [of Walsall] jocularly assert that their shaky knees are caused by ascending so many steps to church. Standing and working at the bench, with bent legs, for ease, is the true cause of the peculiarity others say."

Wash together, wipe together, fall out and fight together. (Northall, 1894).

Wenching it. Having a good time out with the girls; see also **chapping it.**

What don't fatten will fill. Common response to the discovery of an insect or suchlike "in your greens or lettuce" EG "Oh well, what don't fatten'll fill" (Joan Burgess). Win Tainty writes that this phrase was also a stock response to children who refused to eat; see also **you'll eat a peck of dirt before you die.**

What's a penny made of? A street jibe, usually uttered within earshot of a policeman; "The answer is 'Copper!' *Copper*, from the slang verb *to cop*, i.e. catch, signifies constable" (Northall, 1894).

What's the good of a well without a bucket? The 'well' in question here is the *interj.*, rather than the *n.*, and this phrase was usually said mockingly to someone who seemed unsure or indecisive; "'Well' is often the introduction to an excuse or poor argument, and the phrase given is said in reply to this usage" (Northall, 1894);

What the eye doesn't see the heart doesn't grieve. If mother, when preparing food or sandwiches, dropped any of it on the floor, she'd pick it up, dust it down and say, "What the eye don't see the 'eart don't grieve" (Joan Burgess).

What the old lad? What the devil?; used to express great surprise or bewilderment (Raven, 1978).

What you know and tuppence wouldn't get you a haircut. Said of someone a little slow off the mark, or slightly less than bright (K. Carruthers).

When apples grow on orange trees. As in the old song: "I wish, I wish, but 'tis all in vain, I wish I was a maid again; A maid again I ne'er shall be, Till an apple grows on an orange tree" (Northall, 1896).

When Easter falls on Lady Day's lap, beware, old England, of a clap. (Timmins, 1889).

When fools are born they must be reared. (Northall, 1896).

When the Devil's a duck and he hasn't started feathering yet. A humorous response to questions such as "When will you finish . . .?," "When can I have . . .?," etc., (Joan Burgess).

When the monkey jumps. When I feel like it and not before; "when inclination prompts" (Northall, 1894).

When the sun shines on both sides of the hedge. A phrase usually given to mean 'never'; "frequently said to children that inquire when their parents will take them for an outing, or bring presents" (Northall, 1894).

Who marries between the sickle and the scythe will never thrive. An old Warwickshire phrase warning that those who marry between the sickle (symbolising the end of the harvest) and the scythe (symbolising the coming of spring) will not stay together for long (Palmer, 1976).

Who stole the donkey? "Shouted after the wearer of a white felt hat. The idea seems to be that the hide of the animal was used to make the hat" (Northall, 1894); see also **who stole the donkey's dinner?**

Who stole the donkey's dinner? "*Answer.* 'Him with the straw brimmer.' Even in Canada a straw hat is called 'the donkey's breakfast'" (Northall, 1894).

Winking and blinking like a rat in a sinkhole. (Northall, 1894).

Wish in one hand and shit in the other. Said in denial or rejection of a wish, dream or desire (Joan Burgess).

Worcester, poor, proud, and pretty. According to Northall (1894), it was 'proverbial' in the late nineteenth century to speak of Worcester ladies as poor, proud, and pretty.

You can always stoop down and pick up nothing. You can always better yourself (anonymous contributor, Yardley).

You'd make a parson swear. "Said to, or of, any irritating circumstance" (Northall, 1896) EG "Yer enough ter mek a bleedin' parson swear."

You'll be well before you're twice married. Usually said to someone who complains of what appears to be a slight or trifling illness. According to Northall (1894), "You'll be worse before you're any better" was also commonly said "by one woman to another in labour pains."

You'll eat a peck of dirt before you die. Common response to complaints about the cleanliness of food; "if you saw that your lettuce wasn't completely rinsed clean and complained, mother would often say, 'You'll eat a peck of dirt before you die'." (Joan Burgess).

You'll pass in a crowd with a push. "An answer to one who says, 'How do I look?' - in the way of dress, &c." (Northall, 1894).

You look as though you lost a bob and found a tanner. (Win Tainty).

You mean pudding and I mean pork. We're talking at cross-purposes; we're talking about completely different things; derived, perhaps, from the old English proverb "I talk of chalk and you of cheese." There is also a similar expression in Italian: "Io ti domando danari e tu mi rispondi coppe." According to Northall (1894), "in the Midlands, when one wanders into an argument, another replies, "What's that to do with pork?"

You might as well rub your backside with a brickbat. "Said of an action that would cause unnecessary hardship or infliction" (Northall, 1894).

You might put it in your eye and see none the worse. Spoken of anything small or trivial (Northall, 1894).

You must have hollow legs. Said to someone who eats and eats and never appears to put any weight on.

You mustn't expect perfume in a pigsty. Another common variant which shares the same meaning in some Midlands dialects is, "Look not for musk in a dog's kennel."

You must've bin born by a brook. Said of someone who is easily reduced to tears, or who cries too much (Win Tainty).

You're a long time dead.

You're like a fart in colander. Said of someone who rushes hither and thither without accomplishing anything (Dennis Hall).

You're not playing for the Town Hall steps! According to Mary Bodfish, this was often said to a person who appeared to be taking a game too seriously, or was acting as if there was some kind of bet on the outcome.

Your eyes are bigger than your belly. Commonly said to anyone who has eaten too much and can't finish their food (K. Carruthers).

You shouldn't think till the crows build in your bum and then you should wonder how they got the sticks there. According to Northall (1894), this phrase was usually said to someone who apologises for an error and attempts to wriggle out of being blamed for it by exclaiming that they thought something to the contrary.

You sit like Mumchaucer who was hanged for saying nothing. (Northall, 1894).

You've been down the pig market. "[M]eaning that the person to whom the phrase is addressed might well have spent his (or her) time, recently, amongst the dealers, who are generally shrewd of wit" (Northall, 1896); see also **you've been in the knife-box.**

You've been in the knife-box. Your wit is sharper than it usually is (Northall, 1896); see also **you've been down the pig market.**

You must've bin inoculated with a gramophone needle when you was born. Said of someone who is extremely talkative.

You were born in the Wrexham and brought the front out with you. The Brummagem equivalent of "Were you born in a barn?" Used to express mild indignation, esp. when somebody has left a door ajar, causing a draught (anonymous contributor, Kings Norton).

References

Ainsworth, Bill. 1989. 'Brumspeak' in *The Birmingham Historian* 4 (pp.23-6). Birmingham: Birmingham and District Association of Local History Societies.

Alexander, Peter, (ed.). 1951. *The Complete Works of Shakespeare*. London: Collins.

Anderton, John. 1878-9. *Ye old Brum and ye new from a humorous point of view: a complete history of the town, abridged from trustworthy documents by Jayhay*. Birmingham: Houghton & Hammond.

Arkinstall, M. J., and Baird, P. C. 1982. *Erdington Past and Present*. Birmingham: Birmingham Public Libraries.

Bateson, Geoff. 1998. *A History of Castle Vale*. Birmingham: Birmingham Public Libraries.

Beale, C. H. 1882. *Memorials of the Old Meeting House and Burial Ground, Birmingham*. Birmingham: C. Hutton.

Bird, Vivian. 1977. *A Short History of Warwickshire and Birmingham*. London: B. T. Batsford Ltd.

Bird, Vivian. 1974. *Portrait of Birmingham*. Birmingham: Robert Hale.

Bird, Vivian. 1991. *Streetwise: Street Names in and about Birmingham*. Warley: Meridian.

Bloom, James Harvey. 1930. *Folklore, Old Customs, and Superstitions in Shakespeare Land*. London: Mitchell, Hughes and Clarke.

Bosworth, J., and Toller, T. N. 1898. *An Anglo-Saxon Dictionary*. Oxford: Oxford University Press.

Botwood, H. A. 1889. *A History of Aston Manor Past and Present*. Birmingham: H. A. Botwood.

Boyd, A. K. H. 1885. *The Recreations of a Country Parson*. London: W. Ibister.

Brand, J. 1849. *Observations on the popular antiquities of Great Britain*. London: Henry G. Bohn.

Burrow, J. A., and Turville-Petre, Thorlac. 1992. *A Book of Middle English*. Oxford: Blackwell.

Cameron, Kenneth. 1996. *English Place Names*. Nottingham: English Place-Name Society.

Carpenter, Humphrey. 1977. *J. R. R. Tolkien: A Biography*. London: Allen and Unwin.

Carpenter, Humphrey. 1981. *Letters of J. R. R. Tolkien*. London: Allen and Unwin.

Chandler, John. 1993. *John Leland's Itinerary: Travels in Tudor England*. Stroud: A. Sutton.

Chatwin, P. B. 1914. *A History of Edgbaston*. Birmingham: Cornish Brothers.

Chaucer, Geoffrey. 1986. *The Canterbury Tales*. London: Folio Society.

Chew, Linda. 1995. *Images of Stirchley*. Birmingham: Birmingham Public Libraries.

Chinn, Carl. 1994. *Birmingham: The Great Working City*. Birmingham: Birmingham City Council, Department of Leisure and Community Services, Libraries and Learning Division.

Chinn, Carl. 2000. *Brum and Brummies*. Birmingham: Brewin Books.

Chinn, Carl. 1999. *One Thousand Years of Brum*. Birmingham: Birmingham Evening Mail.

Crook, Ronald. 1968. *Kingstanding Past and Present*. Birmingham: Birmingham Public Libraries.

Crystal, David. *The Cambridge Encyclopaedia of the English Language*. Cambridge: Cambridge University Press.

Dent, R. K. 1880. *Old and New Birmingham: A History of the Town and its People*. Birmingham: Houghton and Hammond.

Dobson, Frank. 1969. *Larn Yersel Geordie*. Newcastle upon Tyne: Frank Graham.

Douglas, Alton. *Birmingham At War – A Pictorial Account*. Birmingham: Birmingham Post and Mail.

Dowling, G., Giles, B. D., and Hayfield, C. 1987. *Selly Oak Past and Present*. Birmingham: Birmingham Public Libraries.

Edwards, E. 1877. *Personal Recollection of Birmingham and Birmingham Men*. Birmingham: Midland Educational Trading Co. Ltd.

Edwards, E. 1879. *The Old Taverns of Birmingham*. Birmingham: E. Edwards.

Fairn, Alison. 1973. *A History of Moseley*. Birmingham: Vicar of Moseley.

Farley, John. 1800. *The London Art of Cookery*. London: James Scratcherd.

Fowler, William. 1885. *A History of Erdington*. Birmingham: J.W. Shenton.

Gaskell, Elizabeth. 1848. *Mary Barton: A Tale of Manchester Life*. London: Chapman & Hall.

Gelling, Margaret. 'Towards the rehabilitation of Brummagem' in *The Birmingham Historian 7* (pp.11-12). Birmingham: Birmingham and District Association of Local History Societies.

Gelling, Margaret. 1992. *The West Midlands in the Early Middle Ages*. Leicester: Leicester University Press.

Gelling, Margaret. 1997. *Signposts to the Past*. Chichester: Dent.

Gimson, A. C., and Cruttenden, A. 1994. *Gimson's Pronunciation of English*. London: Edward Arnold.

Gover, J. E. B., Mawer, A., and Stenton, F. M. 1936. *The Place Names of Warwickshire*. Cambridge: Cambridge University Press for the English Place-Name Society.

Halliwell, J. O. 1855. *A Dictionary of Archaic and Provincial Words, Obsolete Phrases, Proverbs and Ancient Customs from the Fourteenth Century*. London: Thomas and William Boone.

Hampson, John. 1936. *Family Curse*. London: Chapman & Hall.

Hancock, Keith. 1954. *Country and Calling*. London: Faber and Faber.

Harman, T. T. 1885. *Showell's Dictionary of Birmingham*. Birmingham: Cornish Brothers.

Harris, John. Undated. *Market traders' back-slang for old money, as told to his daughter Edith in the nineteen-twenties*. Unpublished manuscript.

Harrison, Tony. 1984. *Selected Poems*. Harmondsworth: Penguin.

Hastings, R. P. 1986. *Discovering Northfield*. Birmingham: Northfield Society.

Hawkes-Smith, William. 1831. *The Picture of Birmingham*. Birmingham: James Drake.

Hazlitt, W. C. 1882. *English Proverbs*. London: Reeves and Turner.

Hedges, Martin. 1972. *How Does Your Birmingham Grow?* Birmingham: John Whybrow Ltd.

Hoddinott, G., and Nikitas, E. Undated. *The Vocabulary of Solihull's Household Appraisers*. Birmingham: Solihull History Circle.

Hone, W. 1838. *The Every-day Book and Table Book*. London: George the Elder.

Hopkins, F. E. 1986. *Cotteridge and its Churches before 1911*. Birmingham: Birmingham Public Libraries.

Hotten, J. C. 1887. *The Slang Dictionary*. London: Chatto & Windus.

Houghton, Bob. 1999. *I'll Tell You A Tale Of Birmingham, Mate*. Birmingham: self-published.

Hughes, Arthur, and Trudgill, Peter. 1979. *English Accents and Dialects*. London: Edward Arnold.

Hutton, T. W. 1952. *King Edward's School, Birmingham, 1552-1952*. Oxford: Blackwell.

Hutton, William. 1780. *An History of Birmingham to the end of the year 1780*. Birmingham: Pearson and Rollason.

Jeffrey, G. E. 1868. *A story of old Brum: The avenging hand!: or The lone hut on the banks of the Rea, and the squire of Fuddle-y castle: a short but terrific romance of intense local interest.* Birmingham: W. Willey.

Jones, Frank. 1917. *A Practical Course of Phonetics: with special reference to Birmingham and district.* Birmingham: W. Powis.

Jones, Frank. 1918. *Brummagem English: being an account of the peculiarities of pronunciation commonly heard in Birmingham and District together with a course of phonetic exercises to correct them.* Birmingham: Walsall: W. Powis.

Jones, Frank. 1949. *A Schoolmaster Looks Back.* Birmingham: N. Tiptaft.

Jones, Frank. 1956. 'Old Warwickshire Words' in *The Birmingham Post* 22 August 1956.

Jones, Steve. 1998. *Birmingham: The Sinister Side.* Nottingham: Wicked Publications.

Kemble, J. M. 1876. *The Saxons in England.* London: Quartich.

Kenington, Thomas. 1878. *Drainage of Houses and Ventilation.* Birmingham: Buckler Brothers.

Kersh, Gerald. 1941. *They Die With Their Boots Clean.* London: Heinemann.

Kirkpatrick, E. (ed.). 1993. *Brewer's Dictionary of Phrase and Fable.* Oxford: Helicon.

Laneham, Robert. 1585. *A Letter: whearin part of the Entertainment untoo the Queens Maiesty at Killingworth Castl, in Warwick Sheer, in this Sommers Progress 1575 is signified.* Unpublished manuscript held at the Shakespeare Institute, Stratford.

Langford, John. 1868. *A Century of Birmingham Life or a Chronicle of Local Events from 1741 to 1841.* Birmingham: E. C. Osborne.

Langford, John. 1873-7. *Modern Birmingham and its Institutions: A Chronicle of Local Events from 1841 to 1871.* Birmingham: E. C. Osborne.

Latimer, Hugh. 2000. *Sermons.* Manchester: Fyfield.

Leonard, Francis. 1933. *The Story of Selly Oak, Birmingham.* Birmingham: Birmingham Public Libraries.

Lock, Arthur. Undated. *The History of King's Norton and Northfield Wards.* Birmingham: Birmingham Public Libraries.

Lytton, E. 1853. *My Novel, or Varieties in English Life.* London: Blackwood & Sons.

Mahoney, B. M., Dixon, J., and Cocks, R. 1998. *The Role of Accent and Context in Perceptions of Guilt.* Collected Original Resources in Educaton 22.

Marsden, Bob. 1987. *ABC of Small Heath and Bordesley Green Past and Present.* Birmingham: Birmingham Public Libraries.

Marshall, William. 1796. *Agricultural Provincialisms of the District of the Midland Station.* London: N. Trubner for the English Dialect Society.

Mason, H. W. Undated. *Longbridge Estate.* Birmingham: Austin Village Preservation Society.

Mayell, Leslie. 1982. *Further Memories of Birmingham.* Cornwall: Lodenek Press.

Mayell, Leslie. 1980. *The Birmingham I Remember.* Cornwall: Lodenek Press.

McCrum, R., Cran, W., and McNeil, R. 1992. *The Story of English.* London: Faber.

McCulla, Dorothy. 1973. *Victorian and Edwardian Birmingham.* Birmingham: B. T. Batsford Ltd.

McKenna, Joseph. 1979. *Birmingham As It Was – The City 1857-1914.* Birmingham: Birmingham Public Libraries.

McKenna, Joseph. 1988. *Birmingham Place Names.* Birmingham: Birmingham Public Libraries.

McKenna, Joseph. 1986. *Birmingham Street Names.* Birmingham: Birmingham Public Libraries.

Miege, Guy. 1691. *The New State of England.* London: John Wyat.

Mills, A. D. 1995. *A Dictionary of English Place-Names.* Oxford: Oxford University Press.

Milton, John. 1991. *Paradise Lost.* London: Folio Society.

Montgomery, Martin. 1998. *An Introduction to Language and Society.* London: Routledge.

Moughton, William. 1912. *The Story of Birmingham's Growth.* Birmingham: Davis and Moughton.

Murray, J. 1888. *A New English Dictionary on Historical Principles founded mostly on the materials collected by the Philological Society.* Oxford: Clarendon.

Northall, G. F. 1896. *A Warwickshire Wordbook.* London: Henry Frowde for the English Dialect Society.

Northall, G. F. 1892. *English Folk-Rhymes.* London: Kegan Paul & Co.

Northall, G. F. 1894. *Folk Phrases of Four Counties.* London: Henry Frowde for the English Dialect Society.

Northall, G. F. 1880. *The Momus Miscellanies.* Birmingham: Lawrence & Holland.

Old Sarbot. 1869. *Brum* (1-16). Birmingham: Harris & Co.

Old Sarbot. 1866. *Brum: A Parody.* Birmingham: Harris & Co.

Organ, Alma. Undated. *Aston During the Nineteenth Century.* Unpublished manuscript.

Palmer, A. S. 1882. *Folk Etymology – A Dictionary.* London: George Bell.

Palmer, Roy. 1974. *A Touch on the Times.* Harmondsworth: Penguin.

Palmer, Roy. 1979. *Birmingham Ballads.* Birmingham: City of Birmingham Education Department.

Palmer, Roy. 1976. *The Folklore of Warwickshire.* London: B. T. Batsford.

Partridge, E. 1972. *Dictionary of Historical Slang.* Harmondsworth: Penguin.

Pasquin, Anthony. *The Eccentricities of J. Edwin . . . Collected from his manuscripts and enriched with several hundred original anecdotes.* London: John Williams.

Poole, C .H. 1880. *Glossary of Archaic and Provincial Words of Staffordshire.* London: Henry Frowde for the English Dialect Society.

Preece, V. A. 1990. *Duddeston and Vauxhall Gardens.* Birmingham: Birmingham Public Libraries.

Price, Stephen. 1976. *Birmingham Old and New.* Birmingham: E. P. Publishing Co. Ltd.

Pringle, Roger (ed.). 1980. *Poems of Warwickshire.* Kineton: Roundwood Press.

Raven, Jon. 1978. *A Black Country Word Book.* Birmingham: Broadside.

Raven, Jon. 1977. *The Urban & Industrial Songs of the Black Country and Birmingham.* Wolverhampton: Broadside.

Raven, Jon. 1978. *Victoria's Inferno: Songs of the Old Mills, Mines, Manufactories, Canals and Railways.* Wolverhampton: Broadside.

Renshaw, T. L. 1932. *Birmingham: Its Rise and Progress.* Birmingham: Cornish Brothers.

Reynolds, Mary, and Reynolds, Walter. 1989. *Memories of King's Heath.* Birmingham: Birmingham Public Libraries.

Rhodes, R. C., with notes by Hinton, P.F. 1950. *A Birmingham Glossary.* Unpublished manuscript held at Birmingham Reference Library.

Rosser, A. N. 1998. *The Quinton and Round About.* Birmingham: Quinton History Society.

Rowlands, M. B. 1987. *The West Midlands from AD 1000.* London: Longman.

Rowlands, Samuel. 1620. *The Famous History of Guy, Earle of Warwicke.* London: E. Allde.

Rudland, E. M. 1911. *Ballads of old Birmingham.* Birmingham: E. F. Hudson.

Savage, F. 1923. *The flora and folk-lore of Shakespeare.* Cheltenham: Stone.

Shaw, T. 1930. *A Glossary of Black Country Words and Phrases*. Birmingham: Cornish Brothers.

Sheridan, R. B. 1986. *The School For Scandal*. Basingstoke: Macmillan.

Skeat, Walter. 1911. *English Dialects from the Eighth Century to the Present Day*. Cambridge: Cambridge University Press.

Skeat, Walter, (ed.). 1876. *Original Glossaries*. London: Trubner & Co. for the English Dialect Society.

Skipp, Victor. 1980. *A History of Greater Birmingham*. Birmingham: Victor Skipp

Skipp, Victor. 1970. *Medieval Yardley*. Birmingham: Victor Skipp.

Skipp, Victor. 1983. *The Making of Victorian Birmingham*. Birmingham: Victor Skipp.

Smith, Ron. Undated. *A Paddle in Hockley Brook*. Brierley Hill: Weldon Press.

Southey, Robert. 1849. *The Doctor*. London: Longmans & Co.

Spenser, Edmund. 1912. *Poetical Works*. London: Oxford University Press.

Squiers, Graham. Undated. *Aerbut and Gaertie get Raphaelitis*. Birmingham: Cornish Brothers.

Squiers, Graham. 1917. *Aerbut and Gaertie in War-Time*. Birmingham: Cornish Brothers.

Squiers, Graham. 1916. *Aerbut Paerks of Baernegum*. Birmingham: Cornish Brothers.

Squiers, Graham. 1921. *More about the Paerkses*. Birmingham: Cornish Brothers.

Squiers, Graham. 1931. *The Aerbut and Gaertie Sketches*. Birmingham: Cornish Brothers.

Squiers, Graham. 1927. *The Rotary Bawl*. Birmingham: Cornish Brothers.

Sutclifffe, A., and Smith, R. 1974. *Birmingham 1939-1970*. Oxford: Oxford University Press.

Sweet, Henry. 1897. *The Student's Dictionary of Anglo-Saxon*. Oxford: Oxford Clarendon Press.

Tennant, Ray. 1982. *The Book of Brum*. Birmingham: Westwood Press.

Tennant, Ray. 1983. *The Second Book of Brum*. Birmingham: Westwood Press.

Tennant, Ray. 1984. *The Third Book of Brum*. Birmingham: Westwood Press.

Thornber, Paul. 1999. *Brummy Gems*. Birmingham: Thoro'bred Publishing.

Thorne, Steve. 1999. *Accent + Prejudice: A Sociolinguistic Survey of Evaluative Reactions Towards the Birmingham Accent*. Birmingham: University of Birmingham dissertation (unpublished manuscript).

Thorne, Steve. 2001. *Brummagem English: A Sociolinguistic Study*. Birmingham: University of Birmingham thesis (work in progress).

Timmins, Samuel. 1889. *A History of Warwickshire*. London: Elliot Stock.

Timmins, Samuel. 1866. *Birmingham and the Midland Hardware District*. London: Elliot Stock.

Tomkinson, Kenneth. 1893. *Words of Old Worcestershire*. London: Tomkinson Ltd.

Trudgill, Peter. 1990. *The Dialects of England*. Oxford: Blackwell.

Trudgill, Peter. 1983. *On Dialect*. Oxford: Blackwell.

Upton, C., Sanderson, S., and Widdowson, J. 1987. *Word Maps: A Dialect Atlas of England*. London: Croom Helm.

Ursula. 1988. 'Towards more picturesque speech' in *The Birmingham Historian* 3 (pp.28-9). Birmingham: Birmingham and District Association of Local History Societies.

Walker, Ted. Undated. *The Definitive Black Country Dictionary*. Birmingham: E. Walker.

Wells, J. C. 1982. *Accents of English*. Cambridge: Cambridge University Press.

West, William. 1830. *The History, Topography and Directory of Warwickshire*. Birmingham: R. Wrightson.

White, Francis. 1850. *History, Gazeteer and Directory of Warwickshire*. Sheffield: F. White.

Wilde, Hans-Oskar. 1938. *Der Industrie-Dialekt von Birmingham*. Halle: Max Niemeyer Verlag.

Wilmot, Frances. 1991. *The History of Harborne Hall*. Warley: Meridian.

Wise, J. R. 1861. *Shakespere: his birthplace and its neighbourhood*. London: Smith, Elder & Co.

Wright, Donald. 1981. *An Account of Harborne from Earliest Times to 1891*. Birmingham: Birmingham Public Libraries.

Wright, Donald. 1977. *Bygone Bartley Green*. Birmingham: Birmingham Public Libraries.

Wright, Elizabeth. 1932. *The Life of Joseph Wright*. Oxford: Oxford University Press.

Wright, Joseph. 1898-1905. *The English Dialect Dictionary* (6 vols). London: Henry Frowde for the English Dialect Society.

Wright, Thomas. 1872. *Uriconium*. London: Shrewsbury.

Wrightson, R. 1818. *Wrightson's New Triennial Directory*. Newcastle upon Tyne: Frank Graham.